SAVING SCHOOLS

SAVING SCHOOLS

From Horace Mann to Virtual Learning

PAUL E. PETERSON

The Belknap Press of Harvard University Press
Cambridge, Massachusetts, and London, England
2010

Library of Congress Cataloging-in-Publication Data

Peterson, Paul E.
Saving schools : from Horace Mann to
virtual learning / Paul E. Peterson.
p.   cm.
Includes bibliographical references and index.
ISBN 978-0-674-05011-2 (alk. paper)
1. Education—United States—Philosophy.
2. Education—United States—History.   3. Educators—
United States—History.   4. Educational change—
United States—History.   I. Title.
LA226.P44 2010
370.973—dc22   2009043592

To
the memory of my mother, a public school teacher,
Carol, a former public school teacher,
David, a special son,
Sarah, a school reformer,
John, a techie,
and our grandson, Jack, a schoolboy to be

Acknowledgments

Many have assisted in the production of this volume, though I alone bear responsibility for errors of fact and interpretation. I am especially appreciative of the advice and support received from fellow members of the Koret Task Force on K–12 Education at the Hoover Institution, Stanford University, without which this undertaking would never have begun: John E. Chubb, Williamson M. Evers, Chester E. Finn Jr., Eric A. Hanushek, Paul T. Hill, E. D. Hirsch Jr., Caroline M. Hoxby, Tom Loveless, Terry M. Moe, Diane Ravitch, and Herbert J. Walberg.

I am no less grateful to the many undergraduate students at Harvard University who took my course on the politics of American education or my junior seminar. Equally valuable were those graduate students who served as teaching fellows or participated in my graduate seminar on education policy. In particular, I wish to thank Daniel Nadler, who enlarged my understanding of the legalization of schooling and performed an endless array of research tasks, and Martin R. West, whose ideas and suggestions percolate throughout the manuscript.

Anyone who searches the notes to this volume will realize how indebted I am to my fellow editors of the journal *Education Next:* Chester E. Finn Jr., Frederick Hess, Marci Kanstoroom, Michael Petrilli, and, again, Martin R. West. I extend thanks, as well, to Jay

Greene, William Howell, and Ludger Woessmann, all of whom contributed more than they realize. Antonio Wendland, Mark Linnen, Ron Berry, Ashley Inman, and Mark Isaacson ungrudgingly provided research and administrative assistance even when harassed by other responsibilities.

The Hoover Institution of Stanford University sustained this project in many ways. It provided me with office space and financial assistance, supported the work of the Task Force on K–12 Education, and is the publisher of *Education Next*. I am particularly grateful to Hoover's director, John Raisian, for his unhesitating willingness to back a historical study that did not initially appear to have much policy significance. I am likewise grateful to the Koret Foundation for supporting the K–12 Task Force. The research has also been furthered by grants from several foundations to Harvard's Program on Education Policy and Governance, located in the Taubman Center for State and Local Government in the Kennedy School of Government. These benefactors include the Kovner Foundation, the John M. Olin Foundation, the Lynde and Harry Bradley Foundation, the Thomas W. Smith Foundation, and the Searle Freedom Trust.

Contents

Illustrations

SAVING SCHOOLS

Introduction

Born in 1902, my father, a bright lad, skipped a grade in his country schoolhouse near Watson, Minnesota, but he was perfectly literate and numerate, despite having no more than seven years of schooling. Not far away, my mother (and her sisters) were fortunate enough to attend Marietta High School. Their spelling and grammar were impeccable, their writing exact, their penmanship exquisite, and their literary knowledge adequate, despite the limits on the education available in a small town near the South Dakota border. My mother went on to one year of "normal school" (teachers' college) in order to become a public school teacher of the phonics-and-drill-card method. Her teaching came to an end with her marriage—until she returned to the classroom more than two decades later, after her fourth child had started elementary school.

In the spring of 1946, not long after the end of World War II, now fondly remembered as the good war, I attended kindergarten for six weeks just across the street from my family's home in the small town of Montevideo (Mon-ti-*vid*-eo), Minnesota. Local leaders wanted to put more into their schools, but they had neither the money nor the facilities to do much, so kindergarten, a new experiment that year, was mainly confined to the one-room windowless basement of Henry Sibley School, named after our state's first governor (locally lauded for capturing members of the friendly

1

Chippewa tribe outside our town during the Civil War). Just how the five teachers survived with more than a hundred screaming tots in that cramped, miserable space has not been recorded.

Despite such an inauspicious beginning, my years at Sibley were educationally rewarding. The teachers were all unmarried women. George and Abe hung on the walls. In conformity with the up-and-coming whole-word doctrine, we rote-read *Dick and Jane*, yet phonics card drills were no less a part of the curriculum. As a guide to our penmanship, all the letters of the alphabet, capital and small, ran above the blackboard. Math tables were to be memorized, though not until second grade. We learned long division, fractions, and decimals, again and again. We chanted, "Peter piper picked a peck of pickled peppers." Spelling, grammar, diction, diagrams: all were part of the drill. Though boring, it was certainly thorough. The janitor kept the school sparkling and the grass impeccably green, despite the games of touch football we sneaked in on weekends. Had the baseball diamond been fenced, and had some do-gooder not insisted that the monkey bars be deconstructed (after an arm was broken in a fall), the gravel grounds, if old-fashioned, would have been quite satisfactory for all our needs.

Not until I reached fifth grade did I encounter rampant progressivism. A new teacher—fresh from somewhere advanced, I am sure—wanted us to do projects. She didn't seem to know what else we were to learn. That was the year we shifted from A's and B's to Satisfactory, Needs Improvement, and Unsatisfactory. I got a lot of the middle category on the deportment side of the ledger.

With the arrival of the baby boomers, Sibley became so crowded that the school board shifted my sixth-grade class to Central, a high school enlarged to accommodate the rural students being bused to town now that their little white schoolhouses had been consolidated away. For me, the move to Sibley had its scary moments—an older kid roughed me up for carrying home my French horn in its funny-looking case—but inside the classroom Miss Rice, glasses dangling on her substantial bosom, kept strict order, and learning never skipped a beat.

But in seventh grade, all chaos broke out. Bells rang, we sprinted noisily from one class to another, and, best of all, we held school assemblies, usually rallies for the basketball team. In eighth grade, my European-history teacher spent his time smoking with the janitors, leaving the students to instruct one another. Discussions were lively but not on the topic the school board presumably had recommended. Everyone hated—and many found a way of skipping—health class, during which a new, totally forgettable teacher babbled about disgusting, embarrassing things: pimples, dating, and inappropriate apparel. As a ninth grader, I took a test that said I should become an accountant; it was probably correct, since, unlike most people, I actually like to balance my checkbook. But what a wonderful algebra teacher I had! She made strange facial movements that were of little value in the marriage market, but she taught her subject matter relentlessly. Thanks to her, I still know how to employ x and y.

High school combined the old and the new, the good and the bad. My American-history teacher taught only the facts, giving me a foundation upon which much could be built in the years to come. Our band and orchestra were directed by a clarinetist who had once played under Arturo Toscanini, and he exposed us to some of the more popular classics with an ardor for which I remain forever grateful, despite my continuing embarrassment at having marred a concert by flubbing the high F in the horn solo of Tchaikovsky's Fifth. My Latin teacher, the principal's wife, greatly enriched my knowledge of the English language. Unfortunately, my English teachers tried to teach classics with excerpts and abridged editions. As for the sciences, I am sorry that, to this day, I don't know the formula for anything other than water. I'm proud to say, however, that I undertook my own innovative school project: one day, I stole a substantial batch of sodium out of the chemistry closet and tossed it into the Chippewa River—to the delight of my classmates and the dismay of the local police, who were unable to identify the source of the resulting smoke despite the deployment of advanced interrogation methods.

We said our prayers at home, not at school. To the best of my recollection, a Bible was never opened inside the schoolhouse except on Baccalaureate Sunday, when seniors, if they wished, received an interdenominational blessing from a Protestant minister. Before the practice was abolished, students were excused from classes for one hour a week to receive religious instruction at a nearby church—a ridiculous event except for the year a committed Baptist had us memorize Bible verses, one for each letter of the alphabet. "W: When I walk through the valley of the shadow of death, I shall fear no evil."

The playground of the town's Catholic elementary school—a playground I walked across on the way to my high school—was not quite the valley of the shadow of death that a local Lutheran minister seemed to believe. It was just small and poorly maintained, with only one basketball hoop, often used by the young Merle McClung. I felt sorry for him and all the others who had to go to such an inferior place. What a shock it was to learn a few years later that he was named to Minnesota's All-State basketball team, then admitted to Harvard, and eventually became a Rhodes Scholar.

My experience was of small-town, racially homogeneous, midwestern America. Central High had its social divides, mainly between town and country, Catholic and Lutheran, sports stars and music-minded nerds. The townies were shocked when the outnumbered country kids formed a voting bloc cohesive enough to elect the homecoming queen. Yet divisions were never sharp or deep. Fifty years later, three-fourths of the surviving members of my graduating class happily celebrated their anniversary together. Montevideo did not capture the sophistication of the exclusive suburban school, the vitality of an urban education, or the visible racial separation prevalent elsewhere. It was a middling experience—not the best of American education, but not the worst either.

If my schooling was more or less par for the course, then America's schools at mid-twentieth century, though not unsatisfactory, had hardly reached such a state of perfection that they were not in need of improvement. Schools circa 1950 had come a long ways since their beginnings in the nineteenth century, but they still had a steep hill to climb if they were to become institutions of the first rank.

On my graduation day, our well-trained high school choir sang the soaring opening theme from Beethoven's Violin Concerto in D. A lesser artist had written the inspiring text, which he'd entitled "On the Way to Tomorrow." Our rendition, both enthusiastic and precise, was addressed specifically to the graduates, but it could have been education's song as well. Wherever schooling was headed in Montevideo—in America—it seemed to be moving inevitably forward and upward.

What happened was otherwise. To see why, we must look both before 1958 and afterward down to our present day.

PART ONE

THE RISE

CHAPTER 1

Heroes and History

Men who live in the ages of equality are naturally fond of central power; . . . if it happens that this . . . power . . . exactly copies their own inclinations, the confidence they place in it knows no bounds.

—Alexis de Tocqueville, *Democracy in America,* vol. 2, trans. Phillips Bradley, Henry Reeve, and Francis Bowen (New York, 1945)

In the late 1950s, the American educational system was the envy of the world. Though it had many warts—southern schools were racially segregated, disabled students were excluded, and school facilities were often hopelessly inadequate—the nation's secondary schools could boast a higher graduation rate than that of any other major industrial country. Attendance had exploded in the 1920s and 1930s, so that by 1940 some 72 percent of all teens in the relevant age group were going to high school, a percentage that grew to 90 percent by the mid-sixties. Recipients of bachelor's degrees more than doubled between 1940 and 1970 (see Figure 1 in the Appendix). Schools had helped propel the United States from a developing country to one of the world's superpowers.

Today, elementary and secondary schools in the United States no longer appear exceptional. In recent decades, other countries have been encouraging their young people to remain in school for ever-longer periods of time, but U.S. graduation rates have remained constant. Once the world leader, the United States now stands merely at the average for the industrialized world (Figure 2). Nor are those who remain in school learning more. According to various international measures of high school student performance, America's schools range from just average in reading to well below that level in science and math (Figure 3). White seventeen-year-olds scored little better on reading tests in 2004 than they had in 1971. African Americans and Hispanic high schoolers made noticeable progress in reading during the seventies and eighties, but their performance has slipped since then. The story is much the same in math (Figure 4).

Even the highest-performing students do not excel at the same level as students once did. A hard-nosed but committed mathematics professor at Johns Hopkins University gave his 2006 students the same test in Calculus I that he had given in 1989. The two classes had similar SAT scores, so it is a safe bet that the ability of the students had not changed over time. And it seemed as if they were learning more in 2006 than students had back in the 1980s, because the instructor awarded better grades in 2006 than in 1989. In 2006, he gave 69 percent of the students an A or a B, as compared to 50 percent in 1989. But then the professor ran a check to see what the grades in 2006 would have been if he had been as tough a grader as he had been in 1989. He discovered that in 2006 only 27 percent would have received one of the two top grades, not the 69 percent he actually had awarded. In short, students came less prepared and were as a result learning less, and even an old-time professor was lowering expectations accordingly.[1]

This is only one anecdote, of course. But international studies confirm that even the highest-performing students are learning less than the highest-performing students did in earlier years. The number of students going on to college has been rising, but only 28 percent of those aged twenty-five to twenty-nine actually graduated with a bachelor's degree in 2006, just 5 percentage points higher than in 1978.

These and other signs of educational stagnation abound, despite the following facts: America's parents today have had more years of education and have more money they can spend on their children's education. Per-pupil expenditures for public schools in the United States have more than tripled, in real dollar terms, since the 1960s, and class sizes—as indicated by the number of pupils per teacher—have fallen by a third (Figure 5). Meanwhile, the demand for an educated workforce with highly technical skills that can keep the country competitive in the world economy has never been greater.[2]

Why has a once-dynamic educational system turned stagnant, or worse? Has there been a change in pedagogical practice? Or are resources, though expanding, still inadequate? Has the decline resulted from the racial turmoil accompanying desegregation? Or from the rise of stronger teacher unions and collective bargaining practices? Have school systems become overly centralized, professionalized, legalized, and bureaucratized? These are among the questions I explore as I trace the impact of individuals who have sought to save the schools from the limitations inherited from the past. Their ideas, as well as the vested interests these reformers faced and the ones they themselves created, built a stagnant system that has recently seemed beyond transformation—until perhaps now.[3]

Ideas and Interests

Ideas motivate great undertakings that change the political world. They draw upon people's best impulses and highest ideals—their desire to build a great nation, a better and more wholesome people, a more egalitarian society, or a more democratic polity. Ideas translate those ideals into practical suggestions that have the capacity to direct the energies of large numbers of citizens. At first, only a few have the vision to see how an ideal can be turned into reality. They initially lack material political resources, so they often turn to facts and figures and findings to move their agenda forward. For a shorter or longer period of time, vested interests can ignore them, but good ideas, like a steady rain, eventually wear away long-standing edifices.

A few exceptional leaders had the missionary zeal and reform-minded ideas that motivated many others to try to save the schools from the vested interests of the past. The problematic story of six of these cause-minded leaders, and how their efforts altered America's educational system (though not in the ways they desired), unfolds in the pages that follow. Each of the following reformers, heroic in his aspirations and ideals, had a powerful idea, a loyal following, and an impact that changed the system, but each was frustrated, often for reasons of his own making:

- Horace Mann, the first secretary to the Massachusetts Board of Education, who served in that position from 1837 to 1848;
- John Dewey, the progressive philosopher-educator who founded the Laboratory School at the University of Chicago in 1896, and then concluded his teaching career at Columbia University;
- Martin Luther King Jr., the civil rights leader who challenged school segregation from Montgomery to Birmingham to Chicago, and, through a notable 1963 speech at the Lincoln Memorial, left a spiritual and educational legacy the country has not forgotten;
- Albert Shanker, the head of the United Federation of Teachers in New York City, who revolutionized public-sector collective bargaining;
- William Bennett, Ronald Reagan's secretary of education, who

used the bully pulpit that office provided to make educational excellence a national political issue; and

- James S. Coleman, the University of Chicago sociologist who provided the intellectual underpinnings for the excellence movement that began to question the workings of the school-industrial complex.

The lives of the six men stretch from almost the beginning of the republic to the present day. But despite the historical epochs in which they lived, their upbringing, personalities, and convictions have striking similarities. Most were guided by strong religious or quasi-religious convictions, whether or not they remained adherents of their childhood faith. All had an early education less progressive than traditional, usually in a privileged setting. All were committed to saving the schools as they knew them. All of them altered the future of American education, though none succeeded in realizing his vision.

Each leader was part of a broader wave of forces by which he was shaped and to which he contributed. Mann was the most visible of numerous nation builders who sought to construct schools suitable for a burgeoning democracy. To achieve that purpose, they made elementary schooling universal, compulsory, and free of sectarian influences. Dewey's impact was reinforced by a much broader progressive movement that shifted power from machine-style politicians to professional public servants. King's civil rights group was one of many that extended liberties and more equal opportunities to previously disadvantaged groups and individuals. Shanker marched together with a broader public-sector collective-bargaining movement. Bennett was the most visible personality among many who insisted that schools no longer sacrifice educational excellence to misguided applications of the egalitarian ideal. For him, schools needed clear curricular standards, parental choice, and the willingness to employ new technologies. Coleman prepared the way for the choice movement by exposing the anti-intellectual culture of the high school, by showing that material resources did not matter as much as people had thought, and by identifying the strengths of the Catholic school.

Stakeholders

Change-oriented leaders contend against powerful interests that have a stake in the status quo. Stakeholders resist ideas that threaten their perquisites and their privileges. In the short run, they are very powerful, because they control concrete, material resources that can be mobilized to defend their interests. As a result, reform ideas, when put into practice, can produce unanticipated results. Mann and his fellow nation builders did not expect that the public schools would be captured by ethnic politicians elected by immigrants whose values differed from their own. The new pedagogy inspired by Dewey turned out to be inappropriate for those disadvantaged students about whom he cared the most. The success of his fellow progressives in edging politicians from power left schools isolated from community support at the very time when powerful new demands were being placed upon them.

The civil rights movement set off forces that changed the shape of public education not so much by desegregating pupils as by asking schools to be responsive to court jurisdiction. Shanker created a powerful public-sector labor movement but grew uneasy when teacher unions did not share his own vision of educational excellence. The accountability movement begun by Bennett continues, but its accomplishments have fallen short of the rhetorical goals the secretary of education had proclaimed. Coleman jump-started a movement for school choice, but that movement is still nascent.

Schools as we know them today were not built by six men, any more than the world was created in six days. But just as the story of the Creation is a powerful statement of what it means to be a human on the face of this particular planet, much can be learned by looking at the development of our educational institutions through the ideas and actions of six individuals. As Leo Tolstoy once explained, "History—that is, the unconscious, swarmlike life of mankind—uses every moment of a king's life as an instrument for its purposes." Napoleon did not cause the invasion of Russia in 1812, any more than the "millions of men, in whose hands the actual power lay, the soldiers who shot, transported provisions and cannon." But Tolstoy nonetheless found it necessary, in his account of events, to consider the thoughts and actions of Napoleon and his adversary, the Russian czar Alexander I. So it is with the six men in our story. The "billions of causes [that] coincided so as to bring about what happened" can be elucidated, if not fully explained, by taking a look at their aspirations, ideas, and ideals.[4]

Nor do we wish to suggest that ideas are the driving force in history. Three of the principals—Mann, Dewey, and Coleman—thought deeply about education and society, and their impact was felt primarily through what they said and wrote. The other three—King, Shanker, and Bennett—were mostly men of action. By word or deed, or both, all six played a crucial role in shaping American schools as we know them.

Effective ideas and ideals acquire a force and energy that overwhelm the opposition. What had once seemed impossible becomes reality. Reform movements long in the making succeed in changing the system in one way or another. When stakeholders resist change, they, too must engage in the battle of ideas—often to their disadvantage. As their resistance crumbles, a new arrangement is put into place. An alternative set of interests—some old, others quite different—acquires a stake in the system. What was once an idea becomes its own set of interests.

From Local Schools to Central Control

The system the reformers sought to change was modeled on Scottish and English arrangements marked by voluntary enrollments, fee-based education, religious instruction, and local control. Over the decades, as part of each successive effort to save the schools, the control of education has steadily shifted away from family and community toward more centralized institutions under the control of a professional class. The march toward a more centrally regulated, bureaucratized educational system has taken place through a series of struggles that produced multiple transformations, all of which were gradual rather than immediate, partial rather than complete, and less thoroughgoing than what had been anticipated by those involved. Horace Mann and his fellow nation builders, active in the mid-nineteenth century, used governmental power to impose a compulsory, secular public school system on an immigrant population whose values they wished to shape. But their victory was incomplete, as immigrants and provincials captured control of the local boards responsible for managing the public schools. John Dewey and his fellow progressives of the early twentieth century used the power of state governments to reduce the number of school boards, shift power from politicians to professionals, and introduce a new, child-centered pedagogy. Yet they did not create the efficient, egalitarian educational system they promised.

Martin Luther King and his fellow civil rights leaders exploited the power of the courts and other branches of the federal government to expand not only the rights and liberties of African Americans but also those of linguistic minorities, the disabled, the politically outspoken, public school teachers, and, amazingly enough, the schools themselves. But all those rights did not produce better schools or equal educational outcomes. Al Shanker believed that teacher power would yield educational excellence, yet discovered that his own organization refused to follow him. Bill Bennett and his fellow participants in the excellence movement fought for new state and federal laws that would hold schools accountable for student test performance. Yet they discovered it was easier to prescribe student achievement than to realize it. The school spirit does not necessarily come when ordered.

Each of these struggles shifted control of education away from parents and localities to professionals operating within larger legal entities—large districts, collective-bargaining agreements, state governments, court jurisdictions, and federal executive agencies. Centralization became the almost inevitable byproduct of school reform, simply because reformers sought maximum power to carry their desires into effect.

If the drive to centralize was pervasive, so was the demand for customized education. The early reformers, to be sure, saw no need to fit the schooling to the child. For them, it was the other way around. Horace Mann sought not to adapt schools to the desires of immigrants but to mold children into the rational, tolerant, civilized adults a modern society seemed to require. But those who came after Mann often expressed a stronger commitment to customization than to centralization. They took their cue from their understanding of the French philosopher Jean-Jacques Rousseau, who seemed to want each child to define his own educational experience, the tutor taking his cues from the student rather than the other way around. Profoundly influenced by Rousseau, Dewey tried to replace the standardized rote learning of his childhood with a child-centered system. His less creative followers customized the educational experience by putting students into boxes, giving each one the education they thought the student could profit from. Three tracks—academic, vocational, and general life-adjustment courses—were created. The class size reduction movement also was driven by the idea that teachers could meet the needs of each child more effectively if they had fewer children to instruct.

Customization reached its zenith in 1974, when Congress said that every child with a disability needed an "individualized education plan," a customized set of resources and programs appropriate for his or her particular situation. The idea was also applied to those who came from non-English-speaking families: each was to be taught in his or her native tongue—an extraordinary expectation, given the multiplicity of languages immigrants were bringing to the United States. The accountability movement has had its own approach to customization. The federal accountability law does not just ask for progress by all students on average. Rather, *no child* can be left behind, and it must be shown that all types of students—boys, girls, blacks, whites, Latinos, all other ethnic minorities, the disabled, and even migrants—are moving toward educational proficiency.

Ironically, customization of American education was to be accomplished through centralization, its seeming opposite. Power had to be centralized to save schools from the power of vested interests, as each reform that was undertaken generated its own backlash. When public schools read verses from Protestant Bibles, Catholics built their own schools. When state legislatures abolished local school boards, they did so over bitter objections from rural communities. Machine politicians kept their fingers in the pockets of urban schools for decades after reformers tried to pull them out. When the Supreme Court finally declared segregation unconstitutional, southerners fought a rearguard action that minimized desegregation for a decade, and northerners migrated to suburbs that still remain largely of one skin color. When the courts all but mandated bilingual education in order to sustain immigrant cultures, voters in state referenda reversed the policy. When students were asked to take tests so that schools could be held accountable, teacher unions questioned their accuracy and resisted their use for evaluating teacher performance.

To overcome resistance by vested interests, those who wished to save the schools found it easier to counter opposition by shifting power upward toward more central organs of government. But centralized power did not necessarily yield the customized education reformers desired. Nor did it create the efficient, egalitarian, quality educational institutions they envisioned.

The coming reform struggle holds greater hope, as it appears to meet the long-standing desire for customization by shifting power back to students and families, who are most directly affected by the educational system. It is most unlikely that the coming battle to save American education will yield fairy tale results. But the next direction of change in American education will be quite different from those that occurred in the past. The rapid rise of new educational technologies is subjecting schools to new pressures, creating for the first time the possibility of reform that will decentralize, not centralize, control over the educational system.

The closing chapter will tell the story of Julie Young of Florida Virtual School, because it is her work that best exemplifies the way in which technological advances will likely shape our educational future. If her story is symbolic of what is to come, education will become more reliant on technology and less labor-intensive. As costs continue to rise, school systems will be forced to eliminate those in the middle—the regulators in Washington and the administrator in the central office, for example. Instead, students will find themselves in direct, face-to-face contact with the material to be learned. The student will choose what, where, and when to learn and, one hopes, will be held accountable for knowing it. Teachers will become coaches, not enforcers. Education will become decentralized, personalized, and customized so that schools will look more like those of the earliest years of the republic than the highly structured, professionalized, centralized systems they became in the late twentieth century.

But innovators of the kind that Julie Young exemplifies will be essential in the effort to transform economic and technological necessity into political reality. Reformers will have to articulate ideas so as to overcome the power of vested interests, which can be expected to oppose the introduction of twenty-first-century technologies. Yet if the ideas and the leadership are there, the opportunity to save American education from its historical limitations will arise once again.

preamble speaks of "domestic tranquility" and the "general welfare," but schools are not mentioned. Its Bill of Rights says that Congress shall not "establish a religion," but none of the first ten amendments—or any other amendment—have anything directly to say about our educational system.[2]

The seventeenth-century political theorist John Locke believed that legislative, executive, and judicial powers should be divided among distinct branches of government, a recommendation which left a lasting mark on American democracy. But the work by Locke most widely read in colonial America said less about politics than about the way in which young people should be educated. In "Some Thoughts Concerning Education," Locke, anticipating Benjamin Spock, gave parents advice on how to deal with ill temper, craving, curiosity, sauntering, cruelty, lying, and excuses. He told them how to instruct a child in reading, writing, drawing, French, Latin, history, rhetoric, and much more. He thought children should be educated at home, either by their parents or by a carefully selected, closely supervised tutor. As for schools, Locke could not imagine "what qualities are ordinarily to be got from . . . a troop of playfellows . . . usually assemble[d] together from parents of all kinds." It was one thing to have "two or three pupils in the same house," but quite another to have "three or fourscore boys lodged up and down." According to Locke, "Let the master's industry and skill be ever so great; it is impossible he should have fifty or a hundred scholars under his eye any longer than they are in school together, nor can it be expected that he should instruct them successfully in anything but their books."[3]

Admittedly, Locke had in mind residential boarding schools, so it is not clear whether he would have objected to neighborhood grammar schools over which parents could keep a watchful eye. But colonial Americans generally took Locke's advice. "Whether it was mother or father, it remains the case that the vast majority of children acquired almost all of their formal education and pretty much everything else they learned in the home," says historian Milton Gaither. Girls were expected to stitch samplers that revealed their skills at sewing and displayed such versification as

> When I was young and in my prime,
> You see how well I spent my time.
> And by my Sampler you may see
> What care my parents took of me.

As an almost exclusively Protestant culture, colonial Americans took their Bible reading seriously. Only in the Bible could one learn the "Word of God," and only by comprehending the written catechism could biblical vagaries be resolved in a doctrinally correct fashion. So children throughout the colonies were taught to read. By the time of the Revolution, such education, in the best of families, could be highly elevated. By the age of eight, future president John Quincy Adams was reading portions of Charles Rollin's *Ancient History* to his mother, Abigail.[4]

Schools were adjuncts to the home. In more prosperous homes, tutors would be hired. If the family was struggling to make ends meet, children might be packed off to a neighbor's house, where they were expected to work in return for higher-quality instruction than the parents themselves could provide. Some towns might be visited by an itinerant schoolmaster like Washington Irving's Ichabod Crane. But, increasingly, women were preferred. "Female teachers brought a maternal presence to the classroom, turning the school into an extension of the home." Some women even ventured west, with missionary zeal, to help civilize the frontier. The more responsible families tried to do it themselves. Recalled Charles Weller, whose family settled in Wisconsin: "Our winter evenings were largely spent by the fireside, mother sitting with her sewing and mending, and the boys seated on a brick hearth fashioning with their jackknives cunning little cedar boxes, listening as father read to us." And then there were some astounding young people, such as

Abraham Lincoln, who eagerly read the Bible and Shakespeare and whatever else he could get his hands on, though his own father was illiterate.[5]

If education during the early years of the republic remained largely a family responsibility, schools did not go unappreciated. On the contrary, the Continental Congress in 1785, four years before the Constitution was adopted, made a specific provision for public education: in the new territories west of the Appalachians, it set aside the proceeds of one section of land out of sixteen for the "maintenance of public schools within the said township." But by "public schools" Congress did not mean the type of institution we think of today. Congress had nothing more specific in mind than the locally controlled, faith-based, voluntary institutions of the day, as was indicated by the fact that, in another law passed two years later, Congress affirmed that "religion, morality, and knowledge, being necessary to good government and the happiness of mankind, schools and the means of education shall forever be encouraged."[6]

Even advanced thinkers wanted nothing more than to broaden the availability of the schools already in place. Thomas Paine, in his *Rights of Man,* proposed something more akin to school vouchers than to state-run schools, suggesting that government money help parents send their children "to school, to learn reading, writing, and common arithmetic." To ensure that the money was spent for this purpose, "the ministers of every parish, of every denomination, [are] to certify jointly to an office, for that purpose, that this duty is performed." Benjamin Rush, the esteemed physician who signed the Declaration of Independence (and nearly killed Abigail Adams with the standard treatment of bloodletting when she contracted malaria), recommended "free" public schools funded by a mandate that each "scholar pay the schoolmasters." For Rush, the words "free" and "public" meant only that the school was freely open to all who were willing to pay at least a minimum amount for their child's education. Thomas Jefferson favored a state-run university, but for elementary education he suggested parental choice—for those who were not slaves. "Free" children, he said, should be "entitled to receive tuition gratis, for the term of three years, and as much longer, at their private expense, as their parents, guardians, or friends shall think proper."[7]

Since Calvinists were expected to read the Bible, the Puritan states of New England asked local communities to ensure that children be educated. As George Washington was taking his first presidential oath of office, the Commonwealth of Massachusetts was asking every town "to maintain an elementary school for six months out of twelve," a practice that spread to most other states in the region. Elsewhere, "education was considered a private function of the parent," with the role of the state limited to "providing education for paupers and indigent children."[8]

Haphazard and locally controlled as this educational "system" was, Americans were amazingly literate. Newspapers were the major forum for communication during the Revolutionary period. With dizzying speed, they mobilized the nation against the Stamp Act, the Navigation Acts, and actions taken by the royally appointed colonial governors. During the Revolutionary War, Thomas Paine's *Common Sense* sold 100,000 copies, and it is thought that 25 percent of the white adult population read the book. A study of a Vermont county at the time of the American Revolution found "almost universal male signature literacy," with the rate of female literacy ranging from "60 percent to 90 percent," depending upon the locality's level of commercial development.

Literacy was especially widespread in the Massachusetts Bay colony. In the early seventeenth century, the Puritans had established North America's first institution of higher education, Harvard seminary in Cambridge, Massachusetts; in the eighteenth century, minister Jonathan Edwards in Northampton, Massachusetts, sparked an "Awakening" with his sermon entitled "Sinners in the Hands of an Angry God," which democratized the religious experience in colonial America; during the Revolutionary period, John Adams, in the constitution he wrote for the state of Massachusetts, was the first to make education a public responsibility. It was by no means a coincidence that the Bay State would be the birthplace and home of Horace Mann, the country's premier missionary for state-directed public schooling.[9]

The Nation Builders of the Early Nineteenth Century

Born in 1796, Mann reached political maturity when old New England was being challenged by a large influx of migrants from rural Ireland and Germany, many of whom had fled only when the Irish potato blight reached an intensity that made it cheaper for a landlord to provide passage to America than to hand out minimal food supplies. As Boston's population more than doubled between 1820 and 1840, official voices of concern cried out. "Those now pouring in upon us, in masses of thousands upon thousands, are wholly of another kind in morals and intellect," lamented a joint committee of the Massachusetts state legislature. "Massachusetts seems to have resolved itself into a vast charitable institution," wept the state's sanitation commission. Even worse, most of these newcomers did not believe in the God of the Puritans but confessed to Catholic priests ultimately beholden to their superiors in Rome.[10]

The man chosen to lead the battle against darkness was the younger son of a farmer who tilled fields near Franklin, Massachusetts, not far from the Rhode Island border. As a precocious child, Horace Mann was tormented not by the papist faith of Boston immigrants but by the Calvinist doctrines of his hometown pastor, who preached a "hell and brimstone" doctrine that the bright young lad took so literally it shook his faith in a loving God to its very roots. Then, at the age of twelve, he had a religious experience similar to those described by people who claim to have been born again: "I remember the day, the hour, the place and the circumstances, as well as though the event had happened but yesterday," he recalled much later, "when in an agony of despair, I broke the spell that bound me." Rejecting the Calvinist doctrine of original sin, he embraced a theory of Christian ethics and doctrine not unlike that of the Unitarian church he eventually joined. A year after this religious experience his father died, but his family, though faced with straitened circumstances, secured the help of a private tutor. Horace learned enough Latin to find his way out of Franklin to Brown University and beyond. No zealot is as passionate as a convert. Though the God in which Mann now believed was rational and humane, His servant, Horace, was no less devoted to his calling than missionaries of the past. Yet his church was a schoolhouse, his pulpit a public office, his target not sin but the twin errors of orthodoxy and popery.[11]

Upon his election to the state legislature, Mann first tried to pass laws that imposed the state's will directly upon the drunk and insane. After figuring out that "men are cast-iron; but children are wax," he shifted his attention to saving the young. He spearheaded efforts to create a state Board of Education, and in 1837 he became its first secretary. At that time, Massachusetts schools were locally controlled and church dominated. The state lacked an overarching system, a common curriculum, systematic training of its teachers, and textbooks free of the kind of religious doctrine to which Mann himself had been subjected.[12]

Upon assuming his new responsibilities, Mann traveled to several European countries to inspect their school systems. Ignoring the locally controlled Scottish and English systems that had been the model for colonial schools, he made careful note of the skill with which the Prussians were using public schools to unify the German people. Centralized institutions, a state-directed curriculum, statistical information, and professional cadres were being mobilized to create a unified national spirit, a common language, and an identity that would transcend parochial loyalties.

Horace Mann, secretary to the Massachusetts Board of Education, 1837–1848. Metropolitan Museum of Art, Gift of I. N. Phelps Stokes, Edward S. Hawes, Alice Mary Hawes, and Marion Augusta Hawes, 1937 (37.14.25).

Had Mann attempted to build a Prussian-like system in Massachusetts, where power still resided in the hands of community elites, his reform campaign would have been buried at birth. Instead, he, as secretary, did little more than ask the state Board of Education to approve books for libraries, create normal schools where future teachers could be educated, collect statistics for his reports on the state's educational conditions, and ask local districts to pay for school costs. Mann efficiently wielded those small tools with missionary zeal. State-approved textbooks were limited to those that praised the God of Creation, not the God of Judgment. Teachers were told at normal school the kinds of things that should—and should not—be taught to pupils. Statistics revealed how many teachers were properly trained and which schools used only an acceptable curriculum. Those tools were designed to free schoolchildren both from orthodox Protestant doctrine and from the harsh Catholic beliefs that immigrants were bringing into the Commonwealth.

The reforms encountered such fierce opposition that the Board of Education was nearly abolished just three years after its inauguration. A legislative investigating committee recommended that "instead of consolidating the education interest of the Commonwealth in one grand central head, and that head the government, let us rather hold on to the good old principles of our ancestors, and diffuse and scatter this interest . . . into towns and districts, . . . even into families and individuals." Unless such steps were taken, the committee members feared that "religious liberty" was likely to be endangered, "for there would be but one church." In their view, the elimination of all doctrinal books would turn what remained into a Unitarian-like doctrine of its own. Requiring that teachers be sent to normal school formed "all our teachers upon one model" that "would destroy all competition, all emulation, and even the spirit of improvement itself."[13]

Mann had nothing but disdain for such complaints. The men

"who are assailing me," he wrote privately, were "those who are born orthodox, who are naturally or indigenously so; who, if he had wit enough, would have invented orthodoxy, if Calvin had not. I never saw one of this class of men whom I could trust so long as a man can hold his breath." He courageously fought to keep the state board alive and his reforms largely intact. Though schools remained in local hands, Massachusetts became, in 1852, the first state to introduce compulsory education. A vague "Protestantism" replaced the more sectarian beliefs of Calvinists and other fundamentalists. Teachers began to be trained at normal schools. Mann gathered statistics to make a national case for school reform. By 1843, he was able to claim that "our schools [in Massachusetts] are perfectly free. A child would be . . . astonished at being asked to pay any sum, however small, for attending our Common Schools," though breaches of that principle were detected as late as 1848.[14]

Schools were not for everyone, however, and Mann never called for compulsory schooling. Horace's three children were taught by his wife, Mary. "As a father, he fell back on the educational responsibilities of the family," wrote his biographer Jonathan Messerli, "hoping to make the fireside achieve for his own son what he wanted the schools to accomplish for others."[15]

Schools in the Late Nineteenth Century

The great progenitor of the modern public school died in 1859, just before the outbreak of the Civil War. But once that scorching conflict had begun to cool, Mann's reforms were picked up by a national network of reform-minded educators inspired by his example. In 1870, an agency of the federal government, the United States Office of Education, began to gather statistics on the nation's schools. Normal schools nationwide trained young women—and a few men—in how and what to teach. The National Education Association (NEA) organized teachers and administrators into a political force that could fight for public schools. One state after another decided that most of the costs of schooling should be paid by local districts, not by parents. Compulsory education laws also spread, so that by 1918 every state, the last being Mississippi, had a compulsory-education law. The laws were typically passed in tandem with union-backed laws that forbade children from working outside the family farm or business.[16]

Mann's ideas were powerful, but they ran up against interests and institutions that had had a staying power of their own. Despite nationalizing influences, the many small school districts managed by locally elected school boards gave community elites and ordinary citizens a powerful say in the way schools were run. In 1890, the United States had no fewer than 120,000 school districts, each with its own board or committee. In big cities, the membership on school boards could run into the hundreds, with individual members focused more on the schools serving their neighborhoods than on the system as a whole. Elections were usually held on general-election day and the candidates' party affiliations were listed on the ballot, connecting schools to the patronage-based political party system. All but a tiny portion of the school dollar came from local taxes. As late as 1920, 80 percent of the revenue was raised from local sources. Schools were beholden to city councils for their financing, superintendents were typically recruited from within the community, and principals often had tight connections with ward bosses.[17]

If all of this smacks of politics and provincialism, it provided a robust, democratic base for a rapidly expanding system that commanded broad support throughout the political community. As Tocqueville wrote admiringly, "In no country in the world do the citizens make such exertions for the common weal. I know of no people who have established schools so numerous and efficacious." Both rural Americans and immigrants from abroad saw the schools as vehicles for social mobility. The Irish had a particular advantage, because they could both speak English and relate to other immigrant groups, making them the perfect interstitial group that could bind a diverse nation together. In Chicago, San Francisco, and other big cities, schools were often under the direction of Irish board members and disproportionately staffed by Irish public servants. In New York City, the Jews, with their passion for education, chose teaching as a career and saw schools as an avenue for social mobility.[18]

Popular among immigrants and native-born Americans alike, locally controlled elementary schooling became universal by the late nineteenth century, and secondary education took off at a rapid pace in the early decades of the twentieth century. In small towns, schools became symbols of progress, signs that a community was improving. They were a mark of prosperity and became part of the intense competition among towns and cities for status and advantage.

The competition fueled rapid expansion of a full range of educational services, not least the construction of highly visible public high schools. In Chicago, where the schools were as locally controlled and politically dominated as in any city, the numbers of students in average daily attendance exploded from 25,300 in 1870 to 166,000 in 1896. Despite that growth, expenditures per pupil—in real dollars—nearly tripled, from $39 to $107. The number of pupils per teacher fell from forty-seven to thirty-eight. Politics, competition, decentralization, and democratic control all combined to generate a dynamic, expanding system that gradually acquired an international reputation. In the race to provide secondary schooling for everyone, the United States was leaving the countries of Europe far behind. All of this was being accomplished primarily by local school boards asking local property taxpayers to fund their schools. The price tag seems, in retrospect, to be remarkably small. In 1902, less than 1 percent of the nation's Gross Domestic Product (GDP) was spent on public education.[19]

Following World War I, the nation entered a reactionary, anti-immigrant period when it all but shut the door to those "huddled masses yearning to breathe free." So intense was the nationalistic spirit, and so aggressive the drive for universal, compulsory education, that lawmakers in Nebraska and Oregon attempted to close private schools. In Nebraska, they objected to instruction in any language other than English, while in Oregon the voters, in a referendum organized by the Ku Klux Klan, banned private schools altogether. But even during that xenophobic era, liberty's torch could not be snuffed out. The U.S. Supreme Court, in landmark decisions, declared both laws unconstitutional, saying that the Due Process clause of the Fourteenth Amendment guaranteed individuals the right to send their child to a private school.[20]

That right had been exercised for more than a century, most notably by Catholics offended by Protestant prayers, baccalaureate services, and readings from the King James Bible. Catholic leaders had regularly asked the government to help them pay their educational costs, on the grounds that they, too, were taxpayers, but public school officials, faithful to Horace Mann's legacy—and to their own pecuniary interests—fought back aggressively and usually won, except in a few urban Catholic strongholds. To forestall even those few victories, Maine senator James Blaine, future Republican candidate for president, led a national campaign to enact an amendment to the U.S. Constitution that prohibited any government dollars from going to religious schools. Needing a two-thirds majority in the U.S. Senate, the amendment failed by one vote, but clauses containing similar language (known as "Baby Blaines") were inserted into numerous state constitutions. As a result, the United States, unlike England, France, Canada, Germany, and most other nations, chose not to fund its private, religious schools along with its public, secular ones. Horace Mann's nation builders, though unsuccessful in removing public schools from local control, had at least ensured that they would have no serious private-sector rival.[21]

If Protestants marginalized Catholics, the treatment of the newly freed slaves was much worse. True, northern abolitionists and missionaries created a series of Freedman Schools at the close of the Civil War, but that largely came to an end in 1876, when white southerners succeeded in reasserting their political dominance by electing officials in Democratic primaries that excluded African Americans from voting. After that, black schooling was both segregated and minimal. In Atlanta, one of the most progressive of the southern cities, the number of African American pupils per teacher jumped from 95 in 1878 to 118 in 1895. No secondary school was built for African Americans until 1924, when they demonstrated enough strength in a bond election to force city leaders to establish a black high school, if they were going to extend and rehabilitate Atlanta's white ones. Even the schools for white children in Atlanta were poorly supported. Expenditures were only $25 per pupil in 1878, and failed to increase much above that level for the next two decades. The number of pupils per teacher in white classrooms rose very slightly, from 63 pupils in 1878 to 65 pupils in 1895.

Exclusion and isolation were not limited to the South. In San Francisco, in 1885, only 4 percent of Chinese American school-age children were enrolled in public school and none attended public high schools. As late as 1902, local courts upheld their exclusion from non-Chinese schools, though, under threat of a Chinese elementary school boycott, San Francisco finally opened its high schools to Chinese students in 1905.[22]

Discrimination against minorities—whether Catholics, African Americans, or Chinese Americans—had few immediate political repercussions. But the nineteenth-century school system had other vulnerabilities. Elites in rural areas were provincial, and their economic base, agriculture, was in perpetual difficulty, as technological innovation drove small farmers from the land. In urban areas, school board members were often more gifted in handling patronage and contracts than in designing classroom curricula. In 1884, the San Francisco newspaper compiled a list of the accusations against the school board: teaching positions in the department were sold, janitorships were hawked, textbook purchases were fixed, contracts for merchandise were mismanaged, furniture was used for political and personal purposes, and private homes were built by school carpenters. The "city by the bay" was hardly unique in this regard. According to historian Lawrence Cremin, "corruption reared its ugly—if familiar—head" in urban areas across the country. "Teaching and administrative posts were bought and sold; school buildings . . . suddenly became incredibly expensive to build; and politics pervaded everything from the assignment of textbook contracts to the appointment of school superintendents."[23]

The first transformation of the schools was necessarily gradual, extending over many decades after Horace Mann had first called for compulsory, secular, free schooling. It was necessarily incomplete, because the Supreme Court still recognized that states were sovereign entities independent of the federal government, and the fundamentals of political power remained essentially local. Free, compulsory public schools did not mean that Horace Mann's values would always triumph, because democratic practices had given other groups with their own culture and values the opportunity to shape what was happening in schools and classrooms. The ideas of the nation builders were powerful, but so were the interests they encountered.

Outcomes were a blend of nation-building ideals and pluralistic interests generated by a democratic society. Free, compulsory schooling could not have spread so rapidly if those in rural communities had not seen the local school as a community-building institution, if immigrants in big cities had not seen it as a way ahead for their children, if the trade union movement had not seen it as an alternative to child labor, and if local politicians had not seen it as another source of patronage and perquisites. Horace Mann's ideals, blended with political interests he would have abhorred, created something quite different from anything in Scotland, England, or Prussia.

Yet the ideas of the nation builders were turning into interests of

CHAPTER 3

John Dewey and the Progressives

Experience has shown that when children have a chance at physical activities which bring their natural impulses into play, going to school is a joy, management is less of a burden, and learning is easier. . . .

School facilities must be secured of such amplitude and efficiency as will . . . discount the effects of economic inequalities . . . Accomplishment of this end demands . . . modification of traditional ideals of culture, traditional subjects of study, and traditional methods of teaching and discipline as will retain all the youth under educational influences until they are equipped to be masters of their own economic and social careers.

—John Dewey, *Democracy and Education* (New York, 1916)

By 1900, American schools had gained worldwide renown, but many features—prejudice, patronage, and provincialism, among them—were open to serious criticism. And critics there were, in abundance. An articulate class of educated middle-class professionals—an intelligentsia, as it were—was gathering strength in politics, journalism, the universities, and the professions. Many were themselves educators, building their careers as psychologists, economists, political scientists, sociologists, and experts in pedagogy. It was only a matter of time before schools would capture their attention.

John Dewey

No one person better exemplifies the spirit of the day—or had more influence on the direction schooling would take—than John Dewey. Born in 1859, less than three months after Horace Mann's death, John's early life paralleled Horace's about as closely as any could, given the sixty-three years that separated their birth. Both were born and raised in a small-town New England world ruled by Congregational orthodoxy. John's Congregational minister in Burlington, Vermont rejected literal interpretations of biblical texts, and his father seemed mainly devoted to the family's substantial grocery business, leaving John nearly as fatherless as the adolescent Horace had been. But John's mother, to whom the boy, a shy child, was particularly devoted, stood as "the enemy of all frivolity—drinking, playing, pool, gambling, playing cards, . . . even play[ing] marbles on Sunday." His request to be admitted to Communion was drafted by her as follows: "I think I love Christ and want to obey him"—tentative language that seems well chosen, inasmuch as she subsequently inquired, more regularly than he wished, whether he was "right with Jesus." If the answer did not necessary persuade his dear mother, John was nonetheless an obedient son. Not until his forty-fifth year, when he moved to Chicago, did he drop his Congregational affiliation.[1]

The schools Dewey attended in Burlington had barely been touched by Mann's disciples. The elementary school was not organized into grade levels until he was nine. Instruction focused on the basics and was endlessly repetitive. The building which housed the high school was "condemned as a hazard" not long after he finished. His English teacher's way of explaining grammar was to say: "There is a rule against that." One of his high school teachers "whipped some body practically every day."

That Dewey's child-centered pedagogy owed much to his childhood frustrations is likely, but the importance of two later factors is more certain. In college at the University of Vermont, he was exposed to a Continental philosophy that questioned Enlightenment rationalism, which had shaped Scottish education, and in his first teaching position the young man came to know one of his students, Alice Chipman, a fellow diner at his boarding house. John learned to share her interest in Romanticism, feminism, and early education. In all likelihood, Alice was the one who fostered John's early interest in the labor movement and the Socialist party, though it was not until he arrived in New York City that he became fully engaged in a host of progressive social causes.

In 1885, amid the flush of his first love, he completed a draft of his first major scholarly accomplishment, *Psychology*, which rapidly became the discipline's dominant textbook. As a rising star on the faculty at the University of Michigan, he attracted the attention of William Rainey Harper, president of the University of Chicago, an institution reaching for national prominence with the financial backing of John D. Rockefeller. Accepting Harper's invitation, John and Alice moved to Chicago in 1894, and, for the next decade, they tried out their pedagogical ideas at the "Laboratory School" they founded. Alice served as the principal, while John, the director, developed the philosophical and educational doctrines that would shape the direction of American education.[2]

In 1904, to everyone's shock and surprise, Dewey dramatically resigned. He had long been frustrated by his multiple responsibilities in both the Philosophy Department and the Laboratory School, but what sparked his abrupt resignation was undoubtedly Harper's suggestion that Alice resign as school principal. Teachers had expressed concern about the relationship between the principal and the school's director, Harper explained. Outraged, Dewey gave up his post with no other job prospect on the table—a remarkable decision, given the five growing children in the Dewey household. But

Columbia University quickly scooped up the renowned scholar. In New York, Dewey, without the Laboratory School to occupy his time or to test specific pedagogical innovations, placed his educational thinking in a broader philosophical context, reworking Hegelian systematics into a more practical, if less coherent, pragmatist doctrine better suited to the American milieu. Identifying appropriate educational practices was now left to his disciples, apart from Dewey's periodic bouts of exhortation and encouragement. Alice turned her attention to the needs of their large family.

That Dewey shifted his attention from pedagogy to philosophy seems due less to the loss of the Laboratory School than to his own internal uncertainties and contradictions when it came to things educational. Dewey himself was not much of a teacher. His best students claimed that his "rambling discourse" was actually "very closely knit and carefully thought out," but one wonders whether his absentminded shuffling was truly effective. Max Eastman, edi-

John Dewey, arriving in Cleveland on July 9, 1932, to chair a convention of the League for Independent Political Action, whose purpose was the creation of a third political party dedicated to increasing social planning and control.
Bettmann/CORBIS.

tor of the Socialist magazine *The Masses,* recalled that Dewey
would look out the window or up at the ceiling and "begin to talk,
very slowly and with little emphasis and long pauses. . . . He was
thinking rather than lecturing." If his disciples saw this as the very
personification of progressive pedagogy, the more jaundiced saw it
the other way around: progressive pedagogy was little more than
justification for a disorganized teaching style.[3]

As for administration, Dewey was overwhelmed again and again.
For a small place, the Laboratory School had an unusually convoluted administrative structure. Also, Dewey was swamped by minu-
tiae that absorbed too much of his time as head of Chicago's Philosophy Department. Upon his resignation, he apparently aspired to
become the president of the University of Illinois, but when that position did not materialize, he found he was quite happy at Columbia, where he forswore most administrative duties, focused on his
philosophical writings, and used his New York stage to support a
host of advanced social causes.[4]

Progressive Pedagogy

Dewey's influence was pervasive, far more so than Mann's, probably because his thought was philosophically more deeply rooted
and his writings had implications for a broader range of pedagogical and institutional concerns. Mann's educational agenda had been
shaped by Enlightenment rationalism. He had been focused more
on shaping the character and moral beliefs of the next generation
than on employing a particular pedagogy. His institutional reforms
had been derived not from theory but from observations of various
European practices, especially those in vogue in Prussia and the
Netherlands. Writing more than a half century later, Dewey drew
upon the deeper, murkier wells of later Continental philosophy.
From the ideas of Rousseau, Hegel, Spencer, and Marx, Dewey
fashioned a pragmatist philosophy that had powerful appeal to

American educators seeking a middle way between the dogmatisms of capitalism and revolutionary Socialism. What emerged for educational practice, from Dewey and others, were several not altogether compatible tenets. Two of them emphasized the need for a personalized educational experience customized to the needs of each and every child: (a) accept children as they are, because every child is different; (b) arouse the natural curiosity of the child and use that to motivate learning. But two other tenets implied a need for tight central control in order to achieve a larger public good: (a) socialize the child into the community; and (b) reform the social order.[5]

When Dewey began the Laboratory School, young people were still expected to memorize passages from English classics (Shakespeare's *Julius Caesar,* Eliot's *Silas Marner,* Dickens' *Tale of Two Cities*) or patriotic American poems (Longfellow's "Paul Revere's Ride" and "The Village Blacksmith"), to read character- building homilies put together in the best-selling McGuffey's readers, and to learn to read and calculate by rote methods later characterized as "drill and kill." Sitting stiffly in hard-back chairs at fixed desks or long tables, children were asked to sing, to the tune of "Yankee Doodle," such ditties as "Five times five is twenty-five / And five times six is thirty." Phonics, penmanship, spelling bees, public speaking, punctuation practice, sentence deconstruction, and other boring routines were part and parcel of school life. To improve their diction, children stumbled over "The old cold scold sold a school coal scuttle."[6]

Taking ideas from Rousseau, Dewey sought to change all that. The best education, the French philosopher seemed to say, in *Emile,* was one the child discerned for himself. The tutor was to "do nothing and let nothing be done," so that the child would learn whatever he needed to know without instruction, keeping "the soul idle as long as possible." While Dewey rejected Rousseau's stricture that "reading is the plague of childhood," he readily agreed that no pupil should ever learn anything "by heart." Like Rousseau, Dewey thought that "if one ought to demand nothing from children through obedience, it follows that they can learn nothing of which they do not feel the real and present advantage in either pleasure or utility."[7]

After testing his ideas at the Laboratory School, Dewey, with the help of his disciples, pushed implementation nationwide. Phonics was deemphasized in favor of the "whole-word method," which required no specific instruction but simply the opportunity to see words time and again. "Run, Spot, run," said Dick to his dog in one of the most widely used of the new texts that had come to replace the McGuffey reader. In math, students were no longer asked to learn how to do long division or subjected to drills designed to ensure that multiplication tables had been memorized; instead, they learned fractions by cutting pieces of construction paper into quarters. In literature, students were not asked to memorize Lincoln's "Gettysburg Address"; instead, they were given the opportunity to explore the world about them by completing "projects" about themselves or their immediate surroundings. In place of sterile book learning, students were invited to participate in manual training, vocational education, and life experience courses. Girls learned to cook and sew, while boys did woodworking, metalworking, agricultural studies, and automobile mechanics. Fixed desks screwed to the floor gave way to moveable furniture, rugs, and open space.[8]

Like Rousseau, Dewey objected to the contemporary emphasis on "quantity rather than quality of knowledge." He argued instead for "intimate and extensive personal acquaintance with a small number of typical situations with a view to mastering the way of dealing with the problems of experience, not the piling up of information." Accordingly, some of Dewey's disciples organized themselves into the child-study movement headed by William Kilpatrick at Columbia Teachers College. Kilpatrick concluded that students should not be confined to "customary, set-task, sit-alone-at-your-own-desk procedures." Instead, they should engage in group projects with other children—projects that would help them prepare for participation in the work world. The idea was not unlike the spirit that motivated vocational education, a reform that found favor in the worlds of both business and labor. It was so popular that in 1917 it became the first major educational grant program Congress ever funded. Ninety years would pass before any president dared question the value of federal aid to vocational education. George W. Bush attempted to end the federal funding, but Congress ignored him, leaving the program intact to this day.[9]

Progressive celebration of the natural had its reactionary side, unfortunately. Influenced by Herbert Spencer's social Darwinism, many progressives believed that some children were born to learn more, others less. Along with movable desks and school projects came IQ measurement and aptitude testing. Used in World War I to select men fit to be drafted, the testing movement solidified during the 1920s on evidence that an individual's aptitude had remarkable stability over time. The data were interpreted as proving that only one-quarter to one-third of the population was capable of academic learning. The testing movement reached its apotheosis in the remarkable Scholastic Aptitude Test (SAT), a pencil-and-paper test that could predict students' college readiness regardless of their high school curriculum. With a high enough SAT score, Rousseau's "Emile" could be allowed to matriculate in college without any formal schooling at all.[10]

Those not as talented as Emile needed something else. So concluded leaders of the life-adjustment movement, a progressive spin-off that emerged out of a conference sponsored by the U.S. Office of Education in 1945. According to conference thinking, 20 percent of all students are fit for an academic, college-bound education, and 20 percent more are suitable for the skilled trades, but the remaining 60 percent need something else. It was decided they should learn things that were socially useful and personally engaging. In health classes, students could learn why and when people gossip, why teachers seem old, and how adolescents can gain more self-confidence. Physical education classes would give them the exercise and body tone necessary to live a healthy life.

Not every progressive project managed to make it into the mainstream of American education. Many ordinary Americans—and some contrarian scholars as well—wondered whether learning could be made as much fun as Rousseau, Dewey, and the progressives imagined, so the ideas that were being expounded encountered more than a little resistance. And American schools were too diverse and decentralized for any curricular reform to gain swift, much less universal, acceptance. To carry out their curricular objectives, Dewey's disciples also needed to reorganize the political structures that governed American education.

Organizational Reform

If progressive pedagogical reforms found their way into our schools only fitfully and idiosyncratically, the same cannot be said for the progressives' organizational innovations. Few reform movements have been as successful at changing the educational system's structure of power. The progressives were so effective, in fact, that eventually it became quite unclear whether the schools belonged to the public or to the professionals.

Almost all the organizational reforms had a common purpose: to shift power from misguided, provincial, corrupt political elites to those professionally trained in matters educational. To weaken "friends-and-neighbors" politics and attachments to local schools, the number of school board members was reduced, and citywide (rather than ward-based) elections were held. To weaken the power of political parties, party labels were stripped from the ballots cast in school board elections. By 2002 nearly 90 percent of all U.S. school board elections were said to be nonpartisan. To further weaken party influence, many school board elections were moved from the usual November election days, when political parties were highly visible to—well, just about any other day of the year. In California, for example, local elections occurred in 2005 on any one of twenty-three Tuesdays (see Figure 6 in the Appendix). Nationwide, only half of all school board elections were held on the same day as national or statewide elections. For professional educators, the shift to nonpartisan elections held at odd times made sense. When elections were held on atypical dates, school-based groups had more influence. The more unusual the time of the year, the smaller the electorate, giving those who cared the most—teachers, other school employees, parent activists—a larger voice.[11]

Once board elections were reformed, board members were asked to focus on policy, not on administration. From a professional perspective, most items fell into the second category. Certainly, all personnel questions, save the choice of superintendent, were taken off the board members' plate. Even superintendents were to be chosen upon the recommendation of committees dominated by educators. I learned about this practice in the late 1960s, when, as a novice assistant professor in the University of Chicago's Department of Education, I was asked by Roald Campbell, the chair of the department and an eminent figure in the world of school administration, to help him "survey" the needs of an elite school district so that he could help the district select its new superintendent. Through interviews with community notables and school professionals, I picked up the local gossip and a sense of the issues facing the town. Meanwhile, my boss canvassed his former students to find out which one wanted to take the job. A suitable match was undoubtedly made in this case, as in thousands of similar ones across America.

Transforming board elections and the internal workings of school boards was not enough. In addition, the educational professionals campaigned for larger school districts beyond the ca-

pacity of a lay school board to control. "To have a fully organized school board in every little school district in a county," said
Ellwood Cubberley, dean of the Stanford School of Education in
1914, "a board endowed by law with important financial and educational powers, is wholly unnecessary from any business or educational point of view, and is more likely to prevent progressive action
than to secure it." Few reform proposals have been implemented
more successfully. The number of school districts dropped precipitously, from 120,000 in 1940 to around 15,000 by the century's
end (see Figure 7).[12]

Consolidation enlarged the remaining school districts, creating
the conditions for imposing tighter professional control. When districts had but a couple of thousand students, boards could keep
track of school affairs. But when enrollments climbed into the tens
of thousands, an administrative apparatus headed by a professional
superintendent became essential. The superintendent could then
guide board decisions by invoking professional norms, state laws,
and, eventually, federal regulations. Gradually, school boards became legitimating agencies rather than actual decision makers.[13]

As districts consolidated, small schools were combined into
larger ones, and the little red schoolhouse, with its ungraded classroom, became a thing of the past. Just as Cubberley had expected,
average school enrollment jumped from 85 students in 1930 to
around 300 in 1960. Still, the call for bigger schools continued. After conducting a nationwide investigation in the 1950s, Harvard
University president James Conant cried: "How much of our academic talent can we afford to waste? If the answer is 'none,' then
. . . the elimination of the small high school through district reorga-
nization and consolidation should have top priority." Cubberley
and Conant justified the need for larger schools on three grounds:
(1) big schools were more efficient, as they allowed for more centralized control; (2) schools could group students according to abil-

ity, facilitating efficient instruction of the top 20 percent who were able to take academic courses; and (3) new facilities could be constructed at lower cost. Over the next two decades, average school enrollment increased to 440 (see Figure 8). It would take another fifty years before the educational advantages of personalization and connectedness were grasped by any one other than students, parents, and teachers.[14]

The push for bigger schools and larger school districts came from state education officials. State legislators listened to them because department officers promised fiscal savings. They were particularly eager for any possibility of savings because the state was being asked to assume an increasing share of fiscal responsibility. Whereas localities had been paying more than 80 percent of the cost of education in 1920, by 1950 they were paying only about 60 percent, and by 1980 that percentage had dropped to around 45 percent (see Figure 9). Whether any money was saved is quite another question, as we shall see in Chapter 7.

The rule book followed the dollar. In line with this old edict handed down by Horace Mann, state departments of education now had greater success in limiting the discretion of local school boards. As a guard against patronage and cronyism, states issued certificates that teachers could earn only by completing a program of instruction at what Mann had called normal schools but which were now known as colleges of education. Between 1900 and 1930, the number of states that set up statewide credentialing rules increased from fewer than five to more than forty (see Figure 10). To further limit favoritism, teachers were paid according to a standard salary schedule that varied only with the academic degree a teacher had obtained and the number of years the teacher had been employed. To ensure academic freedom, teachers were granted tenure after only a few years of teaching. To become a principal, one needed first to teach, then to take a properly accredited series of courses in school administration.

Progressive Reforms: Some Questions

Progressive ideas were congealing into a set of professional interests. Teachers and administrators had a set of prerogatives their associations were asked to defend. Teachers' colleges had a vested interest in maintaining their control over access to a large and growing profession. State officials had a vested interest in seeing that state monies were properly spent by local officials. A class of school professionals had a stake in limiting the power of the laity.

The machine politicians and the local notables did not accept defeat gracefully, fighting rearguard actions whenever and wherever they could. Elections in some parts of the country remained ward-based and partisan. To this day, school board members in many communities still involve themselves in personnel matters and other administrative details. Local connections are still very useful if one wishes to become a principal. Repetitive math and phonics drills have not disappeared altogether. The shift of power was partial, not complete. Still, the long-term trajectory favored education professionals. By the end of World War II, the way in which schools were controlled had been utterly changed from the pattern in place a couple of generations earlier.

As a result, professionals were able to direct the enormous educational expansion in U.S. schools that took place when veterans returned to father the baby boom generation. Suburbia needed new schools, creating an opportunity to design classrooms and playgrounds that reflected the latest progressive thinking. New teachers, many with master's degrees and filled with the latest in progressive educational insight, graduated by the thousands from the rapidly expanding colleges of education. New curricular ideas for adolescents blossomed in response to exploding high school enrollments. Guidance counselors were hired to help adolescents adjust to life beyond school. After battling machine politicians for generations, sophisticated administrators found themselves warmly accepted on all sides. Even Richard Daley, Chicago's powerful machine mayor, decided to leave educational matters to the specialists.[15]

The progressives had succeeded in shifting power from rural bumpkins and ward heelers to a new class of educational professionals, and their new pedagogical approaches gradually spread throughout much of the country's educational system. But certain questions began to gnaw. Were the professionals really as public-spirited, politically disinterested, and scientifically grounded as they claimed? Were the schools of education, now in control of the paths to teaching, counseling, and administration, capable of turning out a talented workforce? Would the big, handsome new schools, run by large school districts, acquire capacities that greatly exceeded those of the "little red schoolhouse"? Would advanced pedagogical techniques be as effective in mainstream classrooms as in university imaginations?

Even larger questions loomed. Could schools, even when led by sophisticated professionals, actually change the social order? Or would the ideas of the progressives be transmogrified into a set of well-defended professional prerogatives? Would schools of education seek to protect their control over teacher licensing? Would teacher organizations use tenure and the standardized salary schedule to protect mediocrity? Would lay control of the schools survive the shift of power to larger districts and state authorities?

All such questions were left hanging in the air when another wave of reform, this one of near tsunami-like proportions, fundamentally rearranged the educational landscape.

CHAPTER 4

Martin Luther King Jr. and School Desegregation

Five score years ago a great American, in whose symbolic shadow we stand, signed the Emancipation Proclamation. This momentous decree came as a great beacon light of hope to millions of Negro slaves. . . . But one hundred years later the Negro is still not free. . . . [Yet] I have a dream that . . . little black boys and black girls will be able to join hands with little white boys and white girls as brothers and sisters.

—Martin Luther King Jr., Public address given from the steps of the Lincoln Memorial, August 28, 1963

The origins of civil rights reform can be dated quite precisely: May 17, 1954, the day the Supreme Court decided *Brown v. Board of Education of Topeka, Kansas*. Racial desegregation finally became an idea whose time had come. It had taken nearly a century after the Civil War for the Supreme Court to act, despite the passage of a Fourteenth Amendment to the Constitution that explicitly prohibited states from denying "any person . . . the equal protection of the laws" or denying him or her "life, liberty or property, without due process of law." These two great clauses of the Fourteenth Amendment—known as the Equal Protection and Due Process clauses—seemed to promise racial equality at the time of their enactment in 1868, but not until 1954 did the Supreme Court discover in these words a ban on state-mandated segregation of students by race. Once the decision was made, civil rights groups, including, most

51

notably, the one headed by Martin Luther King Jr., set off a civil rights movement that mobilized African Americans and sympathetic white groups to political action.

In the aftermath of the decision, the school door was opened to political passions that extended well beyond the civil rights movement per se. Rights talk spread from African Americans to other ethnic groups, as well as to the disabled, the politically demonstrative, and public school employees. Each of these extensions of rights affected authority that school boards had once taken for granted—just at the time when schools needed all the legitimacy they could muster to cope with powerful new social forces impinging upon them. In order to accomplish all the objectives of the multiple civil rights movements that unfolded, it was necessary both to attempt a customization of education for individual children and to centralize power in institutions—courts, collective-bargaining agreements, and the federal government—that had previously played little role in the workings of American schools. The rights reformers, no less than the progressive reformers, left a quite unexpected legacy.

To give Martin Luther King Jr. pride of place in this story may seem odd to those who recall Thurgood Marshall's painstaking legal efforts to end state-sponsored racial segregation. As the lead attorney for the National Association for the Advancement of Colored People (NAACP), Marshall argued before the courts, again and again, that the Supreme Court had erred in *Plessy v. Ferguson* (1896) when it found racially separate facilities constitutional so long as they were of equal quality. But the Supreme Court repeatedly found reasons to avoid overturning *Plessy*, usually by deciding cases in ways that excused them from grappling directly with the doctrine of "separate but equal." Even *Brown* itself refrained from directly reversing *Plessy* when it declared that only segregated *schools* were unconstitutional.[1]

For this reason, and for others, *Brown* was less of an end than a beginning, and the story post-*Brown* owes less to Marshall than to Martin Luther King Jr. So it is the eloquent minister, not the dogged attorney, whose birthdate is rightly honored as a national holiday. Of the six noble figures who sought to save the schools, King alone can be identified as a genuine hero in the true sense of the word. He faced extraordinary challenges, he forged a nonviolent strategy to accomplish tasks unfinished since the Civil War, and he willingly sacrificed his life to a cause greater than himself. From the steps of the Lincoln Memorial, in a landmark address comparable to the one Lincoln had given at his second inaugural, King delivered the moving words with which this chapter opens. That marvelous address, together with actions that gave them meaning, have made him central to the American experience. Yet those who do great deeds leave legacies they themselves do not perceive. The movement King led, though triggered by a decision that outlawed segregation of students, had less of an impact on the racial composition of classrooms than on that of workplaces, restaurants, hotels, legislatures, sports arenas, and places of public entertainment. Substantial integration took place nearly everywhere except within schools. Within schoolhouses, whites moved out when blacks moved in.[2]

As for the civil rights movement itself, nonviolent protest regularly threatened to spill over into something more turbulent, with bloodshed initiated first by southern sheriffs and bands of white racists, but eventually also by elements within the black community that were beyond King's control. One city after another was rocked by major civil disturbances. King's assassination in Memphis in 1968 sparked uprisings throughout the nation, leaving whites fearful and African Americans embittered. As whites fled to their suburban enclaves, "equal rights" slogans morphed into Black Power rhetoric. Though formal segregation disappeared, racial integration was not secured. Meanwhile, the forces of change left many schools struggling to maintain an educational focus which even federal dollars could not buy. In the end, the result was not what Dr. King had dreamed.

Martin Luther King Jr.

Born in 1929, on the eve of the Great Depression, the future civil rights leader was baptized Michael King Jr. Fortunately for Michael, his father, like Dewey's, was an acute businessman, though he ran a church, not a grocery store. A rough-hewn, strong-willed, modestly educated, passionate man who had married well above his station, Michael King Sr. succeeded his father-in-law as the pastor of the Ebenezer Baptist Church two years after his oldest son was born. The Great Depression had left the church building on the verge of foreclosure, but the new minister reversed its decline by forceful preaching, centralized control of church funds, and publicly recorded contributions. By 1934, King Sr. was able to travel through the Mideast and Europe en route to a Baptist convention in Berlin. Moved by direct encounters with the very places that had spawned the Reformation, King Sr. changed his name and that of his eldest son to Martin Luther—a renaming that foreshadowed a courage and greatness that would eventually be fulfilled.[3]

Despite his new moniker, M.L., as he was known, had no more commitment to parental orthodoxy than Mann or Dewey had. As a child, M.L. knew every Bible tale, loved to sing Gospel solos, and could, in a teenage oration, passionately compare the sufferings of black people to those of Jesus. Then, at age twelve, King was forced to come to grips with the death of his dear maternal grandmother, in whose home the King family lived. "For days he fell into long crying spells," King's biographer records, and he began to question the family doctrine that his "grandmother still lived." Shortly thereafter, his Sunday school teachers were outraged at his denial of the bodily resurrection of Jesus. It was not only theological issues that

M.L. had with his father. At Morehouse College, which he attended as a teenager, he defied the family ban on social dancing, drawing stern admonishments from "Daddy" King.[4]

Morehouse College was a component of Baptist-connected Atlanta University, a center of southern black intellectual life. Rockefeller family money was critical to its success, just as it had been for the University of Chicago, which had provided a home for John Dewey's Laboratory School. In seventh grade, M.L. attended Atlanta University's own Laboratory School, having skipped a grade at an apparently unsatisfactory segregated elementary school. Unfortunately, financial constraints created by World War II forced the Laboratory School to close within two years, so King returned to public school for a year. Then, at age fifteen, he was admitted to Morehouse College in Atlanta. This posed a challenge for M.L., since he considered himself to have had nothing better than an eighth-grade education. Yet he quickly caught up with his fellow students, became engrossed in philosophical studies, and was asked by the faculty to give the "Senior Sermon," after which he announced to his father that he wanted to go to Crozer Theological School, an integrated, northern, liberal Baptist seminary just outside Philadelphia. His father, delighted that his not altogether perfectly obedient son had chosen the ministry after all, first opposed his attending such a liberal institution, but soon gave up trying to block M.L.'s decision.[5]

A synthesizer much like Dewey, King discerned a middle way between capitalism and communism. At Crozer, he coupled the optimistic "social gospel" theology of Walter Rauschenbusch with Reinhold Niebuhr's more pessimistic assessment of human nature. At Boston University, where he pursued a doctoral degree, King forged his own synthesis of Paul Tillich's remote Deity and Henry Wieman's immanent, personal Heavenly Father with whom an individual could communicate directly. For King, history was not a simple collision of social forces, God was not a mere Creator, progress was not inevitable, and pacifist acceptance of the status quo could not be tolerated. As Mahatma Gandhi had shown, only determined individuals, through strong and loving action, could redeem humans from evil.[6]

It was not all philosophy and theology in Boston. The young, vibrant King charmed many a women during his graduate years. He found his life partner by asking a married friend if she knew anyone she thought suitable. She replied that she did know a quiet student from rural Alabama—a certain Coretta Scott, preparing herself for an opera career at the New England Conservatory. She would be quite suitable indeed, but the friend thought Coretta was probably not interested in meeting a Baptist preacher. Challenged, King proved his friend wrong by displaying for Scott a sociability, erudition, and philosophical understanding of *agape* (altruistic love), all the more impressive when spoken in a rich baritone voice. The couple married in June 1953, when King was twenty-four.[7]

It took a loving action, just nine months later, for Coretta to agree to return to Alabama after Martin passed up professorial positions to accept a call from Dexter Baptist Church in Montgomery. Built during Reconstruction, the church was located immediately across from the state capital, and the congregation was as middle class and forward thinking as the time and place allowed. But no city could have been more rigidly segregated, even though local black leaders claimed that was about to change.

The Supreme Court handed down *Brown* the same month that King preached his first sermon in Montgomery. But the decision's immediate impact was blunted by the fact that the court did not forthrightly bring legalized segregation to an end. To secure a unanimous decision, Chief Justice Earl Warren had written an opinion that avoided directly overturning *Plessy* by limiting it to segregation within public schools, never referring to state-sponsored segregation in general. Citing a study by psychologist Kenneth Clark that showed black children preferred white dolls to black dolls, Warren concluded that segregated *schools* created a sense of inferiority among *children* who were racially isolated. That particular type of segregation was therefore inherently inequitable and violated the Equal Protection clause of the Fourteenth Amendment. Warren said nothing about the feelings of inferiority children might develop from sitting at the back of the bus, a fact duly noted by Montgomery's white public officials. Further, the Supreme Court ruled that desegregation within schools must be accomplished with "all deliberate speed." Many southern whites vowed that such speedy deliberation would persist well into the distant future. Contrary to what Dr. and Mrs. King had been told, they had entered a world determined to resist change.[8]

The Montgomery chapter of the NAACP, which King had immediately joined, interpreted the *Brown* decision quite differently from the Montgomery officials, seeing it as forbidding all forms of state-sponsored segregation. Its opportunity to challenge the status quo came in December 1955, when NAACP secretary Rosa Parks was arrested for refusing to yield her bus seat to a white passenger. Jubilant, the head of the local NAACP cried, "We can go to the Supreme Court with this . . . and boycott the bus line at the same time." To bring ministers and community leaders together to plan the boycott, King offered Dexter Church as a meeting place, despite his status as a young newcomer to Montgomery. The more firmly established ministers deferred to the selection of King as the leader of the Montgomery Improvement Association, perhaps because of mutual jealousies among them, perhaps because each feared the consequences of failure, perhaps because many intuited that this well-educated man from Atlanta, with his rich baritone voice, could galvanize the community—or, most likely, because of all the above.[9]

Desegregation Moves Forward

The choice proved to be inspired, and the Montgomery boycott was so successful that King was immediately transformed into a national figure. For a few years, the Southern Christian Leadership

Martin Luther King Jr. escorts children to a previously all-white public school in Grenada, Mississippi, in 1966, at a time when the civil rights movement was reaching its high-water mark.

Conference (SCLC), which King organized, led a movement that progressed from height to height through Albany, Birmingham, Selma, and on to Washington, D.C., culminating in the mid-1960s with the passage of several pieces of civil rights legislation which racially integrated most of the nation's social, economic, political, and cultural institutions. The Civil Rights Act of 1964 opened all public accommodations—buses, trains, shopping malls, hotels, restaurants—to anyone, regardless of race or ethnicity. The National Voting Rights Act of 1965 gave federal marshals the power to enforce African Americans' right to participate in southern elections. Corporations made serious efforts to recruit African Americans, colleges established scholarships for minority students, the number of elected black officials climbed steadily, black athletes won widespread respect and admiration, African American faces appeared on stage, screen, and television, and an African American with the unlikely name of Barack Obama was elected president. None of those changes have ended more subtle forms of racial discrimination, and racial segregation, as we shall see, would remain strongly entrenched in residential communities, but the progress that has been made is not conceivable apart from the work of Martin Luther King Jr. and other civil rights leaders of that day. King's assassination in Memphis, Tennessee, on April 4, 1968, brought down a great American leader, but it did not stop the processes of racial accommodation and accord.[10]

King's impact on school segregation itself was almost as dramatic, especially when contrasted with the slow pace of reform in the years immediately following the *Brown* decision. Before King mobilized public opinion, desegregation had been implemented only in the schools of Topeka, Kansas (to which the *Brown* decision directly applied), Washington, D.C. (at President Eisenhower's insistence), and the border states of Missouri, Maryland, Kentucky, and West Virginia. Elsewhere, most schools remained as segregated as ever. The states of the old Confederacy formed a stone wall as solid as the line of defense Thomas Jackson had established at the First Battle of Bull Run. They used every social, political, legislative, and juridical tactic available to delay for more than a decade the application of the *Brown* decision to their schools. Only the most token desegregation measures were introduced, and then in just a few symbolic places. Nor had desegregation advanced at any faster clip in the North. The *Brown* decision, northerners thought, applied solely to the South; only there did state laws separate the two races.

The pace of desegregation picked up dramatically in 1968, however. The stone wall crumbled, as courts quickly struck down the repeated southern attempts to evade the requirements of *Brown*. The U.S. Department of Health, Education, and Welfare stated that federal education funding would be granted to southern school districts only if they made clear progress toward a desegregated school system. The Nixon administration asked for—and received from Congress—extra money for any school district undergoing desegregation, sweetening the pill southerners were learning to accept. Northern schools, too, were being pressed by civil rights groups to change school district boundaries and to bus students out of their neighborhoods into integrated learning environments. The proportion of white students at the school the average African American attended increased from 22 percent to 34 percent, and the index of black-white segregation (where 1.0 represents complete apartheid and zero represents the same racial distribution at each school) fell from 0.72 to 0.56. The drop was particularly large in the states of the Southeast, all of whom were part of the former Confederacy. In those states, the segregation index fell from about 0.77 to about 0.35.[11]

The Desegregation Drive Stalls

Just when it seemed that a passion for racial justice would sweep from sea to shining sea, school desegregation came virtually to a halt. After 1972, hardly any additional desegregation occurred. In 2000, more than 70 percent of African American students were still attending schools that had nonwhite majorities. Nearly 40 percent were attending schools with student bodies whose composition was 90 percent or more nonwhite, about the same percentage as in the early seventies (see Figure 11 in the Appendix).

What happened to King's dream? Certainly, it had not stalled for lack of trying. Protests were launched, lawsuits were filed, school desegregation plans were devised, court orders were written and enforced, and some school boards took decisive action when pressed to do so. To provide a more uniform racial mix in schools, attendance boundaries were changed, larger schools were built (so as to include students from both white and black neighborhoods), magnet schools were created to attract a racially mixed student body, and, most controversially, students were bused from their neighborhoods to schools across the city. Yet the more things changed, the more they stayed the same. Whites proved more willing to accept integration in public life than in their homes, communities, and local schools.[12]

In Chicago's liberal, Jewish South Shore community, for example, an interracial group had proposed a two-way busing plan (blacks one way, whites the other) designed to ensure that each school in the neighborhood would be 60–70 percent white, a percentage thought to be enough to avoid the "tipping point" at which whites would leave in droves. The Chicago school board, finding two-way busing too controversial, offered instead a one-way scheme under which only black pupils would be bused. That divided the community group, and the entire busing scheme fell apart. In the words of the community association's president, "If the superintendent's staff had deliberately set out to kill the busing program, . . . it could not have done a better job." Before long, racial transition accelerated on the South Shore, and the neighborhood became almost completely African American.[13]

The South Shore group had at least made a good-faith effort to stem the racial tide. Elsewhere, the migration of whites to racially homogeneous settings continued apace, without much concerted effort to stop it. Since whites were fleeing the central cities for suburban school districts, civil rights advocates proposed to achieve racially integrated schools by way of metropolitan-wide two-way desegregation plans. African American students would be bused to suburban districts in exchange for whites, who would be brought into the central city. When such a plan was proposed for the Detroit metropolitan area, opposition became so intense that plaintiffs had to battle the case all the way to the U.S. Supreme Court, setting the stage for *Milliken v. Bradley* (1974), the most important school desegregation case since *Brown*.

The decision in *Milliken* went against the plaintiffs. The Supreme Court drew a distinction between the *de jure* (that is, legal) segregation in the South and the *de facto* (happenstance) segregation in the North. If schools become racially distinctive as the result of individual decisions, the court ruled, then school boards have no obligation to alter the racial composition of the schools. Writing for the majority, Warren Burger, who had succeeded Earl Warren as chief justice, opined: "Without an inter-district violation and inter-district effect, there is no continuous wrong calling for an inter-district remedy." The lower courts, in calling for metropolitan-wide desegregation, were trying to produce "the racial balance which they perceived as desirable." But, said Burger, the Constitution "does not require any particular racial balance." Replied Justice Thurgood Marshall (whom Lyndon Johnson had appointed to the Court): "Under a Detroit-only decree, Detroit's schools will clearly remain racially identifiable. . . . Schools with 65 percent and more Negro students will stand in sharp and obvious contrast to schools in neighboring [suburban] districts with less than 2 percent Negro enrollment. Negro students will continue to perceive their schools as segregated educational facilities, and this perception will only be increased when whites react to a Detroit-only decree by fleeing to the suburbs to avoid integration." Few predictions have been so on target. Subsequent to *Milliken,* central-city schools throughout the United States became predominantly minority, while most suburban school systems remained overwhelmingly white.[14]

Supreme Court decisions are not written in political isolation. The Court, in *Milliken,* merely codified a new political mood that had strengthened since King's assassination. The turning point had already come two years earlier, when King shifted his focus from the South to northern cities. His initial target was Chicago, geographically the country's most segregated city. Most blacks lived on the south and west sides, while whites lived north of downtown Chicago. Schools were as segregated as the neighborhoods around them. Gangs were well organized, crime rates high, and racial animosities intense, perhaps even more so than in many southern locales. The city was held together by its powerful mayor, Richard J. Daley.

King's decision to challenge Mayor Daley must be judged a mistake, at least in the short run. Though the SCLC demonstrated that segregation was not merely a southern problem, King encountered strong resistance from a powerful mayor. In the process, he alienated previously sympathetic white northerners and triggered civil violence. Even before King arrived in Chicago, a major disturbance had broken out two years earlier in the Watts neighborhood of Los Angeles. Originally thought to be an anomaly, it foreshadowed uprisings in Chicago, New York, Detroit, Philadelphia, and, upon King's assassination, in American cities across the country. The consequences were dreadful. Businesses in black communities were burned out, never to recover. Central-city housing was left to deteriorate, as landlords hoped fire insurance would help them recoup some of their losses. The housing stock for low-income families located within a block of our South Side home, in the same Kenwood neighborhood into which the Obama family would later move, was steadily disappearing because landlords were making no effort to maintain it. Whites fled to suburbia at an ever-faster pace. Our family moved a mile closer to the university, next to the University of Chicago's Laboratory School, where our growing children attended school.[15]

Racial conflicts penetrated into the schoolhouse itself. When a district desegregated its schools, principals were often overwhelmed. So says Gerald Grant, the careful biographer of the pseudonymous "Hamilton High," a racially changing high school in a middle-sized northern city whose history he recorded. When the school board desegregated the school, the longtime principal found the situation beyond his competence and quickly resigned. To succeed him, the school board picked a young, liberal, well-meaning, out-of-town white principal with a doctorate in educational administration.

The new principal discovered that segregation within the supposedly integrated school remained nearly as clear-cut and obvious as in old-time Mississippi. Most whites (along with a few middle-class blacks) took advanced courses from the faculty "old guard" and socialized in the library and in math labs. Most African Americans took less challenging courses and used the cafeteria as their social home-away-from-home. The principal sought to "change the schedule of the entire school and make it student oriented rather than teacher oriented," and the privileges of the "old guard" faculty were stripped away. Despite these and other efforts to reach out to black students, "the school was [soon] in chaos . . . and riots . . . were a way of life." Before long, "turf wars over control of the school" were taking place "not only between blacks and whites but also between blacks." The principal was assigned a bodyguard. If a ruckus broke out, teachers hid in their classrooms. When violence reached the breaking point, the principal closed the school—until he realized that "he was giving the students the power to shut the school down."

In 1971, just as the school was reaching the brink of full-blooded racial conflict, with white students as well-armed as black ones, things finally settled down. But by then, "72 percent of the teachers who had taught at Hamilton in 1966 had resigned, retired, or transferred." The well-meaning, well-credentialed principal, too, had been replaced by a no-nonsense math teacher who freely issued school suspensions until he restored a modicum of order.[16]

Not all desegregation efforts generated the sorts of conflicts that racked Hamilton High. At the University of Chicago's Laboratory School, whose board I was now serving on, the student body was racially balanced, comprising the offspring of University of Chicago professors and administrators, as well as wealthy black doctors, lawyers, and other professionals fleeing South Shore and Hyde Park public schools. Even the son of the future mayor of Chicago, Richard Daley II, came all the way from the white Irish working-class neighborhood in which the Daley clan still lived. In such an upscale, upper-middle-class, carefully controlled private setting, racial integration was working very well. In wealthy suburban school districts, racial integration was also occurring peacefully. But the mere fact that integration was peaceful did not necessarily mean all was well, as is revealed by a closer look at what was happening in Shaker Heights, Ohio.

No place took its responsibilities more seriously than Shaker Heights, a city of approximately 30,000 whose proud history goes back to its founding by the enlightened, if childless, Shaker religious sect. Adjacent to Case Western Reserve University and the symphony hall in which the great Cleveland Orchestra performs, Shaker Heights, in 1961, was described by *Cosmopolitan* magazine as the "wealthiest city in the United States, where nearly everyone belongs to a country club and the typical family has three cars, 'most likely a Jaguar, a Porsche or a Ferrari.'" The district schools were Shaker's pride and joy. Actor Paul Newman, San Francisco 49ers cornerback Nate Clements, and the labor economist Caroline Minter Hoxby are among its proud alums. Well into the 1970s, an annual average of sixty-three students were identified as National Merit semifinalists or commended for their high performance.[17]

But even as the city was enjoying its national reputation, the times were changing. Shaker's housing stock was aging, and prosperous baby boomers wanted newer homes, larger yards, and quieter streets farther from Cleveland, with which Shaker shared a border. So even as the reporter for *Cosmopolitan* was writing, the Moreland and Lomond Association was organizing to prevent "white flight" from two of the city's neighborhoods. In 1964 the city banned residents from posting "For Sale" signs. But try as it might, Shaker could not prevent the processes of racial transition from continuing. Despite the fact that most of the newcomers had become part of the homeowning middle class, the school board felt it needed to take action so Moreland would not have to bear the full brunt of the black in-migration. The district had but one high school, so the focus was on the elementary schools. In 1970, the board allowed the transfer of students from neighborhood schools, provided the transfer enhanced racial balance. When that action proved insufficient, the board turned three of the district elementary schools into magnets that ideally would promote racial integration. When that stratagem failed, the board shut down four elementary schools altogether and created a large citywide school for students in the fifth and sixth grades and another 900-pupil school for those in the seventh and eighth grades.

So positive-spirited were its efforts, Shaker Heights became the subject of a well-received ABC-TV special feature proudly produced by a former Shaker student. "Obviously, Shaker is a model. Obviously, there are a lot of good things that are going on," said commentator Robin Roberts as she introduced the show. Added a colleague: "Trying for that better world, a group of families, both black and white, simply decided to live side by side. They chose integration not only for their school, but for their neighborhood." As in any good documentary, racial cross-pressures were explored, but the documentary's ending note was no less upbeat than its beginning: "It is still [one of a] very few places that you see the mix of people and the quality of education in the schools in the same location." The ABC story has become the conventional wisdom. Even the district's most severe critics admitted that "Shaker Heights continuously struggled to make 'literal integration' a reality." The background music to the documentary could have been set to a tune ending in a resounding C-major trumpet blast.[18]

By 2008, one would have needed to add more than one discordant note to the melody, however. For all of the talk about rescuing the city from white flight, more than 50 percent of the students that year were African American and only 37 percent of the student body was European American. That would not have mattered, had student performance remained at levels achieved in the past. But signs of sliding academic achievement were abundant. To take just one example, the number of National Merit semifinalists and commendations earned annually between 2001 and 2008 averaged thirty-five, little more than half the number chalked up in the early seventies. Even that fall from excellence could be accepted, had there been some indication that both blacks and whites were doing as well in school as could be expected, given their initial skill level. But that was not the case. If one considers only those Shaker students who remained in the same school throughout their first four years of elementary school, African Americans kept pace with white students in math for the next four years, but they slipped nearly a year further behind in reading. Among those who remained in the same middle school between fifth and ninth grade, African American students fell a few months further behind in math performance and nearly two years further behind in reading. As a result, in 2008 only 76 percent of Shaker's African American tenth graders passed the state graduation examination in reading, and just 65 percent did so in math. Meanwhile, virtually all white students passed the test.[19]

More than one scholar attempted to account for the continuing racial education gap in Shaker Heights. Anthropologist John Ogbu attributed persistent racial differentials to the alienation of former slaves from a dominant white culture, while John McWhorter said it was due to the deeply entrenched anti-intellectualism within a black community that attacks its most hardworking young people as "Oreos" (black on the outside, yet adhering to "white" values on the inside). Sociologists Anne Galletta and William E. Cross Jr. qualified these interpretations by rooting them in the racial stereotyping black students perceive in the words and actions of their teachers, black and white alike. As a frank young black man put it, "I think the general judgment is, if you're in, if you're a white kid in CP [colored people's] classes, you're lazy, and if you're a black kid in CP classes—it's expected." Another spoke fondly of his years at predominantly black Moreland school, from which his father moved him when given the opportunity. He had been "proud to be from Moreland" because they were "doing big things there," and he was one of the school's best. After he transferred, his school performance fell. "I felt alienated being 'new kid' but also being 'Moreland,'" he said. Another possibility is that black students are in special need of the informal, settled climate of a small elementary school. When forced to attend large, impersonal middle schools, they feel at a loss and alienated from teachers, and they retreat into an antischool peer-group culture.[20]

One does not need to choose among these or other possible explanations of the education gap to conclude that desegregation, for all of its importance to the well-being of American society, was not by itself, even under the best of circumstances, going to create an effective, egalitarian educational system. Indeed, the Shaker Heights phenomenon was widespread enough to provoke a debate within the black community over whether integration was a goal to be pursued at all.

Integrated or Separate Education: The Theoretical Debate

King—a theologian, not a pedagogue—said little about matters educational, except that black and white children should not be artificially separated from one another. Early African American intellectuals such as Frederick Douglass, Booker T. Washington, and W. E. B. Du Bois also imagined a future without racial distinctions. But other, more marginal figures sought to preserve and extend a black culture they found superior to the dominant white one. Marcus Garvey won a popular following for his campaign to unify all African people under a government of their own. Wallace Muhammad formed the Nation of Islam on the principle that blacks were the chosen people. More important, the Harlem Renaissance, an extraordinary burst of creativity in the 1920s by black artists, writers, jazz musicians, entertainers, intellectuals, ministers, businessmen, and politicians, created a sense of pride among those long treated as inferiors.[21]

That rejected strain in black culture entered the mainstream when Black Power became a major theme of the civil rights movement. Stokely Carmichael, H. Rap Brown, and Malcolm X each defined Black Power in his own way, but together they identified an alternative to the integrationist ideal. White fashions were subordinated to hairstyles, jewelry, clothing, and artwork that reflected African American tastes and culture, just as gospel, blues, and jazz had fostered the Harlem Renaissance. Political goals shifted from equal access to affirmative action, community control, and compensatory education. It was less important that African Americans attend integrated schools than that the schools they entered be controlled and staffed by people from their community. The legacy of inferior schooling should be rectified not by moving black students to white schools but by giving extra resources to schools that served the African American community.[22]

Responses to Black Power theorists were surprisingly timid and uncertain. Exactly why racial integration, and not some alternative reform, was necessary if equal educational opportunity was to be realized was generally left unstated. Into this breach walked a white Johns Hopkins University professor, who provided the most enduring case for school integration, a case taken seriously to the present day. The occasion for his contribution was provided by a little-noticed clause buried in the Civil Rights Act of 1964, which called for a "survey concerning the lack . . . of equal opportunities . . . by reason of race, color, religion or national origin in public education." Though not a prominent public figure, James S. Coleman was the logical choice for directing the survey. He had been trained in survey research, was an acknowledged expert on high schools, and was sympathetic to the civil rights movement—he and his son had been arrested at a demonstration in Baltimore.

Coleman, whose life story we save for Chapter 9, agreed to take on the assignment only after "some hesitation" and "extensive discussion" that transformed what at first seemed to be nothing more than a collection of racial-segregation statistics into the first nationwide study of the factors that affect student achievement. Students at 4,000 randomly selected schools across the country were tested in various subjects. The study also collected information on characteristics of the schools the students attended: racial composition, per-pupil expenditures, the college degrees teachers had earned, teacher ability (as measured by performance on a test), the number of books in the school library, and much more. Family-background information was collected as well.[23]

The study was to go forward with more-than-deliberate speed, as results were expected to reveal a need for federal action to equalize educational opportunity, the keystone of Lyndon Johnson's "Great Society." Imagine, then, the shock inside the White House when a draft of the report began circulating inside the administration. Daniel Patrick Moynihan, one of Johnson's top domestic advisers, gave a sense of the reaction when he recalled being greeted in the spring of 1966 by Harvard professor Martin Lipset with the query: "You know what Coleman is finding, don't you?" "I said, 'What?' He said: 'All family.' I said, 'Oh, Lord.'" The next day Moynihan informed the secretary of Health, Education, and Welfare (HEW) to get ready, as the research project was about to produce findings the administration "was not going to like." The project report, later known as "Coleman I" after two additional reports appeared, was released on Independence Day weekend, 1966. That was thought to be a good time to announce negative news, since much of the press was on holiday. The strategy worked: few but academics paid attention, and only gradually did its message sink in.[24]

To everyone's surprise, Coleman I found that within regions and types of communities (urban, suburban, and rural), expenditures per pupil were about the same in black and white schools. Even more remarkable, students did not learn more just because more was spent on their education. Nor did any other material resource of a school have much of an effect on how well Johnny and Suzy read—not the number of students in the class, nor the teacher's credentials, nor the newness of the textbooks, nor the number of books in the library, nor anything physical or material that schools had for years considered important. What did count were a host of family-background characteristics: mother's education, father's education, family income, having fewer siblings, the number of books in the home, and other factors—all of which together explained more of the variation among students in their reading achievement than any school-related factor.[25]

One finding in Coleman I saved the day for the Johnson administration. The authors found that student achievement was affected by the social composition of the pupils at a school. If a low-income African American child had fellow students who were white or from a higher socioeconomic status, the child did better at reading. The converse was not true, however: a white child did not suffer educationally from having black classmates. In other words, the influence of peers was asymmetrical. Desegregation helped blacks without hurting whites. Many years later, the Nobel Prize–winning econometrician James Heckman and his colleague Derek Neal called that asymmetrical result Coleman's "least robust" finding. But Coleman never doubted it. Testifying before the Senate Select Committee on Equal Educational Opportunity, he said black students at segregated schools were "deprived of the most effective educational resources contained in the schools: those brought by other children as a result of their home environment." Whatever regrets the Johnson administration might have had about some parts of Coleman I, it was pleased by the ammunition the report provided for the ongoing desegregation campaign.[26]

So it was truly ironic that Coleman, the very academic whose work provided the clearest educational justification for school desegregation, would in his next major study, the "white flight" study (known as Coleman II), produce findings that called into question many of the policies being used to desegregate the schools. Using data collected by the newly established Civil Rights Commission, Coleman II tracked trends in black and white school enrollments in cities across the United States. He and his colleagues found that white families were moving outward more rapidly from those central cities where racial desegregation plans were being implemented. Coleman expressed concern that, as a practical matter, busing of students within big cities was self-defeating. Within school districts, to be sure, the segregation index fell from 0.63 to 0.37 in the years 1968–1972. But that only intensified segregation between districts. Said Coleman: "The emerging problem with regard to school desegregation is the problem of segregation between central city and suburbs." Schools were at risk of being as segregated as they had ever been, exactly as Justice Marshall had predicted.[27]

Not since Cleopatra heard about Antony's dalliances has a messenger come so close to being poisoned. Scholars turned on Coleman with an unexpected vengeance that introduced a more virulent tone into the world of education policy research. Well-known Harvard psychology professor Thomas F. Pettigrew claimed that Coleman II "should not be taken seriously." The NAACP general counsel called the Chicago sociologist "without a doubt, a first-class fraud. . . . He is not entitled to any credence or any reliability or any belief with respect to the things he says he has found." A *Washington Post* columnist questioned whether Coleman was mixing research with advocacy, quoting the deputy director of the National Science Foundation (and future president of the University of California) Richard Atkinson as saying, "A lot of what goes under the name of social science is just junk. . . . Too often [when] speaking on issues of education [scholars use] research evidence as a disguise for advocating a particular policy." Atkinson was careful not to mention Coleman by name, but such innuendo by distinguished leaders fed the anti-Coleman fire. It flamed into an effort, led by the sociologist Alfred McClung Lee, then the president of the American Sociological Association (ASA), to censure or expel Coleman from the organization's membership for having spread "flammable propaganda." Though that blaze was contained, "few sociologists ever had to endure the high profile public controversy which swirled around him." Years later, Coleman recalled the ASA plenary session held to debate the report: "The passions generated at that session are hard to reconstruct now, but I still have the posters that were plastered at the entrance to the ballroom and behind the podium, covered with Nazi swastikas, epithets, and my name."[28]

In retrospect, the controversy over the report is difficult to comprehend, since the findings, unlike those in Coleman I, merely confirmed what most people already believed. Coleman II found nothing other than what Justice Marshall had predicted in his *Milliken* dissent. Two scholars who originally claimed to find that white flight was not occurring later retracted their conclusions after additional evidence confirmed Coleman's original findings. Eventually,

Like most federal programs, however, ESEA chugged along decade after decade, tinkered with by one Congress after another, until the law provided the foundation upon which a federal accountability system was built. The program, begun in 2002, was given the title No Child Left Behind (NCLB).[30]

In the meantime, Martin Luther King's life and sacrifice helped to heal, at least in part, the deep wounds inflicted by slavery and segregation. But the healing, to the extent it has occurred, took place more clearly outside than inside the schoolhouse. Yes, careful studies show that school desegregation has had positive impacts on student learning, especially in the South. But those positive results have never been large enough or consistent enough to propel the desegregation agenda forward since that brief halcyon moment from 1968 to 1974. Worse, attempts to integrate schools by crosstown busing and other draconian measures embittered blacks and whites alike, especially in the aftermath of urban racial violence.[31]

Schools came under social pressures they had never previously encountered. Facing insistent demands for civil rights and equality of opportunity from one side, while encountering white protests and white flight on the other, schools were caught in the crossfire. More than ever before, school leaders needed the respect and deference of those in their charge. But just when strong backing was most urgently required, school officials lost much of their legal authority to maintain school discipline. What had begun as a demand for racial inclusion developed into a more general campaign against school authority.

The great alternative to desegregation, the Great Society's compensatory-education program, promised a customized educational experience for educationally deprived children. But it produced instead a host of federal regulations designed to ensure the proper allocation of federal dollars so that the poor, and only the poor, would benefit. In the end, the accounting system overwhelmed the educational objective. Ironically, the impact of the school rights revolution would be greater elsewhere than on black achievement. When it came to desegregation of schools, African Americans met stout-hearted resistance from whites North and South, who feared violence at school and who wished to preserve their homogeneous community enclaves. But once civil rights had been forcefully articulated, others began claiming that their rights, too, were being violated. In the new legal and political climate, they now found it easier to accomplish goals that had previously seemed unrealistic. The rights of the outspoken, the disabled, and those who spoke languages other than English became the school agenda for the 1970s.

PART TWO

THE DECLINE

CHAPTER 5

The Rights Movement Diversifies

The authority of the school continues to shrink.

—James S. Coleman, *Foundations of Social Theory* (Cambridge, Mass., 1990)

"The parents are going to get a lawyer, the kid's going to get off, and you're going to look like a fool," observed a teacher at Hamilton High. A second teacher was asked why she did not report students who made sexually degrading comments to her. "Well, it wouldn't have done any good. . . . I didn't have any witnesses." A third reported that she had taken action: "The truth is I saw the kid cheating. I saw him with his open book on his lap during a test. . . . They wanted documentation. The question now is, 'We've heard John's side of the story, what's yours?' As much as I believe in giving due process to kids something grates when I hear, 'What's your side of the story?' Somehow it felt like I'm part of the crime."

The school's rights policy followed recommendations made by the American Civil Liberties Union (ACLU): "The teacher and administrator should bear in mind that accusation is not the equivalent of guilt. . . . Those infractions which may lead to more serious penalties . . . require the utilization of a comprehensive and formal procedure. . . . At the hearing the student . . . and the administrator should have the right to cross-examine witnesses." Incoming freshmen were given advice through an underground handbook on how to make school rules work for them. Cutting classes is easy, it said, because "no one usually misses you." If you want to make it difficult for administrators to find you, "it's never a good idea to put room numbers on your schedule card. If you must . . . make mistakes." Comments Gerald Grant, the school's historian: "Here was the collapse of adult authority as a standard for children."[1]

Hamilton High had come a long way from the days when an 1859 Vermont court ruled that schools acted *in loco parentis*—in place of the parent—not only at school but in its vicinity as well. The court said, "Most parents would expect and desire that teachers would take care that their children, in going to and returning from school, should not loiter, or seek evil company." For 110 years, that precept did not change. But once civil rights had been placed on the national agenda, it was only natural that the idea would extend itself. Precepts have a way of spilling over from one domain to another, and few are as pregnant with possibility as the principle that individuals have rights. It appeals to every person's sense of autonomy and purpose. In education, it seems only right that each person have personalized instruction adapted to his or her own wants and needs. And it takes a good deal of thought to realize that when one person has a right, another acquires a duty. In this case, the duties would accrue to teachers and other school officials, who all of a sudden no longer had the responsibility to act *in loco parentis* but now had the duty to take care that all due process was followed before exercising school discipline. Rights talk, once unleashed, is not easily bounded, least of all when judges are involved.[2]

The connection between the rights of African American students and those of other students was more than conceptual. Rights extensions were advanced by specific individuals and groups closely associated with the civil rights movement. Many of the attorneys involved had received their law degree from Yale, a fountainhead of new rights thinking. Many Yale grads and other Ivy Leaguers were finding employment within the Legal Services Program (LSP) of the Office of Economic Opportunity (OEO), the principal bureaucratic arm of Lyndon Johnson's antipoverty program. The LSP had been set in place in 1964, the very year the civil rights movement reached its height. According to one of its directors, the law would be the principle instrument of educational reform: "Legal Services constituted a better investment in education than Head Start which absorbed most of OEO's 'education' budget." The program was committed to putting into practice principles set forth by Minnesota's up-and-coming senator Walter Mondale. In his 1970 "Justice for Children" address, the senator called for the expansion of the "rights of children vis-à-vis institutions—[including the] rights of children in school to engage in free expression and not to be subjected to discipline without due process."[3]

Working together with the Ford, Rockefeller and other foundations, as well as with newly formed action-oriented interest groups, the LSP pushed the rights agenda in multiple directions. In addition to securing due process for all students, its work helped win the right to equal educational opportunity for the disabled and appropriate education for linguistic minorities.

The movement gained most of its strength from rights talk, but it also capitalized on society's desire to have a more customized educational system. Just as John Dewey's plea for a child-centered educational system resonated with families and educators alike, so the claim that each student had certain rights at school was essentially an insistence that schools accommodate the specific needs and wants of each individual. A rising professional class resented its children's entrapment in regimented schools run by officials insistent upon their authority. Even after the Vietnam War came to an end, the suspicious, antibureaucratic spirit of the times remained intact. Similarly, the creation of an individualized program for each disabled person went beyond the mere the right to attend school to a right to an appropriate program specifically designed for a certain student's needs. And those who came from a non-English-speaking home needed a culturally sensitive, bilingual instructional program suited to their situation.

Customization by right differed from Dewey's child-centered ideal, however. To realize his vision, Dewey relied on a cadre of progressive professional educators, not on attorneys, courts, and bureaucrats. The new customization, paradoxically, had to be standardized so that it could be enforced. Instead of customizing schooling, the legalization of American education merely added another layer of centralized controls over its practice. Despite the attractiveness of each legal step, the overall march threatened the local vitality and spirit that for more than a century had been the hallmark of the American system.

Due Process Rights

In 1969, three high school students in Des Moines, Iowa, were suspended for wearing black armbands to protest the Vietnam War. Relying on long-standing precedents, lower courts rejected student claims of a right to free speech at school, but the U.S. Supreme Court, in *Tinker v. Des Moines,* overturned those rulings, saying, "It can hardly be argued that either students or teachers shed their constitutional rights to freedom of speech or expression at the schoolhouse gate. In our system, state-operated schools may not be enclaves of totalitarianism. School officials do not possess absolute authority over their students." Especially noteworthy in the quoted passage is the fact that the court treated "students" and "teachers" as having equivalent free speech rights inside the schoolhouse. *In loco parentis* no longer.[4]

The *Tinker* decision might have remained a relic of the Vietnam era, with no particular consequences for school life once that divisive war had come to an end. Instead, it became enshrined in law, not to be overturned when a more conservative Court was installed. Nor did the Court limit itself to ensuring the right to free speech at school. In addition, students could not be asked to wear school uniforms unless parents gave their consent, and appropriate procedures had to be followed before students could be subjected to disciplinary actions.

Even as conservative a court as the one sitting in 2007 was unwilling to overturn *Tinker* when it had the opportunity to do so, the day the "bong hits" case arrived on its desk. In 2002, as the Olympic torch was passing through Juneau, Alaska, Joseph Frederick

In an incident that initiated a Supreme Court decision denying students the right to advocate illegal activities at school events (*Morse v. Frederick*, 2007), high school students in Juneau, Alaska, held up a banner advocating drug use as the Olympic torch approached on its way to Salt Lake City in 2002.

Clay Good / ZUMA Press.

had lofted a sign proclaiming "Bong Hits 4 Jesus" above the cheering crowd outside the local high school. The meaning of the sign had been a matter of dispute, except for the generally known fact that marijuana can be smoked with a water pipe known as a bong. Deborah Morse, the principal at the school, had suspended Frederick for advocating "substances that are illegal to minors." But a federal court, relying on *Tinker,* had found the suspension to be a violation of Frederick's free-speech rights.[5]

Justice Clarence Thomas wanted to use the occasion to reverse *Tinker.* But no court majority could be found for so draconian a ruling. Instead, by a 5–4 majority, the Supreme Court reversed the lower court on the narrow ground that Frederick had no school-yard right to advocate illegal activity. In his opinion, Chief Justice John Roberts made it clear that the court was not stripping from students the right to comment "on any political or social issue." That reassurance did not satisfy the Supreme Court's four-member minority, however, who remained disturbed that "the Court does serious violence to the First Amendment in upholding—indeed, lauding—a school's decision to punish Fredrick for expressing a view with which it disagreed."[6]

The minority must have been at least partly reassured, however, by a subsequent rejection of a Napa Valley, California, school board's decision to order all lettering removed from students' clothes and backpacks. The board wanted to discourage the formation of gangs and eliminate other educational distractions. Still, some students insisted on wearing "Tigger" (of *Winnie-the-Pooh* fame) socks, "Jesus Freak" T-shirts, and promotions of breast cancer awareness. When the ACLU filed a lawsuit on their behalf, the district judge declared that such slogans were protected speech, so long as they did not "materially and substantially disrupt the work and discipline of the school." As a nod to the school board, the judge said he would allow school uniforms—so long as parents could opt out of conformity with such a policy.[7]

Protecting student speech and clothing from school authorities is not the only issue involved. School suspensions of any kind must be administered with the greatest care. In *Goss v. Lopez,* a 1975 case, several students in Ohio had been suspended from school for ten days without being given a hearing. The Supreme Court objected, reasoning that students have a right to a public education, a right that cannot be withdrawn "on grounds of misconduct, absent fundamentally fair procedures to determine whether the misconduct has occurred. . . . Where a person's good name, reputation, honor, or integrity is at stake, proper procedures must be followed." Since only ten-day suspensions had been imposed, the Court ruled that legal formalities were not required in this instance, but "longer suspensions or expulsions . . . may require more formal procedures."

That same year the Supreme Court, in *Wood v. Strickland,* had held school board members liable for the violation of the rights granted in *Goss.* An Arkansas board had expelled three girls for bringing intoxicating drinks into the school, and the board had done so without first giving the defendants the right to dispute the evidence upon which their expulsion was based. "A school board member is not immune from liability for damages . . . if he knew or reasonably should have known that the action he took . . . would violate the constitutional rights of the student affected," opined the Court majority. In response to this ruling, school systems elaborated complex procedures to protect themselves. A former superintendent noted: "In Fairfax County [Virginia], not unlike any other place, a youngster who is suspended from school for one day [can appeal] from the school to the area office to the superintendent's office to a three-member panel of the . . . school board, and then to the full board."[8]

Goss and *Wood* were decided at a time when school discipline cases were being appealed to higher-level federal courts with increasing frequency, rising to a high of sixty cases decided in 1974, mainly as a result of the stout efforts of OEO's Legal Services

Program. After the program was curtailed by a Republican White House, the number of cases fell to twenty to thirty cases a year for the next two decades, but during the 1990s legal activism increased once again and the number of cases filed rose sixty-five a year in the first decade of the twenty-first century.[9]

Due process rights are not as thoroughgoing as some advocates would like. The Supreme Court has refused to extend to student lockers the same protection from searches as those given a private home; nor has it banned random testing for drugs; nor has it ever forbidden paddling junior high students on the grounds that spanking is "cruel and unusual punishment." Instead, it has been left to lower courts and broader changes in social norms to greatly reduce the number of recorded instances of the exercise of corporal punishment.[10]

Even so, court-ordered rights and duties penetrated the thinking of teachers and students alike, shaping the ways teachers and students related to one another. According to one national survey of teachers, half of them did not think they could lower a student grade for disciplinary purposes; and of the remaining half, a third said that it could be done only if a formal hearing were held. A survey found that 60 percent of students felt themselves entitled to formal due process protections, including the right to cross-examine witnesses, if faced with an expulsion or long-term suspension. A third thought similar protections were available if they were suspended from extracurricular activities or had their grades lowered for disciplinary reasons.[11]

Some of the changes were undoubtedly for the better. Even that old Victorian Winston Churchill, who as a schoolboy had been ruthlessly beaten for his misbehavior, could hardly have objected to the demise of corporal punishment. But how much educationally is lost when the authority of the teacher in the classroom is systematically undermined? Do teachers ask less of their students in order to minimize potential sources of conflict? Even as schools were addressing such questions, they had to turn their attention to still another set of litigants demanding their constitutional rights: the disabled.

Disability Law and Practice

Ideas are particularly compelling when vested interests are not concentrated in opposition. If an idea costs the taxpayer but no one else, it has a decent chance of being taken seriously. If costs are fairly small (or seem to be), all the better. If the idea can be humanized through personal stories, the cause is further advanced. If the human drama can be told in a courtroom as a civil rights violation, victory is near at hand. That, in a nutshell, explains how special education came quickly out of the closet in the early 1970s, to become a component of the country's educational system.

Just as it is almost impossible today to imagine the racial segregation of the early 1950s, it is difficult to comprehend the widespread exclusion of the disabled from public schools of the early seventies. The science of IQ testing developed during the progressive era legitimated a practice that was thought to be practical, not inhumane. Those with profound mental deficiencies were identified as "cretins" or "idiots" beyond educational remediation. The less severely retarded were called "feeble-minded" and assigned to custodial institutions.

New ideas were in the air, however. As early as the Eisenhower years, federal agencies were encouraging new research on the education of the disabled. John Kennedy, whose sister Rosemary had been identified as mentally retarded, appointed a presidential commission that argued for "a new legal, as well as social concept, of the retarded." The number of colleges and universities offering programs in special education went up from forty in the late 1950s to around three hundred by 1970.[12]

That year my wife and I celebrated the arrival of our eldest son.

When we learned he was autistic, we were told that public schooling might not be appropriate for him. At the time, only half the disabled population was participating in a publicly provided educational program. Fortunately, a broader conception of the educational rights and needs of the disabled was drawing nigh.[13]

Death by fire provided the human drama which initiated far-reaching change. A boy had died at Pennhurst State School, an institution in Altoona, Pennsylvania, that offered care for the mentally retarded. Officially, the death, never reported to his mother, was caused by pneumonia, but an investigation undertaken a year later identified burns on his body. One of the boy's friends said, "Johnnie died in a fire." The truth of the matter is still unknown, but the tale was enough to persuade the Pennsylvania Association for Retarded Children (PARC) to pursue a legal case against the school. Attorney Thomas Gilhool took on the case as a pro bono assignment. Drawing upon a strategy he had learned as an LSP employee, he recommended that PARC file a federal lawsuit "based on the claim that residents enjoyed a constitutional right to an education that was being denied them on the spurious grounds that they were uneducable."[14]

PARC v. Commonwealth of Pennsylvania had few precedents to draw upon. But one overwhelmingly significant fact worked to its advantage: the state was unwilling to defend itself. From the beginning, Pennsylvania's director of special education, in theory a party to the defense, was giving plaintiffs information and advice through an intermediary. With his help, the plaintiffs were able to recruit experts who testified at a preliminary hearing that all retarded children could learn at least "some degree of self-care." That was enough to persuade the state to drop its defense and, in 1971, consent to an agreement requiring that all disabled children be provided with a free, appropriate public education in as normal a setting as possible with whatever special assistance they required. The judge later provided a constitutional basis for the agreement. He said the plaintiffs' right to an education had been denied without due process. In short, a constitutional right had been constructed by a consent decree agreed to prior to trial.

Meanwhile, there were parallel developments in Washington, D.C. Two advocacy groups for the disabled, working with a recent Yale Law School graduate, filed a suit against the District of Columbia's school system. Once again, they had the cooperation of district officials, who failed to appeal a trial court's decision that went against the schools.

The facts of the case were not contested. Students such as twelve-year-old Peter Mills, who were identified as mentally retarded, autistic, or otherwise disabled, were being denied access to public schools on the grounds that education was inappropriate for them or because they were a "behavior problem." The school district defended its actions on the grounds that it lacked the funds necessary to provide the requisite facilities. Rejecting that claim out of hand, the court said all children were entitled to an appropriate education, which could not be denied on the grounds of inadequate resources (*Mills v. Board of Education*, 1972). The judge based his ruling on the Equal Protection clause of the Fourteenth Amendment. Despite the large constitutional implications of the judgment, the school district did not appeal.

So at this point two courts—one in Pennsylvania and another in the District of Columbia—had found that the disabled had some kind of constitutional right to education. Still, the right was hardly secure. One judge discovered the right in the Fourteenth Amendment's Due Process clause, while the other rooted it in the Equal Protection clause. Success in both cases had been facilitated by a cooperative defense, and no higher court had made any ruling. At this point, the disability advocates had two choices. Either they could continue filing suits in one state after another until a case finally reached the Supreme Court, as the civil rights movement originally had done over the many years before the *Brown* decision was handed down; or they could try to secure the rights of the disabled by means of a federal statute. The court-focused strategy might have made sense at the height of the Warren Court. But President Nixon had already appointed four new justices—Warren Burger, William Rehnquist, Harry Blackmun, and Lewis Powell Jr.—all of whom were casting more conservative votes than their predecessors had. In light of these changes, a legislative strategy was more appealing. Democrats still controlled Congress, and many were eager to place the Nixon administration on the defensive.

It made good political sense then for advocates to forgo a legal strategy in favor of a march on Washington—"march," that is, if phone calls and backroom meetings with subcommittee staff members on Capitol Hill can be given that label. A near-silent revolution was about to take place. The campaign did not bring students in wheelchairs to Washington, and no nationwide letter-writing campaign was ever mobilized. The bill progressed without opposition from the school districts that eventually would have to underwrite much of the cost. No partisan cleavage opened up. Teacher unions rather presciently worried about the provision of the bill that said disabled students should be taught in the "least restrictive environment" feasible, but they never mobilized their members against it. The closest thing to a real fight was the struggle between two congressional staff members over which senator was to get credit for the law. The senators themselves didn't seem to care all that much. In the end, the law sailed through Congress with overwhelming support, in a form that came close to a virtual restatement of the rights the judges had set forth in *PARC* and *Mills*. President Gerald Ford signed the bill into law, despite his own misgivings concerning its fiscal impact, in part because his own special-education expert refused to write a veto message. Here was an idea no vested interest seemed willing to oppose.[15]

The Education of All Handicapped Children Act, later known as the Individuals with Disabilities Education Act (IDEA), the moniker we shall use here, broke new ground in multiple ways. For the first time, states were asked to provide "free appropriate education" for all children with disabilities from ages three to twenty-one. No longer could a person be deprived of an education because school officials did not think he or she could learn.[16]

Also for the first time, federal sanction was given to parents' deeply held desire to provide their children with a customized education. What had been theorized by Rousseau and championed by Dewey now became federal law. Appropriately enough, the education to be provided was called "special." Each student diagnosed as disabled was someone special who needed a distinctive educational program. The Individualized Education Plan, as it was called, was developed by school professionals in consultation with family members. Children were to receive both an appropriate education and all other needed services, such as counseling, medical attention, therapy, and the like. If the parents did not agree with the plan, they could appeal to a hearing officer and ultimately to the courts. In its first decision interpreting the law, the Supreme Court identified customization as one of the statute's key components. "A free appropriate education" was provided, so long as the school district offered "personalized instruction with sufficient support services to permit the child to benefit educationally from that instruction." Further, "Congress placed every bit as much emphasis upon giving parents and guardians a large measure of participation at every stage of the administrative process as it did upon [any] substantive standard." Legalization now meant customization and attention to the wishes of the client.[17]

IDEA broke further new ground when it declared that cost considerations were irrelevant. Following *Mills,* it prohibited districts from denying a disabled person an appropriate education simply because the district could not afford it. Congress itself appropriated only limited funds, foisting the bulk of the costs onto the states and districts. Those costs rose steadily, in part because the percentage of students enrolled in special education increased from 8.3 in 1977 to 13.6 in 2007. That increase was largely due to the identification of more students with specific learning disabilities. The percentage of students suffering from more serious disabilities remained fairly constant, with the important exception of autism, the detected incidence of which increased from 0.1 percent to 0.5 percent in the decade 1997–2006.[18]

Rising costs have created tensions between advocates for the disabled and those responsible for general school operations. But both sides agree that the federal government should pick up a larger share of the cost. In response to such pressures, federal funding for the disabled increased to the point where it became the largest component of the K–12 education budget during the George W. Bush administration, and in the Obama stimulus package it doubled beyond its previous high.

The fiscal debate receives more attention than it perhaps deserves. Those who have examined the issue carefully have concluded that special education explains "only a small portion of total spending and of spending growth" that occurred during the late twentieth century. According to one study, districts agreed to private-sector placements in fewer than 2 percent of all special-education cases, and the amount used for that purpose in 2000 constituted only 0.24 percent of the total K–12 budget. Overall, the special-education share of total revenue for public education did not change in the quarter-century of 1977–2003. Costs of special education rose, but at the same rate as all other school expenditures.[19]

Rising costs are not the main challenge that special education poses to the functioning of American schools. Much more significant is the requirement that each eligible student be educated in the "least restrictive environment" feasible. No official interpretation of this phrase has ever been handed down by the Supreme Court. But special-education advocates, federal bureaucrats, and state officials have increasingly interpreted it as requiring instruction in regular classrooms whenever possible, a practice known as "inclusion" or "mainstreaming."

Three factors have facilitated the drive toward mainstreaming. For one thing, it is often the least expensive option. As one special-education attorney put it, "Many school districts are using it as a pretext to avoid having to pay for appropriate special education." Second, some parents insist that their disabled child be included in a regular classroom, because they believe that in this environment the child will learn more, educationally and socially. Other parents worry, however, that their child may receive inappropriate instruction or be harassed by other students, so they prefer customized instruction in a separate setting. Third, advocates argue that the disabled child and the African American child both have the same right to inclusion. If the disability is mild, that argument can be quite persuasive. It makes little sense to separate out students with moderate dyslexia, speech deficiencies, learning problems, and other mild disadvantages. Also, most of those with physical disabilities, even severe ones, need not be separated if schools are architecturally well designed. But in other instances, the disabled child needs the personalized attention of specialists familiar with his or her specific disability. What may be needed can vary enormously, depending on whether the child is autistic, brain damaged, blind, deaf, mentally retarded, dyslexic, hyperactive, mentally disturbed, suffering from severe attention disorder, or otherwise challenged.[20]

Determining what is best for each child requires thoughtful consideration by trained professionals, and school districts try to personalize their special-education offerings. But in making the mainstreaming decision, schools cannot—at least not officially— consider the well-being of the other students at the school. To consider impacts on other students runs against the *Mills* rule, which requires that each special child receive all appropriate educational and related services. Yet the impact on schools and classrooms can be severe if the mainstreaming requirement is applied by rule rather than according to the specific situation at hand.

Such was the experience on September 29, 2006, when the high school principal of Cazenovia, Wisconsin, a quiet village populated by some 300-plus residents a couple of hours' drive northwest of Madison, was killed by a fifteen-year-old boy. The alleged assailant, Eric Hainstock, was seriously troubled, a person who had been identified in second grade as having Attention Deficit Hyperactivity Disorder. Because of his repeated classroom outbursts and unpleasant encounters with peers, the school psychologist had recommended he be placed in a private school. But school policy in Wisconsin, as in many other states, is to try to keep students mainstreamed. A student is deemed to have a disability that requires a separate setting only if a behavior problem is detected somewhere other than at school—a policy instituted, apparently, because the school situation might be the fault of the teacher or the principal, not the student. Hainstock did not qualify for a special setting because his family insisted he had no problems at home or in the community. In any case, the school district serving Cazenovia tried, according to its superintendent, to "adjust and monitor so as many students as possible remain mainstreamed."[21]

That same year, an autistic sophomore in a well-heeled suburb of Boston stabbed a fellow student to death, and a high schooler with mental illness in Tacoma, Washington, used a gun to murder a fellow student. According to a General Accounting Office report, fifty out of every one thousand students in special education engage in serious misconduct (carry a weapon or engage in violent behavior), as compared to fifteen out of a thousand students not so classified.[22]

Cazenovia is not the only town where interpretations of federal law lean heavily toward mainstreaming special-education students whenever possible. Of the nearly six million students diagnosed as being in need of special education, fewer than 2 percent are placed in a private school. The percentage of students considered to be "fully mainstreamed" rose from little more than 30 in 1989 to nearly 55 in 2005. The percentage of "emotionally disturbed children" who spend more than 80 percent of their time in a regular classroom jumped from 17 to 35 during the decade ending in 2005.[23]

For classroom teachers, the challenges can be enormous, especially since pupils in need of special education cannot be suspended for actions beyond their control. In Scranton, Pennsylvania, teacher Patricia McDermott discovered she had five disabled first-graders in her class of nineteen. One was known for having frequently disrupted kindergarten class, so the teacher decided to have the child sit immediately next to her desk. According to a newspaper account, "The strategy backfired. One morning, Andrea swept an arm along the teacher's desk, scattering framed photos of Ms. McDermott's family across the classroom. A glass frame shattered, and another hit a student in the arm. Though no one was hurt, Ms. McDermott says she lost hours of instruction time getting the children to settle down after the disruption." Mainstreaming became a collective-bargaining issue for the Scranton chapter of the American Federation of Teachers. The president of a local parents group was no less concerned: "The general consensus is that it doesn't work having all these kids together."[24]

Of all the rights reforms in American education, those pertaining to the disabled have been among the most consequential. Classroom practices have become customized to individual needs, and public awareness of and sympathy for those with disabilities has been enhanced. In the movies, it's no longer the basketball hero but the boy sensitive to the oddities of the disabled who gets the girl. Personally, I am most grateful. I can now take my autistic son to the annual Thanksgiving high school football game without worrying that his perpetual motion will evoke catcalls and unreasonable stares. Yet a single student who needs extra attention can affect the learning of an entire class. For example, a careful study of Florida classrooms found noticeably lower overall student performance if a class had one or more students at risk of abuse at home—abuse being a frequent source of emotional and behavioral disability. Impacts on the boys in the classroom were greatest, especially if the student at risk was also a male.[25]

A more general risk is that good intentions can be taken too far. When mainstreaming decisions are made with only the needs of the disabled child in mind, the consequences for others can become problematic. When those needs are defined as much by a bureaucratic rule or a professional ideology as by assessment of the situation at hand, the risks to teaching and learning are all the greater.

From Bilingual Education to English-Language Learners

The rights of the disabled constituted a new idea, which was not articulated on a national scale until the latter decades of the twentieth century. Bilingual instruction, on the other hand, was an old idea that had been flatly rejected. Immigrants time and again tried to preserve their languages in the New World, but that world, once it began to age, had little time for a welter of immigrant languages— at least not until the rights movement created new sensitivities. Even then, bilingual education proved to be a delicate flower. English has been one of the few things that held Americans together, and it has become the language of international commerce. Efforts to preserve other languages make little sense, even to many immigrants themselves.

Yet language preservation was at the very heart of the original American experience. My children were told at the Thanksgiving table that the Pilgrims had come to America in search of religious freedom. That tale was not the whole story, however, as the Pilgrims had already succeeded in securing their religious liberties on their prior move from England to Holland. Their migration across the Atlantic was motivated as much by the fear that their children would forget the English language and acquire Dutch habits and customs.

Immigrants ever since have sought to protect their home cultures. Among the most successful were the Germans, who in late-nineteenth-century America established private schools in which their native tongue was the language of instruction. Even some public schools did the same. In 1866, the Chicago school district offered courses in German whenever 150 people in a part of the city requested it, a quota easily met. The practice was defended as a recruitment strategy for the public schools. Said the chairman of the German-language committee on the school board, "The number of private schools now to be found in every nook and corner of the city will decrease, and the children of all nationalities will be assembled in the public schools, and thereby be radically Americanized." Bilingual instruction became common throughout the German-speaking Midwest.[26]

The idea of German-language instruction in the public schools met increasing resistance, however. In the 1890s, the Republican-controlled Illinois legislature tried to ban it from the state altogether. Enough Germans switched parties in 1892 to elect a German-speaking Democrat as governor, so the practice was retained until the United States was drawn into World War I and tolerance of German evaporated altogether. Illinois, along with Texas, Nebraska, Oregon, and many other states, enacted legislation stipulating that the language of instruction in public schools had to be English. It took a U.S. Supreme Court decision to keep Nebraska from banning bilingual instruction from *private* schools.[27]

As anti-immigration sentiment rippled across the country, bilingual education virtually disappeared. An American could be of any race or creed—but to be an American, he or she had to speak English. To pass the nationalization examination, an adult had to know the U.S. Constitution and take the test in English. Similarly, a child, to succeed in school, had to speak the country's dominant language. Thus, my father, born into an entirely Danish-speaking home, learned English so well after seven years at school that by midlife he could no longer understand his native tongue. Teachers in those days did not leave the learning of English to chance. When children drifted off into their native tongue, reprimands were in order. In enforcing Texas law, one teacher went beyond the call of duty: the young Lyndon B. Johnson whipped his students if he heard them speaking their native Spanish.[28]

Laws mandating instruction in English are not entirely unjustified, from an educational point of view. In the case of young migrant children, complete immersion in the dominant language of their adopted society may be the quickest means to help them acquire the new tongue. That was teacher Lyndon Johnson's theory, and not a few specialists in language acquisition endorse it today. A case can also be made for teaching content in a student's native tongue, along with English as a second language, especially if the student arrived in the United States past the age of childhood. Students can learn substantive material in their native tongue even while learning English as a second language. Some excellent U.S. schools take pride in simultaneously teaching Spanish to their English-speaking students and English to their Spanish-speaking students. In this way, instruction and peer-group culture reinforce each other. The best rule on language acquisition is probably to avoid having any strict one, and instead to customize the situation to the particular circumstances.

This was not the theory that motivated the legalists responsible for developing bilingual policy, however. For them, it was a matter of rights and wrongs, not of flexibility and choice. The bilingual legal operation got underway when the Ford Foundation asked the NAACP's Legal Defense Fund to help develop a similar legal arm for Mexican Americans. By 1968, a new entity, the Mexican American Legal Defense and Educational Fund (MALDEF), had set up shop in San Antonio, Texas, with a $1.2 million Ford grant. It recruited a corps of OEO volunteers and began filing suits, including one that proposed bilingual education as a remedy for unequal educational opportunity afforded to minority language groups. Within three years, the fledgling organization had persuaded a federal appeals court to order "a form of bilingual instruction that would celebrate cultural diversity."[29]

Meanwhile, another group of attorneys, also working with OEO help, filed a much more significant suit, *Lau v. Nichols* (1973), on behalf of Chinese American parents whose children attended the San Francisco public schools. The parents complained that their children had been denied equal educational opportunity because the district had not provided them with a more customized instruction that took into account their native tongue. Lower courts rejected the petition, but, ironically, the Supreme Court reversed that decision after listening to Richard Nixon's solicitor general, Robert Bork (later rejected by the Senate as too conservative to serve on the Supreme Court), argue in favor of bilingual educational requirements.

The Supreme Court was persuaded by Bork's argument, saying, "There is no equality of treatment merely by providing students with the same facilities, textbooks, teachers, and curriculum, for students who do not understand English are effectively foreclosed from any meaningful education." Preferring to find educational rights in statutory law rather than in constitutional clauses, it based its *Lau* decision on a clause in the Civil Rights Act of 1964 that forbade discrimination on the basis of race or ethnicity, thereby making explicit the connection between the triumphs of the civil rights movement and the new rights of linguistic minorities. To provide equal opportunity, the Court required only that schools effectively address the linguistic challenges minority students faced. The ruling did not say whether this required bilingual instruction or whether this could be done by immersing children in the English language. The latter option was excluded, however, by the interpretation given to *Lau* by the Office of Civil Rights (OCR) within the U.S. Department of Health, Education, and Welfare. To understand how that happened, we have to go back to 1968, the year the Ford Foundation gave MALDEF its initial grant.[30]

The weary Johnson administration was then in its closing months. Seeing an opportunity, the president's Texas rival, Senator Ralph Yarborough, proposed giving Spanish-speaking students the right to instruction in their native tongue. Maine's influential senator, Edmund Muskie, a presidential hopeful, found that too parochial a perspective and altered the bill so as to cover all linguistic minorities. Soon legislators had passed a law requiring localities to "develop forward-looking approaches" that would ensure equal educational opportunity for linguistic minorities. Although curricular approaches were not specifically stated, it was generally understood that Congress had decided that "non-English speakers be taught in their own language until they were fluent in English." Most states rescinded the old World War I laws that forbade instruction in any language other than English. In other words, the practices that teacher Lyndon Johnson had quite ruthlessly enforced were now all but outlawed by legislation that President Lyndon Johnson had signed into federal law. Yet he seems to have done so reluctantly, agreeing to a funding level of only $7.5 million.[31]

Richard Nixon was no more enthusiastic about bilingual education than his predecessor, but he could see the political advantages of appealing to a rapidly growing ethnic group that might be edged away from the opposition party. Asked to do something that could be sold as responding to the needs of the Hispanic community, he allowed the new federal program to expand to $35 million in 1974, and, more important, he looked the other way when liberal Republicans in HEW's Office of Civil Rights issued a directive ordering districts to "take affirmative steps to rectify . . . language deficiency." Clarifying what this phrase meant, HEW secretary Elliott Richardson said in testimony before Congress that districts must "affirmatively recognize and value the cultural environment of ethnic minority children so that the development of positive self-concept can be accelerated." In other words, a Republican administration was endorsing bilingual education as an end in itself, not simply as a means for immigrants to become proficient in English. OCR all but insisted that federal law required bilingual instruction. Under heavy pressure from above, districts hired a new corps of teachers with Spanish-language skills. Once hired, the bilingual teachers became a potent force for perpetuating the practice.

Bilingual education implied the customization of the educational experience to fit the specific language background of each child. But in the process of implementing the policy, the government introduced changes with a conviction that paid more attention to a larger cause than to the needs of any one child or, indeed, to the evidence that the innovation was beneficial on average. Asked about the likely effectiveness of bilingual education, a key OCR official remarked that "there aren't any federal studies worth a damn"—an odd thing to say when the federal government was asking districts across the country to revamp their educational offerings.

Despite energetic advocacy, the bilingual idea did not, in the long run, become as deeply institutionalized as mainstreaming did. If ideas are to take hold, they must resonate with the needs and thinking of the larger society, something that bilingual instruction never achieved. It is true that languages other than English appear with more frequency in the wider American society today. Technology allows customers to draw money from an automatic teller machine in whatever language they wish, and TV channels provide access to mass entertainment in the language of the viewer's choice. Machines can talk on the telephone in multiple tongues. But all of these devices are tolerated by the English-speaking majority because they hardly inconvenience anyone. Otherwise, American public opinion today differs but little from the opinions of those who approved the English-only laws in the aftermath of World War I.

In retrospect, it appears the bilingual movement conducted a stealth attack, winning court cases and legislative victories below the public radar. But as the rates of undocumented immigration rose, the English-speaking majority began to take notice and bilingual instruction became a full-blown political issue. Not surprisingly, the issue first surfaced in California, the state where money for political causes is plentiful and initiatives and referenda are a way of life. In 1998, voters were asked whether they wanted to ban all bilingual instruction not specifically requested by a child's parent or guardian. Rattled by the state's flood of Spanish-speaking immigrants, voters were no longer in a mood to sanction "cultural maintenance" by their public schools. Similar referenda succeeded in Arizona and Massachusetts as well. The passage of the referenda issue was not entirely motivated by anti-immigrant sentiment. A majority of Hispanic voters themselves favored the California proposition (though they would come to resent the Republican governor who backed it). Apparently, many who settled in the United States in the late twentieth century were more eager to have their children learn the language of their new country than to preserve the language of their homeland. Unlike the Holland-based Pilgrims, they seemed to feel their native culture was hardly in danger of being obliterated.

In the years that followed the enactment of California's new law, bilingual teachers recruited parent signatures for the alternative they favored. But the bilingual option faded steadily from sight, as evidence accumulated that immersion theory was at least as good a way—and probably a better way—for young children to learn English. When No Child Left Behind was enacted, it did not refer to bilingual education but instead required that all English-language learners had to be proficient in that language by the year 2014. The right of linguistic minorities to equal educational opportunity was still intact, and families could still opt for a bilingual solution. Yet English would remain the country's dominant language. Voters insisted on that, regardless of what courts or federal bureaucrats had said. An idea can win in court without surviving in the court of public opinion, especially if opposing interests are aroused.[32]

Ideas and Interests

The judicial branch is the "least dangerous" branch, Alexander Hamilton explained in his classic essay in *The Federalist*. Unlike Congress, it lacks the power of the purse, and unlike the executive branch, it cannot wield the sword. A court can have an effect only by its "judgment." If the suggestion was entirely correct when those thoughts were penned, they acquired an ironic meaning in the late twentieth century, when the judgments handed down in courtrooms altered classroom practices in ways unanticipated when the drive for racial justice first began. When a teacher had to defer to the due process rights of students, he or she could no longer act as the personification of the rule of law. When federal laws were interpreted as requiring the mainstreaming of emotionally and behaviorally disturbed students, classrooms were subjected to events over which teachers had little control. When Supreme Court decisions were understood as insisting that the language of immigrants be protected, a large cadre of new teachers, with bilingual skills, was recruited to carry out the policy.

The new legalism in American education was inspired by noble ideals. Public-interest lawyers, backed by foundations, antipoverty agencies, and civil rights groups, combined legal and legislative advocacy. Their tactics were crafted to the circumstances at hand. Student due process rights were best introduced not by winning congressional majorities but by appealing to the highest court in the land. Rights for the disabled were better secured by new federal legislation than by hoping for a victory from a Supreme Court that was moving in a more conservative direction. In the case of bilingual education, a federal bureaucracy interpreted a vague Supreme Court opinion in ways that served the cause. But in all three cases, it was the law and its interpretation, not pedagogical ideas or insight, that transformed the schools.

Still more was to come. Capitalizing on the country's anti-authority mood, teacher organizations began making their own civil rights claims. For generations, public school teachers had docilely accepted the principle that salaries and conditions of work were matters to be decided by democratically elected officials. A new set of ideas was about to alter that principle, too.

CHAPTER 6

Albert Shanker and Collective Bargaining

"A standard day shall be defined as 435 minutes, excluding lunch but including a morning homeroom period of 7–15 minutes. . . . The teaching day shall not exceed 349 minutes of classroom teaching. . . . Up to eighteen (18) hours per year . . . an average of six (6) minutes each day . . . may be assigned each teacher for supervisory duties."

Such precise language in a collective-bargaining contract is not limited to school districts in small midwestern towns such as Eau Claire, Wisconsin (the passage just quoted is from its 2003 teacher contract). In New York City, high school teachers "cannot be asked to teach for more than 3.75 hours per day." Nor can a teacher be asked to "help supervise a lunchroom or study hall, help special-education students on and off the bus, . . . or write truant slips." In Milwaukee, the collective-bargaining agreement grew in length year by year from eighteen pages in 1965 to no less than 119 pages in 1997 (see Figure 12 in the Appendix). In New York City, the agreement is 200 pages long; with supplements, it expands to 600.[1]

Historical Practice

Before 1960, very few school boards were bound by such agreements. At that time, almost no public employees had the right to bargain collectively. If they went on strike, the law stipulated that they were to be fired. When Boston police officers went on strike in 1919, Massachusetts governor Calvin Coolidge broke a silence with words that rang across the decades: "There is no right to strike against the public safety by anybody, anywhere, any time." At Coolidge's insistence, the strikers never wore a Boston police uniform again. Coolidge's actions won overwhelming public approval, catapulting an unknown governor to the vice presidency. When President Warren Harding died a couple of years later, "Silent Cal" assumed the nation's highest public office.[2]

For nearly forty years, public-sector unions, and any potential allies they might have had, treaded carefully. Franklin D. Roosevelt, the greatest presidential friend the House of Labor has ever enjoyed, signed the Robert Wagner Act (named after New York's pro-labor senator), which protected private-sector workers' rights to bargain collectively. But he rejected altogether any form of public-sector bargaining within the federal government: "All Government employees should realize that the process of collective bargaining, as usually understood, cannot be transplanted into the public service. . . . The very nature and purposes of government make it impossible for administrative officials . . . to bind the employer in mutual discussions with government employee organizations. The employer is the whole people, who speak by means of laws enacted by their representatives in Congress." The head of the American Federation of Labor (AFL), George Meany, did not disagree. As late as the 1950s, he said quite simply that "it is impossible to bargain collectively with the government." Those representing federal employees took the position that collective bargaining was demeaning for civil service professionals. The National Education Association, by far the largest of all teacher organizations, was firmly opposed to the idea.[3]

Laws against strikes and collective bargaining remained in effect well into the 1950s. But during the next decade, school districts across the nation were repeatedly hit by illegal strikes like the ones that had once cost Boston police officers their jobs. Before long, most districts found their policies circumscribed by formal agreements with teacher organizations. Many factors precipitated that profound change in board-teacher relations, not least the effective use of nonviolent disobedience by the civil rights movement. Yet the introduction of collective bargaining cannot be explained by impersonal forces alone. Events were driven by the resourcefulness and energy of Albert Shanker, head of New York City's United Federation of Teachers. Writes Richard Kahlenberg, Shanker's biographer: "If Horace Mann was the key educational figure in the nineteenth century and John Dewey in the first half of the twentieth century, Albert Shanker has stood as the most influential figure since then." Biographers often exaggerate the influence of their subject, but in this case many agree that public-sector collective bargaining changed American education forever.[4]

Albert Shanker

Shanker was born in 1928, to Orthodox Jewish immigrants whose marriage had been arranged after their families fled anti-Semitic pogroms in Poland. He was raised in a crowded, ground-level apartment in a nondescript, Depression-ravaged section of Queens, New York, with his sister, parents, and grandmother. His father had hoped to be a rabbi but instead sold newspapers, a job he hated. Its only virtue, it seems, is that it gave him an escape from Al's mother, who worked long hours as a seamstress and was an enthusiastic member of the left-leaning International Ladies' Garment Workers' Union. As distant from his father as Mann and Dewey were from theirs, Shanker also tried to elude his mother's sharp eye, though he, like King, adored his grandmother, who encouraged the gangly, socially isolated boy, fearful of anti-Semitic neighbors, by telling him: "You are very special. You're exceptional. You are going to be a great man."

In his early years, Al took seriously the family's Orthodoxy, but when a rabbi told the teenager he should not read the New Testament, Shanker, suspicious of such dogmatism, explored "humanistic and Unitarian" services. At about the same time, he escaped from his detested neighborhood school by taking an exam that won him admission to Stuyvesant High School, the city's premier public school for boys. He was a solid student, excelling especially at debate. When his application to Harvard was rejected, he pursued philosophy at the University of Illinois, reading works by Hegel, Marx, and Dewey. Outside class, he participated in sit-ins led by the local Unitarian church in still-segregated Urbana-Champaign and became an active member of the Young People's Socialist League. As soon as he graduated, at the age of twenty-one, he married a fellow student, Pearl Sabath, who became a teacher in the New York public schools while Al continued his studies at Columbia University, in a philosophy department dominated by Dewey's followers.

As with many a philosophy student, the years spent writing the doctoral dissertation were rough going. For someone as energetic as Al, examining the thought of an obscure Dewey acolyte could hardly have been scintillating, especially given his dependence upon spousal income. To assist with family finances, Shanker took a job in nearby East Harlem as a substitute junior high school math instructor, teaching out of his field, with no pedagogical credentials. The young scholar was no happier in the classroom than his father had been peddling newspapers. Shanker's pay was poor, he was subjected to demeaning duties, and he received little guidance or support from school administrators. "Here I was, gone to college, very close to a Ph.D., and there I was locking myself into a room with kids who were exactly the kids I was trying to run away from," he later recalled. Life was spiraling down in other ways as well, as Shanker's marriage was turning sour, ending in divorce a few years later.

Shanker was able to transfer to a junior high school in Queens in September 1953. There, after encountering a difficult assistant principal, he decided that teachers, no less than seamstresses, needed union protection. He joined the same New York Teachers Guild to which John Dewey had belonged, a small, left-leaning but anti-Communist organization affiliated with the American Federation of Labor. Young Shanker became an energetic member of the union, but the guild, despite its prestigious connections, had only a couple of thousand members (less than 5 percent of the city's teaching population) and its leadership seemed more interested in debating the fine points of Socialist doctrine than organizing colleagues.

Albert Shanker, waving to the crowd protesting the decentralization of the New York City school system, at a 1968 rally at New York's City Hall.

William E. Sauro / The New York Times / Redux.

In fact, it was not the guild but a quite different group of some 800 nighttime high school teachers who, in 1959, were the first to walk out of the classroom. Other guild leaders refused to back the illegal strike, but Shanker rallied to the night-teachers' cause, winning plaudits when the strikers doubled their pay while keeping their jobs. The incident showed how ripe for action the situation had become.

Civil Rights for Teachers

Before the Montgomery bus boycott, illegal action by public school teachers would have been inconceivable. But the civil rights movement had changed the rules of political discourse. Thereafter, if the goal was honorable, court orders could be disobeyed, regulations against street parades could be violated, and public employees could ignore laws against withdrawing their services from the public. Shanker himself had participated in "illegal" sit-ins that helped desegregate public accommodations in Illinois. The New York Teachers Guild had given its John Dewey Award to Thurgood Marshall, and labor unions were speaking of a broad new political coalition of labor and civil rights groups. "Teachers, like blacks," said Shanker, had been "treated in a second-class way" and were engaged in "an honorable struggle for a legitimate place."

It was not just within Shanker's own political circle that opinion was changing. Robert F. Wagner Jr., the son and namesake of the senator who had introduced the most important labor legislation enacted during Franklin Roosevelt's administration, had become the mayor of New York. He had already agreed to accept a union contract as part of the city's takeover of a privately owned but bankrupt subway system. "All of a sudden," said Shanker, "you had government involved in a collective bargaining relationship." Shortly thereafter, the city granted collective-bargaining rights to sanitation workers.

As Wagner was signing those bargaining agreements, the AFL, which had joined with the Congress of Industrial Organizations (CIO) to create the AFL-CIO, was dropping its own opposition to public-sector bargaining, and a CIO affiliate gave the Teachers Guild monies to hire additional organizing staff, opening up a job opportunity for Shanker. Relieved of classroom drudgery, Shanker threw himself into the struggle. His first big success was to pull off a merger with the militant High School Teachers' Association (HSTA)—no easy task.

New York teachers were split among multiple organizations. The HSTA, predominantly male, found its *raison d'être* in its objection to a New York policy that put secondary school teachers on the same rigid salary schedule as elementary and junior high school teachers. Meanwhile, the Teachers Guild, as a left-leaning, labor-affiliated trade union consisting mainly of elementary and junior high school teachers, stood solidly behind the uniform salary schedule. Against all odds, the two organizations merged in the spring of 1960 to form the United Federation of Teachers (UFT). Shanker and his colleagues had devised a compromise formula that would resonate through the country's educational system. The uniform salary schedule would remain intact, but teachers who had a master's degree or better (like Shanker) would receive extra compensation. At the time, high school teachers were more likely than others to have the higher credential. Despite the seemingly favorable compromise, high school teachers in the long run got the short end of the stick (see Chapter 7). For union leaders, however, the compromise made sense. Wagner soon promised what presidents from Coolidge to Roosevelt to Eisenhower had long denied: an agreement to allow collective bargaining if just 30 percent of the teaching staff voted for the idea.

Precisely when victory seemed at hand, it all but vanished. When legal advisers told Wagner the city could not hold a vote on collective bargaining because the practice was contrary to law, the mayor withdrew his commitment. Incensed, Shanker and his fellow UFT leaders decided to call their own illegal strike—on the day before the 1960 Kennedy-Nixon presidential election. The risk was great, since teachers had been told they would be fired if they walked out. But union leaders reminded members that night school teachers, by striking, had both won a hefty salary increase and kept their jobs.

On the appointed day, approximately 5,000 teachers failed to show up for work, just 10 percent of the teaching force but enough to cause havoc should they all be fired. That, at least, is what Mayor Wagner, no Calvin Coolidge, believed. Striking teachers were quickly reinstated, and the mayor, despite the advice of his attorneys, agreed to collective bargaining after all. Teachers voted for collective bargaining by a wide margin, despite the desperate, feeble opposition of the hapless local chapter of the National Education Association, the city's largest teacher organization. In a subsequent election, the UFT won the right to bargain on behalf of the teachers. Almost overnight, the Teachers Guild had gone from a tiny fringe group to the city's teacher powerhouse. Like King's victory in Montgomery, Shanker's masterstroke in New York seemed to come out of nowhere. Furthermore, in March 1961 Shanker had happily married union activist Edith ("Eadie") Gerber, a graduate student turned English teacher, who remained his partner to the end.

More victories came in rapid succession. On January 17, 1962, President Kennedy issued an executive order granting federal workers the right to bargain collectively. Fiscal decisions were still reserved to Congress, but, otherwise, representatives of employees could negotiate the terms of their work situation. Though strikes remained unlawful, negotiations were subject to binding arbitration by independent experts. Many years later, New York senator Daniel Patrick Moynihan, who had been the assistant secretary of labor who prepared the order, spoke at an occasion celebrating Shanker's life and contributions: "If as Emerson wrote 'an institution is the lengthened shadow of one man,'" he memorialized, "the public employees' [unions] of our nation are singularly the mark of Al Shanker's inspired life and work."

Still, there was one more terrestrial river to cross. When the UFT sought its first collective-bargaining agreement, the district declared that it had no money for anything other than a trivial salary increase. Shanker and his colleagues again called a strike, and nearly half of the city's teachers walked out. Within days, the Democratic mayor, with the help of Republican governor Nelson Rockefeller, found the money to give teachers the "largest raise in New York City school history."

Such success proved contagious. Big-city unions across the country demanded the right to negotiate, and, when granted it, secured higher salaries and greater worker protection. School boards quickly learned that the public wanted strikes settled quickly, children returned to school, and teachers rehired. The number of strikes escalated from 9 in 1964 to 107 three years later, though that number later fell as unions, once entrenched, found ways to reach favorable agreements without relying upon their ultimate weapon. Affiliates of the American Federation of Teachers (AFT) won recognition rights in Philadelphia, Chicago, Boston, Cleveland, and many other large cities, despite the fact that in most places it had once represented only a sliver of the teaching profession. "For the first time since 1918, the AFT threatened to surpass the NEA," one historian noted. That changed when the NEA, seeing its membership slip away, gave up its principled opposition to collective bargaining and entered the fray. In the end, both organizations prospered: NEA membership climbed from 700,000 in 1960 to 3.2 million in 2007, while the smaller AFT grew from under 60,000 to 1.3 million during the same period. Collective bargaining, hardly known in education before 1960, became pervasive in most states outside the South.[5]

So prevalent is collective bargaining within the public sector, few today can remember Franklin Roosevelt's objections to such a practice. It is not only union leaders who think collective bargaining for teachers is as much a civil right as are African Americans' demands for school desegregation. The few remaining critics say it disturbs the democratic relationship between government and citizens by privileging a particular set of interests: those of government employees. Only union representatives have the right to meet formally with elected officials, usually in secret sessions, to negotiate a set of agreements that then become binding on all citizens. Government sovereignty has been partially handed over to a union that has not been democratically chosen by the citizens at large.

Critics draw a distinction between public- and private-sector bargaining. Within the private sector, workers need to join together to protect their interests from a profit-seeking management that might otherwise exploit its disproportionate power vis-à-vis each individual worker. When a tough union bargains with tough management, each protects its own vital interests in the collective-bargaining process. Within the public sector, such a balance of power and interest cannot be assumed, especially when the managers are elected school board members. Unions contribute heavily to school board campaigns. School employees are well represented among the few who turn out for school elections, which are often low-visibility, nonpartisan affairs held on an odd day of the year when only the most interested parties are paying attention. Dollars and votes together give employees special influence over the school board with which they negotiate. If teacher unions are not quite negotiating with themselves, neither are they negotiating with a hostile private management whose interests run counter to those of the employee.[6]

Bargaining agreements have extended unions' political power in other ways as well. In many districts, contracts require that districts deduct from employee paychecks an amount equivalent to union dues, which is then at the disposal of the organization. Unless a member specifically objects, the deduction includes fees that may be used for political purposes. With these resources, teacher unions have asserted disproportionate influence over state policy. In a 1985 nationwide survey of informed observers, "teacher organizations" were identified as the most powerful interest group in state politics; in 2002, they were found to be second only to chambers of commerce. In both surveys, they outranked such powerful groups as utility companies, insurance companies, hospitals, trial lawyers, manufacturers, and representatives of local governments more generally.[7]

Rights in Conflict

No sooner had Shanker consolidated his power in New York City and jump-started a transformation in union rights nationwide than he faced his most brutal political struggle of all. As the UFT was settling into its undisputedly authoritative role at the collective-bargaining table while enjoying the applause of right-thinking liberals as a newfound fighting force for education, its organizational status and prestige were threatened by those who had helped catapult it to power in the first place. The right of the union to control the hiring and firing of those who worked for the schools was trumped by those who claimed an even more fundamental right: that of African Americans to control their own schools. In the end, the UFT would demonstrate overwhelming political and economic power—but so vicious was the clash that teacher unions would never again hold the moral high ground in education. The UFT was doomed to fighting a defensive position, hanging on to a status quo that became increasingly difficult to justify.

The reforms of the progressives had laid the trap. As part of their effort to drive political patronage from the schools, progressives in New York had instituted a set of procedures that determined the selection of school principals. Instead of leaving the choice up to the school board or the superintendent, who were assumed to have dubious political motives, progressives saw to the enactment of legislation that forced the selection of principals from among those who scored the highest on a civil service examination. The law was sacrosanct, despite the fact no one had ever shown that the skills needed to run a school can in any way be detected by performance on an examination. As the civil rights movement unfolded but New York schools remained as segregated as ever, those progressive regulations came to be seen by black activists as nothing other than a thin disguise for white power. Those who had sufficient years of experience in New York schools to be eligible to take the principal's examination were almost always whites, as were those who scored well enough to pass the examination at the highest levels. Nor was the composition of the teaching force significantly better. In 1965, the schools in many parts of the city were overwhelmingly African American but only about 10 percent of teachers—and fewer than 2 percent of New York's principals—were black.[8]

As racial integration stalled, those gnawing facts became intolerable to activists within the African American community. The issue boiled over in the very East Harlem community where Shanker had had his initial, unhappy teaching experience. In September 1966, a group of parents boycotted a new school, demanding that it be either integrated or placed under community control with a principal whose racial background reflected that of the neighborhood. Unable to find a black principal high enough on its civil service examination list, the school district gave a nod to Black Power by asking a white liberal Jewish principal, along with a black assistant principal, to implement an Afrocentric curriculum. Not satisfied, East Harlem parents boycotted again, forcing the principal to resign and leave the assistant in charge. In response, the school's teachers, with the help of the UFT, went on strike, forcing the return of the Jewish principal. "The very integrity of the school system was at stake," Shanker later wrote, "for if we had not prevailed, we would enter an era where only a Jewish principal could be appointed in schools located in a predominantly Jewish neighborhood, Italians in Italian neighborhoods, Irish in Irish."[9]

But no sooner had Shanker spoken than the community struck back. Students mounted within-school disruptions that were so effective the principal resigned. Battling back again, Shanker demanded a clause in the next union contract that would allow teachers to suspend disruptive students, only to hear complaints from the NAACP and a Harlem parent group that such a clause invited white teachers to discriminate against blacks. Unable to get their demands accepted, the teachers went on strike. Only then did the warring factions reach a convoluted compromise. It created "local discipline review boards, consisting of teachers, board members, and outside child experts," along with a set of procedures for removing children which was, according to Shanker, "so cumbersome that 'it was never used.'"[10]

Far from ending the dispute, the agreement took it to a new level, as minority activists proposed a new system of community-controlled schools that would shift power from New York's centralized bureaucracy to neighborhood activists. Mayor John Lindsay, Ford Foundation president (and former Kennedy adviser) McGeorge Bundy, and New York State's Republican legislators all, for their own reasons, saw promise in the concept. The state legislature promised funding if the mayor submitted proposals for replacing the current mammoth-sized school district. At the invitation of the mayor, a "Bundy plan" was devised that broke up the New York City school district into many locally controlled ones. In the meantime, the school district itself agreed to set up in the Ocean Hill–Brownsville neighborhood a "demonstration project," an unusually prescient moniker.[11]

The demonstration board asked Rhody McCoy, an African American, to be its director. He, in turn, appointed black principals, some of whom had close ties to the Black Power movement. He ignored the civil service examination list, on the grounds that demonstrations were exempt from district regulations—a decision challenged in the courts by the Association of School Administrators, with the help of the UFT. (The challenge won in the lower courts but lost in the New York State Supreme Court). All of that was controversial enough. But on May 9, 1968, McCoy asked eighteen white educators to seek assignment in other parts of the city the next fall. Outraged, Shanker asked teachers to go on a series of strikes, first at the demonstration schools but, when that proved insufficient, then throughout New York City. The citywide strike lasted for five weeks. Shanker emerged victorious: a trustee replaced the governing board for Ocean Hill–Brownsville, and a special committee was created to ensure that teacher rights were protected. In Albany, Shanker was able to water down community-control legislation so that local boards had only limited powers, with no control over teacher recruitment, compensation, or dismissal—or any other policy subject to collective bargaining.[12]

Shanker obviously won the battle, but it was less clear that he'd won the war. "The Ocean Hill–Brownsville strikes of 1968 left an indelible mark on New York City and to a certain degree on American liberalism itself," concludes Shanker's biographer. Organized labor and civil rights leaders no longer walked side by side. Many African Americans came to believe that half-hearted efforts to integrate schools were a mere mask for continued white control of the levers of power. In New York and elsewhere, attention turned to questions of affirmative action, community control, autonomous black schooling, and parental school choice. Even Kenneth Clark, the Harlem author of the famous "doll study" cited in the *Brown* decision, now advocated community control. Worst of all, "Shanker" became a term of abuse in popular culture. In Woody Allen's movie *Sleeper*, a character wakes up after sleeping for two hundred years to learn that "a man by the name of Albert Shanker got hold of a nuclear warhead." Shanker was kicked upstairs to lead the nationwide American Federation of Teachers, a more visible but less powerful position than running the biggest local union in the country.[13]

Unions on the Defensive

That the organized teaching profession should become something other than the leading force for educational reform is more than mildly ironic, for teachers are critical to the success of a child at school. Now that scholars have begun to track student performance in specific classrooms, they have been able to quantify something that parents—indeed, all those who reflect upon their own education—have known intuitively, namely that a teacher can dramatically affect the amount a student learns. Students in classrooms taught by the very best teachers (the top 20 percent) acquire approximately an extra year's worth of learning annually, compared to students taught by the lowest-performing teachers (the bottom 20 percent). Or, to put it another way, if identical twins attending the same school are assigned to different classrooms for several years, and one has a consistently top-performing teacher while the other has a consistently low-performing teacher, by the eighth grade the difference in their performance will be comparable to the difference between the average fourth-grader and average eighth-grader. If school districts could double the size of the teaching force now considered the top 20 percent of all teachers, and if they could encourage the bottom 20 percent to leave teaching for other professions, student achievement would take a quantum leap to levels rivaling the world's highest.[14]

Unfortunately, the quality of the teaching profession, far from shifting upward, has steadily deteriorated over the past fifty years. The percentage of students with high SAT scores saying they plan to become teachers dropped precipitously from the 1960s to the 1990s. So did the percentage of teachers coming from selective colleges and universities. In 1990, a group known as Teach for America (TFA), founded by a Princeton graduate, Wendy Kopp, dedicated itself to reversing the decline in teacher quality by building connections between students attending selective colleges and urban school systems suffering from teacher shortages, especially in math and science. TFA provides intense preparation over the summer before the new graduates begin their teaching. The program initially met with indifferent success, but it has constantly searched for ways of strengthening its ability to identify quality teachers, preparing them for the classroom, and supporting them once they're engaged. Many of its alumni have moved into leadership positions within the education reform movement.[15]

TFA practices what Shanker preached when he called for reforming American education through the collective-bargaining process. But when the NEA and AFT won the right to help shape the destiny of the schools, they used their newfound political power to block such promising innovations. When Boston's school superintendent tried to alleviate a shortage of math and science teachers by hiring TFA recruits, the local AFT president publicly told the TFA teachers they were not wanted. Instead of leading the profession to new heights, as Shanker had promised, union leaders focused on increasing membership, controlling grievance procedures, and extending worker benefits and pensions. Many collective-bargaining negotiations were successfully conducted, and many union-backed laws passed through state legislatures, but unions never convinced very many for very long that their first concern was the welfare of the American schoolchild. Even on matters peripheral to the organization's own interests, unions took a defensive position. Teacher certification policy was the most obvious case in point.[16]

Teacher Certification

The passage of state laws requiring certification as a prerequisite for teaching took place long before unions won collective-bargaining rights. A progressive favorite, the laws shifted control over teacher recruitment from the hands of local politicians to professors in state teachers' colleges. Future teachers had to take thirty or more courses in such subjects as educational history, psychology, pedagogy, and practice teaching. As certification rules proliferated, schools of education developed specialties for particular subjects and for children at different stages of their education. The rules became byzantine, as individual specialists fought to create their own specific credentials. In Missouri, for example, laws and regulations provide for more than 200 distinct teaching certificates, each for a specific type of teaching and, no less important, each protecting some specific pattern of college coursework.[17]

All of this could be justified if it could be shown that certified teachers were more effective than those lacking the credentials. Yet numerous studies, dating back to Coleman's original 1965 report, reveal nothing of the kind. In one of the best of the recent studies, Harvard economist Thomas Kane and two colleagues compared the effectiveness of New York City teachers with four different types of certification: (1) those with traditional certification; (2) uncertified teachers trained by TFA; (3) alternatively certified teachers (expected to take courses while they teach); and (4) uncertified teachers of minority background recruited through a program designed for this purpose. Which type of teacher was, on average, the most effective? The race ended in a photo finish. Students learn as much, on average, from teachers with one type of educational training as they do from teachers with a different type of training. Teachers vary enormously in quality, but, on average, the credentials they can pin on their sleeves tell us next to nothing about the level of that quality.[18]

Quite apart from certification rules, seventeen states insist that districts pay extra to those teachers who hold a master's degree. In the districts of many other states, collective-bargaining agreements require extra pay for those with advanced degrees. In Denver, for example, a collective-bargaining agreement reached in 2007 said that teachers with ten years of experience would earn an extra $3,500 over and above their base salary of $45,000 once they acquired an M.A. diploma (see Figure 13). The practice of paying more for extra credentials was initiated by progressives and has since been concretized in collective-bargaining contracts. Teachers responded avidly to the financial incentive, so by the beginning of the new century almost half of elementary and secondary public-school teachers had earned a master's degree or better. All of this would be well and good if one could show that teachers become more effective once they earn an extra diploma. But scholars who track student performance within individual classrooms have been unable to identify any benefits to students from the additional credential.[19]

Inasmuch as credentials are not a guarantee of—or even correlated with—effectiveness, those seeking to reform the teaching profession say it should be open to any college graduate, so long as local administrators deem the teacher qualified. Kate Walsh, president of the National Council on Teacher Quality, says that the certification process has only a "crude capacity for ensuring" quality teachers, because pedagogical "knowledge can be acquired by means other than coursework." Teachers learn to teach by practicing the craft, not by taking courses in its history or psychology. Accordingly, teachers should be able to obtain certificates through routes alternative to traditional coursework. More than half the states now offer teachers alternative certificates that limit the number of required education courses. The policy has opened the door to TFA recruits and more teachers of minority background. The idea seems popular: according to surveys, nearly half the American people support the concept and only a third oppose it.[20]

Alternative certification has nonetheless been vigorously opposed, most especially by those who represent schools of education. The head of the National Council for the Accreditation of Teacher Education, justifying the group's opposition to alternative certification, insists that "rigorous teacher preparation is key to ensuring that no child is left behind. . . . Content knowledge is only one indicator of readiness to teach." Unions have been no less opposed to the reform. In 2007, NEA president Reg Weaver objected to alternative certification as a way of mitigating a current teacher shortage, saying, "The solution is not to . . . increase the supply of recruits by allowing prospective teachers to skip 'burdensome' education courses or student teaching. The solution is to show a little R-E-S-P-E-C-T, and show us the money."[21]

It is not clear exactly why unions feel they must oppose alternative certification. Admittedly, any state licensing law restricts the supply of teachers, thereby creating shortages in certain subjects, which can drive up the price that districts need to pay teachers. And it is also true that union support for certification helps to sustain the symbiotic relationship between teacher unions and schools of education. Still, nothing in teacher certification law is vital to the organizational interests of teacher unions. Their power rests fundamentally on their collective-bargaining agreements and on the dues that teachers are required to pay, not on restricting the labor supply or carefully managing ties with schools of education.

Teacher Compensation

The unions also take a defensive posture toward the uniform salary schedule. Aside from getting a master's degree, individual teachers can do little to lift their salaries beyond the normal increment they receive from one year to the next. In Denver, a city with a typical salary schedule, all teachers in 2007 who had a B.A. degree earned $32,490 the first year, $34,457 the third year, and so on, up to $47,500 in their fourteenth year (see Figure 13). Teachers can earn extra pay by taking on an additional assignment, but they are not rewarded for superb teaching or compensated for working under particularly onerous conditions. Nor do physics, math, or special-education teachers earn extra money, despite the shortage of qualified personnel in these areas.

The uniform salary schedule predates collective bargaining. Another progressive pet, it was expected to keep school board members from rewarding political favorites. The practice was codified in collective-bargaining negotiations, as unions saw the advantages of uniform schedules for unifying the organization. When everyone received the same increment, the only way to get better pay was to support union leadership.

In the private sector, professional salaries are not uniform but depend on the difficulty of the assignment, the scarcity of the skill, and the quality of the professional's performance. Accordingly, school reformers propose modifications of the salary schedule that would permit extra compensation for those assigned difficult tasks (such as teaching in the inner city), higher salaries for those teaching technical subjects (math, science, and computer science, for example), and merit pay for those who perform at a high level. Once the idea of a small band of conservatives, the notion of replacing the uniform salary schedule with a more differentiated set of policies has been gathering wider support. In 2007, 45 percent of the American public said they supported extra pay for high performance, while only 31 opposed it. Shortly after taking office, President Obama expressed his support for paying math and science teachers more money in order to alleviate teacher shortages and promised policies ensuring that "good teachers will be rewarded with more money for improved student achievement." His secretary of education, Arne Duncan, has insisted that states, if they are to receive extra federal dollars, must design merit pay plans.[22]

Union opposition to merit pay and nearly all other forms of differentiated pay has been intense, however. Late in life, Al Shanker expressed support for schoolwide teacher bonuses, if schools were high-performing, but even he did not favor paying individual teachers for performance. "You don't see [secretary of defense] Caspar

Weinberger saying that good generals should get paid more than lousy generals," he declared. Merit pay policies have been defeated or rendered meaningless in Rochester, Columbus, and Denver. In Little Rock, the school board accepted a philanthropist's offer to give bonuses to effective teachers, but then reversed the policy when the board members were defeated by union-backed candidates. But the most dramatic merit pay initiative was mounted by the superintendent of the District of Columbia's predominantly African American school system, Michelle Rhee, with the full support of the district's mayor. She offered high-performing teachers the opportunity to earn salaries as high as $135,000 annually, provided they gave up tenure. When the union mounted an all-out defense of existing practice, it underlined the growing divide between the teacher union and the black community.[23]

Union opposition to merit pay gives the AFT the appearance of an intransigent, defensive organization whose interests run counter to those of minority students, an image that conjures up memories of the Ocean Hill–Brownsville debacle. In 2008 a group calling itself Democrats for School Reform received the backing of a number of black political leaders when it raised the merit pay issue at the Democratic National Convention. The open conflict between minority groups and teacher unions opened the door for the Obama administration's efforts to promote merit pay.

Less controversial but no less troubling has been union support for generous health, pension, and other benefits. Districts and state legislatures have been enticed into making significant pension concessions, since the cost of paying for the benefits can be put off to the future, while the political credit can be claimed immediately. As a consequence, teachers receive a relatively high percentage of their total compensation in benefits rather than salary. According to calculations by economists Robert Costrell and Michael Podgursky, public school teacher pension benefits climbed from less than 12 to more than 14 percent of salary in the years 2004–2008, outstripping by a sizable margin the 10 percent share received by private-sector professionals more generally.[24]

When benefits constitute a disproportionate share of professional compensation, they introduce their own rigidities. If pensions are defined-benefit plans, as they usually are for teachers, the lion's share of the benefits go to the relatively few who remain in teaching for a long period of time, at the expense of young people who teach for only a few years. Benefits are often calculated on the last few years of teaching, so not a few teachers earn a master's degree shortly before retirement as a way of boosting their pension. The costs are further driven up by policies that allow for retirement after twenty-five or thirty years of teaching, enabling teachers to retire in their mid-fifties. In Denver, the average retiree participating in the state's K–12 pension system received 35 percent of his or her lifetime professional compensation in pension benefits over and above reasonable interest from their own contributions.[25]

If retirement benefits supplemented all teacher salaries by 35 percent, teachers would be better-paid professionals. Unfortunately, those who do not teach more than four or five years typically receive no benefits at all from defined-benefit retirement plans. By concentrating resources into defined-benefit plans instead of putting them directly into salaries, states and districts have made it more difficult to set salaries at a level that's rewarding enough to attract high-quality new teachers. At the same time, dissatisfied, unproductive, long-time teachers are discouraged from seeking alternative work even though they might otherwise prefer to do so, because they can lose considerable pension benefits if they leave prematurely.[26]

Teacher Retention

Teacher tenure is still another legacy of the progressive era. Introduced as a way of preserving academic freedom, and championed by progressives as a way to keep teachers free of political pressures, tenure guarantees teachers a job unless malfeasance or moral turpitude can be shown. When unions won collective-bargaining rights, they extended the concept by insisting that districts follow complex grievance procedures before dismissing a teacher. As a way of recruiting members, unions guarantee teachers full legal assistance if a district attempts to dismiss them.

In view of the grievance procedures that have been negotiated, dismissal cannot take place unless administrators can provide detailed documentation of malfeasance that can withstand the scrutiny of union attorneys. Since the dismissal process can take an inordinate amount of a principal's time and can spread over several years, principals are extremely reluctant to initiate a request for dismissal. An enterprising reporter in Illinois, Scott Reeder, took it upon himself to check out how many of the state's school districts had dismissed a teacher for poor performance. Over an eighteen-year period ending in 2004, only two per year were let go—out of a teaching force of 95,000. Only sixty-one of the 876 school districts examined had "ever attempted to fire a tenured teacher." In the state of California, only thirty-one teachers with tenure lost their jobs over the most recent five-year period for which information is available.[27]

Tenure laws are often set by states, an inheritance of their progressive past. The length of time it takes before a teacher can be eligible for tenure varies from one to five years, during which time the teacher must have a received satisfactory rating from his or her principals, a rating generally given with little hesitation. When Obama's secretary of education, Arne Duncan, was superintendent in Chicago, he encouraged principals to review all teachers in the early years of their teaching so that ineffective teachers could be weeded out, and principals there seem to have made well-informed decisions. He took that idea with him to Washington, and President Obama declared early in his administration: "If a teacher is given a chance . . . but still does not improve, there is no excuse for that person to continue teaching."[28]

But once again, unions have adopted a defensive position. In 2008, the New York school system was considering asking principals to use information on a teacher's classroom effectiveness, as measured by student learning gains, when deciding whether or not to grant teachers tenure. To forestall such action, the teacher union persuaded the state legislature to forbid principals from using test score data for this purpose. "There is no independent or conclusive research that shows you can accurately measure the impact of an individual teacher on a student's academic achievement," said AFT president Randi Weingarten. New York's mayor, Michael Bloomberg, begged to differ: "All of us are judged on whether or not we do a good job, and to not judge teachers the same way, it's an insult to the teachers." In Los Angeles the school district asked that the state tenure law be revoked—but "it has no chance of passing," observed one school administrator, because similar attempts in the past had been regularly defeated by the California Teachers Association.[29]

Teacher Union Reform: Class Size Reduction

On many issues affecting the teaching profession—alternative certification, merit pay, tenure, and dismissal policies—unions are challenged by energetic opponents who appear to have at least passive public support. But on one issue—class size reduction—unions have the clear advantage. Unions have successfully campaigned for smaller classes in many states and school districts. In 1996 they persuaded the California legislature to withhold funds from districts that did not limit class size to twenty for students in grades K through 3, and later a similar law was passed for students in high school. In Florida, class size reduction was mandated by nothing less than a state constitutional amendment, which says that the maximum number of students in core-curricula courses assigned to a teacher in 2011 cannot exceed eighteen students in grades K–3, twenty-two students in grades 4–8, and twenty-five students in grades 9–12. Nationally, the number of pupils per instructor declined from twenty-six in 1960 to nearly fifteen in 2005 (see Figure 5).[30]

The benefits of smaller classes seem obvious to teachers, parents, and students alike. Everyone enjoys the intimacy, friendliness, and conversational pace of a smaller class. Whether students learn more in smaller classes is less certain. Many studies show little, if any, benefit, though there is one high-quality experimental study of class size reduction in Tennessee that indicated substantial benefits for children in grades K–3. The one thing certain about class size reduction is its expense. A reduction in the size of a class from 24 to 16 (approximately the reduction in the pupil-teacher ratio nationally since 1970) increases the number of teachers needed by 50 percent—from two teachers to three teachers for every forty-eight students. The number of rooms must also increase by 50 percent. If we assume that half the cost of schooling is driven by such classroom costs, the increase in expenditure would be 25 percent.[31]

If resources are scarce, reductions in class size necessarily limit the amount that can be spent on teacher salaries. Presumably, most teachers prefer larger salaries over smaller classes, but union leaders may prefer the latter, as the additional employees that must be hired are potential union members. Is the vigorous union support of class size reduction placing organizational interests ahead of the teachers' own concerns? That possibility exists, but a more generous and perhaps more plausible interpretation would take note of the broad public support for class size reduction. When Americans were asked whether "increasing teacher salaries or decreasing class size" was the "better use of our educational dollars," 77 percent selected the latter option. When unions pushed on the class size door, they found it unlocked, oiled, and ajar. It was hard not to walk in.[32]

The fight for higher salaries was not so easy. It is the supreme irony of the teacher rights movement that on the issue of presumably the greatest importance to teachers—their compensation—the unions did not deliver. The AFT and NEA successfully fought off community control, protected teacher tenure, enhanced health and pension benefits, defeated many efforts to weaken teacher certification rules, and kept intact the uniform salary schedule. But when it came to the most important issue—maintaining teacher salaries at the level needed to keep jobs in the industry competitive with other jobs—the collective-bargaining rights Al Shanker won for teachers failed to bear fruit. Just how and why that happened is the topic to which we now turn.

CHAPTER 7

Money and the Adequacy Lawsuit

Education is very labor intensive. We may be getting to the point where there will have to be some basic changes in the model.

—Mark G. Yudof, president, University of California, *New York Times*, November 8, 2008

Consider the following two paradoxes: (1) School expenditures have tripled—in real dollar terms—over the past fifty years, but, relative to other employees who hold college degrees, teachers today are not as well paid as they were in 1960. (2) Legal efforts to bolster educational expenditures have succeeded in dozens of state courts across the country, but the overall fiscal impact of the litigation has been almost nil.

Resolution of both paradoxes requires a glimpse into the economics of industries that become increasingly labor intensive as the rest of the economy is becoming capital intensive. Those industries are doomed to become more expensive, or to decline in the quality of their workforce, or both. Education provides a spectacular example of a truth better known to economists than to educators. In this chapter we'll explore why schools always get more money but never seem to get enough.

Rising Expenditures but Declining Quality

For those outraged at the rising cost of education, nothing is more telling than the events that unfolded in 2008 in prosperous, upscale Newton, Massachusetts. Town aldermen approved the mayor's request for the construction of a new building for North High School, to the tune of $197.5 million—approximately $100,000 for each of the nearly 2,000 students in attendance. One state official dubbed the school the state's "Taj Mahal." The design featured a "new outdoor stadium, an indoor swimming pool, state-of-the-art vocational education workshops, a glass-walled cafeteria, a restaurant, and an architecturally trendy zigzag shape." Newton's prestigious shopping mall would no longer be the city's longest building.

As the price tag escalated, the high school became a matter of public controversy—even in that education-enthralled city. Was it necessary to have an irregular shape? Departures from right angles require expensive construction techniques. Was an angled roof essential, when flat roofs cost less? Did the school really need a "Main Street," a wide, compelling corridor that ran down the middle? Is a two-tiered theater crucial for learning? Taxpayers across Massachusetts wanted to know the answers, for they were being asked to bear a healthy share of the cost.[1]

Newton's North High is not an isolated example. Shortly thereafter, a neighboring community, my hometown of Wellesley, embarked on a project almost as ambitious. But pricey construction projects for well-heeled towns funded in part by taxpayers statewide are not the primary source of rising education costs. The bigger impact comes from the cost of the personnel hired to operate the schools. Nationwide, the average cost for educating a student has risen steadily for more than a half century—even after the figures are adjusted for inflation. When calculated in 2002 dollars, expenditures in 1940 amounted to just short of $2,000 per pupil. Twenty years later, when the civil rights transformation was just beginning, annual costs were approaching $3,500 per pupil, and they rose to $4,000 by 1970. Ten years later, in 1980, the rights revolution had run its course and the country was on the eve of its excellence reforms. By this time, annual expenditures had reached $6,000 per pupil. One might have thought that President Ronald Reagan would find a way to brake the trend. Instead, expenditures exploded over the next twenty years, rising to over $11,000 per pupil by 2007.[2]

Expenditure growth has been driven in part by the rising cost of labor. In 1960, teacher salaries averaged nearly $35,000 a year (as calculated in 2007 dollars in order to adjust for inflation). Salaries rose to $46,000 annually by 1975, then fell to around $42,000 in 1981, as the value of nominal salary increments was eaten away by rampant inflation. Once inflation was contained, salaries took off again, climbing to $50,000 in 1990, then rising slightly to nearly $51,000 in 2007. Overall, salaries climbed about 20 percent in real-dollar terms between 1960 and 2007. To that figure, one must add about 5 percentage points to cover the growing cost of teachers' health, pension, and other benefits. So overall teacher compensation rose by about 25 percent, over and above the cost of living, between the early 1960s and the end of the century.[3]

Even as the price of labor has risen, the number of laborers relative to the number of students has turned north as well. One professional employee served seventeen pupils in 1960. Professional "administrative" and "instructional" employees, as defined by the U.S. Department of Education, include not only administrators and teachers but also guidance counselors, librarians, and the many other professional educators employed in the school system. By 1970, one such employee was present and available for every fourteen students. In 1980 that number fell to ten students, and in 2005 it was eight. In other words, for each student in 2005 there were more than twice as many educational professionals as there had been in 1960, at the beginning of the rights revolution. The impact on expenditures was profound. Even if professional compensation had remained completely flat, the personnel costs still would have doubled.

Only around half the administrative and instructional employees in 2005 were teachers—a fact that explains why the pupil-teacher ratio is 15:1, while the "pupil-professional" ratio is 8:1. So while the class size reduction discussed in the previous chapter contributed to the growth of the administrative and instructional staff, it is by no means the only factor at work. Indeed, it explains less than half the total growth in the number of professional employees.[4]

The greatest growth in administrative and instructional employees occurred among nonteachers. Guidance counselors were employed to help students choose among the multitude of high school courses available and to assist with the preparation of college applications. Multimedia centers hired staff, curricular experts were needed to define and implement state standards, and professionals were called in to design and administer the tests that determined compliance with accountability legislation. Instructional aides—an idea sparked by the War on Poverty as a way of hiring lower-income personnel in the schools—were also employed by the thousands. Finally, many new administrators were needed to oversee policies that had been created by the rights revolution—ensuring compliance with judicial decrees, administering disciplinary actions in an appropriate way, negotiating and implementing collective-bargaining agreements, designing school attendance plans that conformed with judicial guidelines, putting into place special-education and English-language learner programs, and administering the lunch program, the breakfast program, the medical services program, and a host of other federally funded programs.

The increase in personnel was not limited to instructional employees. Relative to the number of pupils, the support staff (everyone not defined as an instructional employee) was also doubling. People were needed to operate the buses, supervise children crossing busy intersections, prepare breakfast and lunch, type reports, handle communications, organize meetings, and perform the myriad other tasks a complicated bureaucratic system must perform. The ratio of pupils to support staff fell from 59:1 in 1960 to 44:1 in 1970, then to 30:1 in 1980, and, finally, down to 27:1 in 2006. In other words, the number of support staff relative to the number of pupils was growing as fast as that of instructional staff. In some districts, the parallel growth may have been shaped by local politics. In the Edgewood school district in San Antonio, Texas, the district that became the centerpiece for the legal-equity movement, the school board required that one new support person be hired for every additional teacher. The policy was locally popular, because support staff had to live in the community, while most teachers lived elsewhere.[5]

Altogether, personnel costs constitute approximately 80 percent of a school district's budget. Doubling the number of adult employees relative to the size of the student population between 1960 and 2005 meant doubling the personnel expenditure, even if salaries had remained flat in real terms. Inasmuch as salaries and wages rose faster than the rate of inflation, the real expenditure growth rate nearly tripled.

Even while money flowed so freely, schools still appeared to have insufficient funds. For one thing, the salaries needed to recruit quality teachers—the most important educational ingredient a school can provide—were not climbing at a rate needed to attract the kind of talent that schools had recruited in the past. The remarkable salary leaps won by Al Shanker in New York City in the early seventies drove the collective-bargaining movement forward. But initial successes did not translate into long-term gains. Instead, gains in average teacher salaries nationwide merely kept pace with overall salary and wage growth, so twenty-first-century teachers are no better paid, relative to other workers, than Shanker's colleagues were when he was teaching in East Harlem. Indeed, teachers, relative to other college-educated workers, are paid less than they once were. In 1962, teachers were being paid about the same as all other people with a college degree. But by the year 2000, the salaries of teachers were 30 percent lower, on average, than those of other employees with college degrees (see Figure 14 in the Appendix). The drop-off was especially large among secondary school teachers, the very teachers who were the most enthusiastic supporters of Shanker's drive for collective-bargaining rights.[6]

Changes were most dramatic for women. In 1950 the salaries of women teachers under the age of thirty were right at the median for all college-educated women in that age category. But fifty years later, two-thirds of all young college-educated women were earning more than a teacher of that age. For men, teaching has always been less financially rewarding than other professional occupations. In 1950, more than 60 percent of all young college-educated male employees were paid better than teachers; by 2000, this was true of nearly 70 percent.[7]

So the vast growth in expenditure for the nation's public schools did not translate into enough resources to pay young teachers salaries equivalent to levels in the past or build an educational system that was any more equitable or effective than the one in place prior to the civil rights revolution. For all the money that was being poured into the nation's schools, they remained unable to keep pace with changes elsewhere in society. Apparently, even more money was needed.

Fiscal Equity

It was in this context that the notions of fiscal equity and, later, fiscal adequacy were born. At a time when all problems had the potential for becoming constitutional issues, school expenditures became the subject of legal action. If students had rights, and the disabled had rights, and linguistic minorities had rights, and teachers had rights, perhaps public schools themselves had certain constitutionally protected rights. Although the idea of asking courts to order school expenditures challenged the ancient practice of leaving money questions to school boards, city councils, and elected legislatures, the undertaking made extraordinary headway, if only to leave even staunch advocates disappointed in the end.

Historically, school finance rested on the local property tax. Each community was responsible for the construction and maintenance of its own school system. Communities varied in their wealth, however, because some were composed of low-income households while others, like Wellesley and Newton, had prosperous homeowners or were the site of major commercial centers whose valuable properties could be taxed. The resources available for public education expenditure could thus vary by an amount that educator Jonathan Kozol said was beyond belief: "In 1989, Chicago spent some $5,500 for each student in its secondary schools. . . . Some $8,500 to $9,000 [is spent on] each high school student in the highest-spending suburbs. . . . The gulf . . . seems so blatantly unfair that it strikes many thoughtful citizens . . . as inexplicable."[8]

What Kozol found incomprehensible, states had long been aware of. Most of them had created a "foundation" program whereby the state would allocate to every district the funds deemed sufficient to create a basic school system. Local districts could top up the fundamentals as they wished. Defining "foundation" was a messy political process, and the end-product usually defied all reason, other than the basic democratic principle that the outcome could command a majority of the legislature. Yet the idea took hold in one state after another because it served as a pragmatic compromise that let each district define its own educational needs and aspirations, while assisting with the finances of schools in very poor districts.

Generally speaking, foundation programs grew in size and scope. The steady drift in finance was toward the state and away from the locality. Even so, 1960 data indicate that at the dawn of the rights revolution 57 percent of the revenue for public schools came from local sources. The state paid most of the balance, and the federal government made only a token contribution (see Figure 9).

In the wake of the *Brown* decision, district variation in school expenditure per pupil came under attack. In 1967, Arthur Wise, a student in the Department of Education at the University of Chicago, defended a doctoral thesis arguing that geographic inequities were as unconstitutional as racial inequities. I was asked to serve as Wise's external examiner—the one faculty member participating in the examination who had not served on the dissertation committee. As a junior faculty member, I was expected on such occasions to avoid disturbing a consensus the committee had already reached. I dutifully performed the expected role, since it was easy to be impressed by the force of Wise's legal suggestion. Why should the amount spent per pupil vary by geography any more than by race? One category seemed as irrational as the other.[9]

Wise's idea traveled to the University of California at Berkeley, where John Coons and his students built an even more persuasive case for fiscal reform. They showed ways in which local districts could preserve their autonomy yet still obtain adequate resources. Coons's ideas were reframed for legal purposes by Sidney Wolinsky, a Yale Law School graduate and volunteer for the War on Poverty's Legal Services Program. Wolinsky found a plaintiff, John Serrano, whose son had transferred from a poor Latino high school in Los Angeles to a school in the suburbs. Serrano had little to do but let his name be used, so he agreed to participate, though he later confessed to thinking it was "a pretty hopeless court complaint." Wolinsky and Coons soon proved otherwise, helped along by a state supreme court filled with judges one police chief described as "legislative sociologists." The California Supreme Court, in 1971, found that district spending disparities were in violation of the

U.S. Constitution's Equal Protection clause. "Quality is money," the plaintiff's legal team argued, and the court agreed.[10]

With *Serrano* tucked comfortably into place, the equity lawsuit bandwagon shifted into high gear, fueled by the Legal Services Program, as well as by support from the Ford and Rockefeller foundations. Within a year, five additional equity suits found success at trial. Even the Nixon administration seemed favorably disposed. Its commissioner of education declared it a "very fundamental breakthrough in the concept of state educational system," a positive-sounding, if somewhat incomprehensible, sentiment. In more direct language, the president himself declared it "a shocker, in a way," but still a "good thing." The groundswell seemed powerful enough to win a Supreme Court case, as the equity argument could cite a pregnant passage from Earl Warren's opinion in *Brown:* "It is doubtful that any child may reasonably be expected to succeed in life if he is denied the opportunity of an education. Such an opportunity is a right which must be made available to all on equal terms."[11]

But although the idea resonated, political clouds hovered over the country's high court. Warren was no longer chief justice, and the Burger court, while not reactionary, was hardly ready to embrace the full agenda of its activist predecessor. The disabled community, for example, was doing its best to get congressional action that would render moot any need for a Supreme Court decision. The fiscal-equity advocates were no less worried about their prospects. One Washington attorney warned against the "danger of an over-zealous, over-optimistic dash to the court." But even a nationally organized legal campaign cannot necessarily control the pace and timing of legal developments. Lawsuits can be filed by anyone, and those cases can acquire a life of their own, as *Rodriguez v. San Antonio Independent School District* would prove.

As a concomitant of its growth and boundary expansion, the

City of San Antonio had inherited multiple school districts which remained independent entities within the city's boundaries. Many of them, like the Edgewood School District, consisted of low-income, mostly Latino neighborhoods with few commercial resources to tax. As the civil rights movement spilled over into the Latino community, activists had complained about the quality of their schools and called for the removal of the district's white superintendent. Their attorney, Arthur Gochman, persuaded them to dig deeper into the issue and fight for the fiscal resources any superintendent, of whatever ethnicity, would require to staff an effective school system. Familiar with developments in California, he proposed a federal lawsuit and even approached the Mexican American Legal Defense and Educational Fund, which was initially based in San Antonio. The organization deemed the case not promising enough to be worth the required investment in time and money. So Gochman, working with Edgewood community activists and finding a San Antonio resident named Demetrio Rodriguez willing to serve as the lead plaintiff, took the case at his own expense even before the *Serrano* decision had been handed down.

As an individual attorney without statewide or national standing, Gochman did not cut a wide swath. Texas state attorneys rejected his equity claims out of hand, saying they were based on socialist doctrine. But the federal district judge was persuaded enough to hold the case open until the state legislature had time to consider possible remedies. As the case dragged on and the Texas legislature did nothing, *Serrano* was decided, bolstering Rodriguez's claims. To the state attorney general's surprise, the judge found Texas school finance arrangements in violation of the Fourteenth Amendment to the federal Constitution. Not surprisingly, the state appealed, and the U.S. Supreme Court agreed to hear the case. All of a sudden a fly-by-night lawsuit by a local attorney had become the vehicle for a decision on a question of national significance by the country's highest court.

Here the balance of legal power shifted. To the horror of the nationwide equity movement, Gochman seized the moment as his opportunity for glory, a chance to argue his first case before the highest court. Texas, chastened by its lower-court defeats, turned to University of Texas law professor Charles Wright, a friend of several justices and a respected legal mind who had successfully argued many a case before the highest court. Wright crafted a brilliant defense that highlighted the difficulties with fiscal-equity claims. Poor children lived in many places besides poor districts. Those with special needs required more than just equity. Equity could be achieved more easily by leveling down than by leveling up. If every school district was to have equal funding, then local communities would have to have equal funding for their police, fire, and sanitation needs, as well as for all other public services. Persuaded by such considerations, the court ruled against Rodriguez by a 5-to-4 margin. Writing for the majority, Justice Powell concluded that nothing in the Constitution identified education as a fundamental right requiring the highest level of judicial scrutiny. So long as states did not discriminate by race, they could allocate their educational dollars among districts as they saw fit.[12]

Rebuffed at the federal level, equity advocates turned their attention to state constitutions. If educational equity was not a fundamental federal right, perhaps it was guaranteed by state constitutions, which had similar equal protection clauses. Here they had greater success, especially in California. Though the Supreme Court had found that unequal funding was not a violation of the U.S. Constitution, the Golden State's high court decided it still violated the identically worded clause in the state constitution. A number of other state courts followed California's lead.

Yet the fiscal-equity movement gradually ran out of steam. By 1990, when the dust had more or less settled, plaintiffs had lost just as many cases as they had won (see Figure 15, Part A). As Wright had argued in the *Rodriguez* case, "fiscal equity" was easier to say than to define specifically. Should resources be the same when children are different? How about the needs of those in special education? Don't urban districts need more money per pupil than rural ones? So numerous were the ways in which "equity" could be interpreted, many judges concluded that the question could not be adjudicated.[13]

Even when such difficulties were overcome and plaintiffs were successful—New Jersey's 1973 case being the most celebrated example—implementation of court orders proved to be a political challenge. In New Jersey, the state's high court decided in 1973, in *Robinson v. Cahill*, that state aid to wealthier districts should be cut in order to give more aid to poorer ones. Such Robin Hood court decisions created antagonisms within legislative bodies. High-spending districts did not like to be told they had to decrease their educational offerings to the level set by lower-spending ones, nor did they appreciate large buckets of state aid going to other districts when they got none. New Jersey governor James Florio lost his re-election campaign shortly after pushing for school finance reform that met court equity requirements. Whether or not that issue was the deciding factor in the election can never be known, but legislators from high-spending districts took notice, and the courts and the legislature embarked on a continuing confrontation that lasted for more than a decade. And even when legislatures were compliant (as they were in California), the result did not necessarily yield more fiscal resources. One can level down more easily than one can level up. In the original home of the equity lawsuit, spending increases failed to keep pace with those in other states.[14]

In short, equity advocates discovered that ideas can fall short when they run up against entrenched interests. Arthur Wise and John Coons had conceived a powerful idea: equal protection before the law implies that all school districts within a state should have the same fiscal capacity. But that idea came up against the basic fact that those with more money want to spend more on their children's education, just as they want to spend more on housing, transportation, and all the other good things in life. To be told that their child's school shall have no more resources than any other school in the state runs counter to the desire of virtually all educated, prosperous parents to see their own children given every educational advantage. Fiscal equity was divisive. Some communities could get more only if other communities got less. Robin Hood makes for a good story—so long as it is set in thirteenth-century Nottinghamshire.

Fiscal Adequacy

One might say that the shift from equity to adequacy occurred by accident, were it not for the fact that it developed precisely at the time the country, tiring of equity talk, was becoming concerned about the adequacy of the American school. The spark was the 1983 report "A Nation at Risk," by the National Commission on Excellence in Education, whose work I will examine in the next chapter. Here I need only say that the study prompted many states, especially in the South and in border states such as Kentucky, to assess the quality of their schools. Commissions were formed, governors made pronouncements, business leaders convened, reports were composed, newspaper editorials were written, and, in Kentucky, a group of school superintendents, calling themselves the Council for Better Education, filed a lawsuit. To keep their coalition together, the superintendents eschewed a Robin Hood approach in favor of asking for more taxpayer dollars for everybody. For them, the real issue was not inequities among school districts but the minimal spending on education statewide. Despite their pleas, the Kentucky state legislature—though overwhelmingly Democratic—had refused to enact the desired tax increases. And so it was that in 1989 *Rose v. Council for Better Education* arrived at the doorstep of Kentucky's court of last resort, with broad political backing not only from school superintendents but also from business leaders, newspaper editors, and the governor himself. Though the lawsuit asked the court to take on a fiscal job usually reserved for the legislature, Kentucky's judges, aware of the groundswell of support for the idea, felt empowered to conclude that "the entire Kentucky education system was unconstitutional." The state had not lived up to its constitutional obligation to provide for an "efficient system of common schools throughout the state." The court decision, it said, applied "to the entire sweep of the system—all its parts and parcels." The legislature was ordered to provide "funding which is sufficient to provide each child in Kentucky an adequate education."[15]

Kentucky might have been a "one-off," an isolated case produced by peculiar political circumstances. But equity advocates, seeking new ammunition for their legal guns, quickly grasped its national implications. If state constitutions mandated "adequate education," lawsuits could be filed that could ask not just for equal funding but for more dollars altogether. By 2006, advocates had gone to court in thirty-nine states, with one or another combination of adequacy and equity arguments. Armed with photographs of rundown school buildings and evidence of abysmal and unequal student performance, teams of lawyers alleged that schools lacked sufficient funding to provide children with the quality of education guaranteed by the state's constitution. As a remedy, they asked courts to mandate large increases in state aid for public schools. In the vast number of court cases, the decision went to the plaintiffs (see Figure 15, Part B).[16]

Victories came one after another, despite the fact that the adequacy idea was not nearly as substantively convincing as the equity one. It is difficult to find in most state constitutions anything that says a legislature must spend a specific amount of money on state schools. It is true that almost every constitution does refer in some way to a statewide system of schools, but the language is typically as general and vague as the Kentucky requirement that there be an "efficient system of common schools throughout the state." New Jersey's constitution mandates a "thorough and efficient" system for "all" children, a popular phrasing that many state constitutions employed. Minnesota's says the state should have a "general and uniform system of public schools." Arizona's is phrased almost identically. Florida's actually uses the word "adequate," saying that "adequate provision shall be made by law for a uniform . . . system of free public schools." But none of these clauses, or those of any other state constitution, mention how much money should be spent. Thus, they provided only a very thin foundation upon which plaintiffs could seek to substitute court authority for that of the legislature.

Philosophically, the adequacy concept is more difficult to define than its sister concept, equity. Whatever difficulties the court had in defining "equity," the concept at least implied treating everyone more or less in the same way, unless a good reason could be given for doing otherwise. Adequacy, on the other hand, resembles beauty—something pretty much in the eye of the beholder. To determine adequacy, judges had to calculate what teachers should be paid, the optimal class size, the curriculum that should be taught, and many other specifics. To calculate what was "adequate," plaintiffs hired experts who gave their considered opinion on how much money was needed to obtain the requisite teachers and the quality of the space to bring student performance up to an adequate level. But the science upon which these experts relied scarcely went beyond astrology and tea-leaf reading.

In fact, even the best available evidence finds virtually no connection between additional school expenditures and gains in student performance. James Coleman's path-breaking study of the causes of student achievement found little correlation between expenditure and achievement, and subsequent studies confirmed Coleman's results time and again. Inasmuch as a large share of the growth in expenditure simply went to salary increases, adding support staff, or hiring administrators and others who never worked inside a classroom, the weak connection between expenditures and student achievement is not quite as surprising as it might seem.[17]

This is not to say that schools can be run without money; it says only that increments in expenditure do not appear to yield much in the way of higher levels of student achievement. Nor does it say that increased expenditures can never yield positive benefits for student performance. If additional monies were used to attract a higher-quality teaching force, or to retain especially effective teachers, or to take other steps that might make for more productive schooling, then court-ordered expenditure increments might have beneficial consequences for students. But judges, when handing down adequacy decisions, simply left it to local school districts to figure out how best to spend the money the court had awarded.

The most persuasive argument available to defense attorneys, however, had less to do with money per se than with the proper constitutional responsibilities of courts and legislatures. Precisely because no one can know just what it takes to create an adequate school, funding levels for education have always been set by elected officials, not by judicial fiat. Ever since the British Parliament snatched taxing authority away from the Crown, control over the power of the purse has been jealously guarded by legislatures as fundamental to democratic practice. To shift that power to un-elected judges is an extraordinary act. It may be justified in extreme circumstances as, say, part of the reforms necessary to remedy racial segregation. But for that authority to be extended to the determination of the level of funding it takes to have an adequate school is a bold grasp for power by an institution assigned the task of applying existing laws to particular situations, not creating new ones.

Philosophical and constitutional arguments are not necessarily the decisive element in court decision making, however. The balance of political power is often a good deal more important. In this regard, plaintiffs had big-time advantages over the defense. For one thing, they could pick the trial court, which meant they could choose one with a particularly inadequate school district and a judge with a particularly friendly judicial philosophy. A case brought before a trial judge in New York City fetched a ruling at trial that said New York State had to give the city's schools another $5.6 billion dollars annually in operating costs and another $9.2 billion dollars in construction costs. That would bring school expenditures up to $18,000 per pupil. According to the ruling, the state had to pay the full cost; the City of New York need not contribute an additional dime. Excluded from the handout, other New York State school districts wondered why *they* hadn't found some equally creative plaintiffs—and judges.[18]

Despite the over-the-top remedy, the suit received favorable treatment in the New York City press, perhaps because the money was to come from a source other than local taxes, but also perhaps because spending more on education is quite popular in the court of public opinion. In a nationwide poll conducted in 2007, 51 percent of those surveyed favored increased spending on education, while only 10 percent thought budgets should be cut. Another 38 percent favored keeping spending at current levels. Building on that base of public support, plaintiffs were able to dramatize for the press horrific stories of dilapidated schools with leaking roofs and antiquated plumbing. The defense might argue that such horrors were highly unusual or due to bad administrative practice. But such claims don't translate easily into television visuals.[19]

To respond effectively to plaintiff arguments in the court of public opinion takes strong action by a leading political figure. Seldom will that figure be the state school superintendent, almost by statute an advocate for his constituency. The office of the state attorney general has the constitutional obligation to fight suits filed against the state, but lawsuits can be fought aggressively or hardly at all. Ambitious state attorneys general (few are not) typically find little political advantage in taking a strong stance against public education, and as a result many an adequacy lawsuit has been weakly defended. Similarly, it takes a bold—or very conservative—governor to challenge an adequacy lawsuit.

So although the defense had the separation-of-powers doctrine on its side, plaintiffs had the political advantage once the debate turned from equity to adequacy. If equity lawsuits divided rich districts from poor ones, adequacy brought educational interest groups together against a diffuse, inchoate opponent: the taxpayers. As a result, it was easy to rally supporters and neutralize potential opposition. From 1990 to 2005, the plaintiffs won thirty-nine out of fifty-three cases (see Figure 15).

Despite winning many favorable judgments, plaintiffs still found the path from courtroom to classroom long and uncertain. The most powerful force was not a sophisticated defendant but the mere passage of time. Cases decided in trial court had to be taken to the appeals court and then to the state's court of last resort. All of that took years, and even when plaintiffs won, legislatures did not necessarily comply with court orders, requiring another round of court action. Meanwhile, the cost of living rose, and educational costs climbed at an even steeper rate, so remedies that originally seemed large turned out to be modest by the time they were actually implemented. Like hamsters on a treadmill, the plaintiffs often found themselves spinning in circles but never getting anywhere. On occasion, the legislature simply refused to comply, leaving the courts caught between sending legislators to jail or backing themselves out of the corner they had wound up in. That happened in Ohio, when the state supreme court, having found unconstitutional inadequacies time and again, finally shrugged its collective shoulder and said it was up to the legislature to resolve the question. In New York, the suit won spectacularly at trial, but the result handed down by the state's highest court was so modified and so long in coming that it fell far short of the plaintiffs' expectations. Nationwide, adequacy lawsuits did not lift educational expenditure any more in states where judgments were won than in other states.[20]

As the twenty-first century arrived, plaintiffs were encountering greater skepticism for their basic claims. Amazingly enough, the turning point came in Massachusetts, allegedly the country's most liberal state. It had climbed on the adequacy bandwagon as early as 1993, when the wheels were just beginning to turn. Advocates won a spectacular victory in *McDuffy v. Secretary of the Executive Office of Education,* which was immediately put into law by a friendly legislature. A decade later, adequacy advocates plotted a second try. But this time, in *Hancock v. Driscoll* (2005), they were handed a surprise defeat by a liberal state supreme court unconvinced that the state's schools were inadequate, despite a carefully written decision by the trial court judge. In contrast to the situation in 1993, the governor's office put up a stiff defense, and the highest court was presented with persuasive testimony that the state had in recent years funded the schools very well. In the wake of the *Hancock* decision, other courts retook the temperature on adequacy, and the idea floundered in one state after another, in part because of its own intrinsic lack of merit. Constitutions created school systems, but they also separated power between the courts and the legislatures. Judges did not have the power of the purse. Finally, in 2009, the U.S. Supreme Court weighed in on adequacy issues, finding in an Arizona case that the state need not spend more on English-language learners simply because their performance lagged behind that of other groups. The adequacy lawsuit tide was clearly ebbing.[21]

The Iron Law of Ever-Increasing Centralization—and Cost

The adequacy lawsuit has left one important legacy, however: it further shifted the burden of financing schools from local school districts to the state. When states were ordered to increase their spending, local districts cut their contribution, leaving the net impact roughly unchanged. The further centralization of school finance paralleled the larger shift in power away from local boards to higher levels of government. As districts oriented themselves to federal and state regulations, ties between schools and local communities weakened, making it more difficult for boards to raise revenue from the local property tax. Voters in California, Massachusetts, and elsewhere passed referenda limiting the rate at which the property tax could be increased, unless voters gave specific approval in referenda. In 1960, 57 percent of the revenue for public schools had come from local districts, mainly from the local property tax. That percentage fell to 44 percent by 2006. Offsetting the local contribution was a growth in the federal share from 5 to 10 percentage points. That number is set to rise steeply with the passage of the federal stimulus package of 2009. Prior to that event, the biggest increments had been coming from state treasuries. By boosting their income and sales tax rates, state legislatures found the monies to boost their contribution to public-school costs from 39 to 47 percent of the total (see Figure 9). As more centralized institutions—states, courts, and federal agencies—were taking control, revenue could be more easily obtained at higher levels than from local taxpayers.[22]

The centralization of finance was probably inevitable, given the economic reality that schools were facing. As a labor-intensive industry, education is doomed to a treadmill of rising costs and declining adequacy. Any industry that fails to keep pace with productivity gains in the overall economy will necessarily become more expensive or decline in quality, or both.

William Baumol and William Bowen set forth the economic logic behind this reality in a classic 1966 publication devoted to the economics of the "live-arts industry." To simplify the presentation of their basic point, they asked readers to imagine a world that has only two industries: makers of automobiles and producers of live string-quartet performances. In the automobile industry, inventions have made it possible to build better cars with fewer workers. But the number of person hours it takes for four people to play Franz Schubert's String Quartet in D Minor remains the same today as in 1824, when Schubert wrote the composition. No productivity increase is possible, apart from enlarging the concert hall, which can be done only up to a certain point without harming the listening pleasure of the audience.

In the auto industry, constant increases in productivity allow each worker to be paid more while the overall price of a car remains constant. But since live performances of string quartets cannot be produced at a faster pace, ticket prices must rise if violinists are to be paid salary increments that keep pace with those in the auto industry.

For this reason, live performances of string quartets, symphonies, theatrical productions, ballets, and operas are endangered species. As the economy becomes more productive, the salaries paid to performers must increase to keep pace with other wage growth. As prices rise, audiences diminish. Symphony deficits grow, and performing-arts institutions serving smaller cities close their doors. Repertory theaters struggle to fill their seats. When hard times arrive, the live-arts industry is one of the most badly damaged. The recession of 2008–2009, for example, left the industry in a state of near panic, with even major symphony orchestras at risk.

Baumol and Bowen said their analysis applied no less to education than to the live arts: "Education, like the arts, affords little opportunity for systematic and cumulative increases in productivity. The most direct way to increase output per hour of teaching—an increase in the size of classes—usually results directly in a deterioration of the product, which is unacceptable to much of the community. Thus, the financial problems which beset education are, at least in part, another manifestation of the fundamental relationship between productivity and costs."[23]

The education industry may be even worse off than the performing arts. Opera companies and symphony orchestras can subsidize live performances with income derived from the distribution of performances through compact discs, DVDs, and radio and television performances, and by giving popular concerts in large arenas that use loudspeakers which emit sounds that seem ugly only to the trained ear. Family foundations, local firms, and wealthy individuals have been willing to make large donations to sustain the live arts in their community. And the public is willing to pay more than twice as much of its income to attend live performances as it was when Baumol and Bowen did their study. The amount spent on legitimate theater and other live performances more than doubled, from 0.05 percent of Gross Domestic Product in 1966 to 0.11 percent in 2006. And if money simply cannot be found, artists may be willing to accept salaries well below what is paid for equivalent talent in other sectors, simply because the intrinsic rewards from performing are so great. Few things are more thrilling than performing Shakespeare on stage or playing a Beethoven symphony for an appreciative audience![24]

Schools have few of those advantages. Classroom teaching may have its own intrinsic rewards, at least for some, but the thrill of the classroom, day after day, can hardly compare to the applause that crowns a successful performance. So when the salaries of teachers fail to keep pace with those in other industries, the quality of available personnel declines. Capable math, science, and computer science teachers, always a scarce commodity, have become as hard to find as a spotted owl in daylight. Nor have schools yet found a way to subsidize live performances with products sold to mass markets. Unlike the opera companies that broadcast live concerts in movie theaters or on television, public schools have historically not put classroom events online. Businesses and foundations do make substantial contributions to public education, but donations still constitute only a trivial percent of total expenditure.

At one time, taxpayers were willing to spend an ever-higher percentage of their income on public education. Throughout the first three-quarters of the twentieth century, spending on public schools as a percentage of GDP crept steadily upward. From 1902 to 1920, it edged up from 1.0 to 1.5 percent, and then up to 2.2 percent by 1930. It then slipped to 2.0 percent by 1950, as the Great Depression, the baby bust of the 1930s, and World War II took their toll. But in the years that followed the war, American taxpayers more than doubled their commitment to K–12 public schools. The share of GDP grew from 2.0 percent in 1950 to 2.8 by 1960, to 3.9 by 1970 and to 4.5 by 1975.[25]

That period of increasing commitment to education has come to an end. Indeed, the share committed to K–12 education was just 4.1 percent of GDP in 2006—less than in 1975. One cannot attribute that slippage to Ronald Reagan, George Bush, or any other president, since the federal share of spending on education—10 percent of the total—was higher in 2006 than it was in 1975 and the Obama administration promises to lift the percentage even higher. States also have been willing—or forced by court decisions—to spend more money on schools, so the state share of the cost of education has increased as well. But all of those efforts by states and the federal government have been offset by a steady decline in the share of costs that local districts have been contributing. What may be gained in Washington or state capitals has been offset by decisions made by property-tax payers in 14,000 local school districts.

When the public limits its support for a labor-intensive industry, the quality of the services will decline. Salaries simply cannot keep pace with those being paid in the more productive sectors. When that happens, the quality of those working in the industry will slide. In education, it has already happened. The percentage of students with high SAT scores saying they plan to become teachers dropped precipitously from the 1960s to the 1990s. So did the percentage of teachers coming from selective colleges and universities.[26]

Ironically, school districts have aggravated the situation by becoming aggressively more labor-intensive. As mentioned, the number of employees relative to the number of pupils—instructional and support staff—doubled between 1960 and 2000. Teachers were given responsibility for fewer students, and many other staff members were added to execute administrative duties and provide ancillary services. This at a time that other industries were becoming more efficient by eliminating the person in the middle and asking consumers to become their own store clerks and bank tellers.

So long as the public was willing to commit an ever-higher percentage of its income to the provision of K–12 education services, schools could become more labor-intensive without undermining their quality. But around 1975, society—acting through its governments—chose to contribute no more than 4.5 percent of GDP for K–12 public education. Given that decision, schools could not continue to add more employees and at the same time pay the salaries it would take to attract high-quality teachers. In the event, districts chose quantity over quality.

It was left to others to call for a renewed emphasis on excellence in education. Though that effort has been long and convoluted and has yet to bear much fruit, it provides some hope for the future. Yet the main thrust of the excellence movement, by emphasizing standards and accountability, created still more bureaucracy and still more centralized control.

CHAPTER 8

William Bennett and
the Demand for Accountability

Our Nation is at risk. . . . The educational foundations of our society are presently being eroded by a rising tide of mediocrity that threatens our very future as a Nation and a people. What was unimaginable a generation ago has begun to occur—others are matching and surpassing our educational attainments.

—U.S. National Commission on Excellence in Education, April 1983

Accountability is the linchpin, the keystone, the *sine qua non,* of the reform movement. . . . Schools that produce good results should be rewarded; those that do not should face penalties that will spur them to improve.

—William Bennett, U.S. secretary of education, April 5, 1987

As was the case with the rights reform movement, the beginnings of the excellence movement's efforts to save the schools can be tied to a particular moment: the day the National Commission on Excellence in Education, appointed by President Ronald Reagan's secretary of education, issued its report "A Nation at Risk." The report's impact on the federal system would prove to be quite ironic, for Reagan's educational vision, like that of the country's founding fathers, expected states and localities to run their schools with no direct help from the federal government. Indeed, Reagan had promised to eliminate the same Department of Education over which Secretary Terrel Bell presided, and had refused the secretary's request to appoint a presidential commission. So Bell's group was only a "national" commission, with few prominent members and little chance of getting much attention.[1]

Yet the report proved to be the match that lit the kindling that fueled the excellence movement, a triggering event that mobilized national dissatisfaction—and, ironically, one that would extend still more centralized control over American education. The commission stressed that average SAT scores had fallen by more than ninety points between 1963 and 1980. "Average achievement of high school students on most standardized tests is now lower than twenty-six years ago, when Sputnik was launched," it lamented, concluding that "for the first time in the history of our country, the educational skills of one generation will not surpass, will not equal, will not even approach, those of their parents."

The commission's indictment was better defined than its solutions, which were little more than platitudes about the need for greater commitment and dedication. But so sweeping and credible was its critical assessment, the report set off another wave of school reform. Secretary Bell himself was too bland a figure to cut brave new swaths through American education, however. It would take a more articulate, more colorful figure who could use a Washington-based bully pulpit effectively, if the Reagan administration was to reverse direction, give up its attempt to eliminate the federal role in education, and spark a nationwide school excellence movement. For this task, it made much more sense to hand over the federal education reins to William J. Bennett, an outsider who believed that "education has deteriorated in America" because "our schools were systematically, culturally deconstructed. They were taken apart. Many of the things which mattered most in our schools were removed, and they were set adrift." Bennett, by preaching the "three C's"—content, character, and choice—would join the quieter and more academic James S. Coleman in becoming a high priest of the excellence movement.[2]

Theoretically, the excellence movement's two central thrusts—accountability and parental choice—are complementary strategies designed to enhance school quality: information supplied by an accountability system can be made available to parents, who can then make intelligent choices among schools. To win parental support, schools will provide an educational experience that results in high achievement. Just like love and marriage, choice and accountability go together like a horse and carriage.

But the way in which accountability and choice impact school operations is entirely different. Accountability requires the setting of standards, the measurement of performance against those standards, and the disciplining of states, districts, schools, and teachers who fail to meet those standards. As districts are asked to meet state requirements, and as states are asked to meet federal rules, the schools are subjected to still more bureaucratization and centralization. A uniform system that meets common standards becomes the ideal. But inevitably, the regulations at times become inappropriate, teachers become unhappy, and unions fight to minimize their effective application. To protect their most vital interests, teachers become even more dependent on unions. The complex of interests that runs the schools becomes ever more convoluted and entrenched.

The logic of parental choice is quite the opposite. Parents select their children's schools. Schools compete with one another for a clientele. To compete effectively, each school must have the autonomy to define its mission, recruit its teachers, and establish its ethos. Centralized directives interfere with efforts to satisfy parents.

When choice and accountability are pursued simultaneously, they operate on a collision course. Choice-based institutions need autonomy to win support, but accountability systems must be applied uniformly, if they are to be applied at all. This is the dilemma that has come to challenge the excellence movement: try to master the education complex, or else reconstruct it from the bottom up. Mastery via state and federal power seems easier to accomplish, and for that reason excellence reform became, in the first instance, accountability reform.

William Bennett

Bennett was hardly the first to notice the boredom and complacency in America's schools, but he did more than anyone else to broadcast the fact by trumpeting his three C's—content, character, and choice. Directly changing the state of American education was not his contribution, however. Just as Dewey did not do much more than encourage the progressive movement, so Bennett was more a cheerleader than the manager of the drive for excellence. Although Bennett wanted schools "to teach what we ourselves have loved— *The Call of the Wild, Treasure Island, Swiss Family Robinson, Huckleberry Finn"*—as secretary of education he never tried to establish a set of national curricular standards. Nor did he offer legislation asking that students be tested annually, much less hold them or their teachers accountable for their progress, though he asked states to do so. Federal direction of the nation's schools was unnecessary, Bennett said, because education was a state and local responsibility. It was the secretary's job to visit schools, identify problems, and issue calls for action. Bennett tired even of these activities, resigning as secretary of education before Reagan's term was up, though he later became the country's "drug czar."[3]

That said, Bennett must be credited with raising the profile of the excellence movement beyond the realm of a few nerdy professionals. He was the first to discern potential in the title "U.S. secretary of education," created when President Jimmy Carter persuaded Congress to elevate the Office of Education to departmental status. The first person to hold the office, Shirley Hufstedler, was a civil rights attorney who laid little claim to being the nation's first educator. The second secretary, Terrel Bell, was a virtual unknown, even after "A Nation at Risk" appeared. It was Bennett who transformed a virtually invisible position into one of the best-publicized jobs in the president's cabinet. After Bennett captured the public's attention, the state of American schools would never disappear as a national political issue.[4]

For decades, Democrats had "owned" the education issue in national politics. Democrats in Congress had fought hard to overcome Eisenhower's opposition to most forms of federal aid, and Kennedy made education a key plank in his campaign against Richard Nixon. Johnson had signed into law the first major school aid program, while teachers swarmed to the Carter candidacy when he promised to establish a Department of Education. Reagan foolishly sought to dismantle it.

"A Nation at Risk" often gets credit for changing the Republican party's direction. But the document needed a personality to give it life and meaning, something "Big Bill" Bennett was exceptionally capable of doing. Once he had done so, Republicans remade themselves into champions of educational quality. In 1989 the newly elected president, George H. W. Bush, met with the nation's governors, who agreed upon a set of national education goals to be reached by the year 2000. Although the goals were not met by the turn of the new millennium, Bush did see his son elected president on a platform that featured strong accountability and school voucher planks. During the campaign, the younger Bush mentioned education in half of his advertisements, whereas Al Gore's ads referred to it only a third of the time. Upon assuming office, Bush signed into law the country's first comprehensive federal school accountability law, No Child Left Behind.[5]

A movement can't possibly gain such momentum without attracting support from across the political aisle. The way was eased by Albert Shanker in his emerging role as national educational statesman. He endorsed George H. W. Bush's initiatives both in his weekly editorials and through his service on national committees. With that kind of support from organized labor, Democratic gubernatorial candidates—Ann Richards in Texas, James Hunt in North Carolina, Michael Dukakis in Massachusetts, and Bill Clinton in Arkansas—could confidently back student testing and tighter school accountability. President Clinton also pushed the federal agenda forward by signing legislation asking states to set standards and begin testing their students. In 2002, Democratic senator Ted Kennedy played a crucial role in assembling the coalition that passed NCLB by an overwhelming majority.[6]

The way forward was not as smooth as it sounds. The accountability road had many bumps and detours—so many, in fact, that the country ended up with a system of accountability that was more apparent than real. But let's not get ahead of our story. For now, it is enough to say that many leaders, Republicans and Democrats alike, responded with alacrity once Bennett, by campaigning tirelessly for the "three C's," placed accountability on the national agenda.

Bill Bennett was born in the Flatbush section of Brooklyn, New York, in 1943, not far from the Queens neighborhood where Albert Shanker had spent his childhood some fourteen years earlier. When Bill was still a toddler his parents divorced, though divorce went against their Catholic heritage. Young Bill attended Holy Cross Boy's School. After he moved with his mother, brother, and Hungarian grandmother to Washington, D.C., he attended a Catholic high school, Gonzaga College. Never forgetting that his football team had won two city championships, Bennett often referred to football and coaches when making points about American education: "I still watch the Gonzaga College High School football team and compare it to the one I played on thirty years ago. . . . The current team would have beaten our brains out. . . . Sports performance has improved because coaches did not stop doing the right things or stop having high expectations. They did not ask, 'Let's see, who will be coach today?'"[7]

That a U.S. secretary of education would have attended a Catholic, not a public, school defied all precedent. Ever since the days of Horace Mann and presidential candidate James Blaine (who in 1875 proposed that religious schools be barred from receiving government funds), public schools had been expected to rid education of sectarian influences, while Catholic schools were generally deemed to be educationally inferior. But their cachet had been enhanced by James Coleman's finding that students learned more in Catholic schools than in public ones (see Chapter 9). Bill Bennett did not need to apologize for his educational background.

That background was greatly enhanced by the Williams College diploma awarded to Bennett in 1965. A scholarship recipient, he had served his college as interior lineman, toyed with joining the leftist Students for a Democratic Society, and taken a philosophy course. "We did Plato's *Republic,* and I really got hooked on those things—questions of right and wrong, good and bad, justice and injustice," he later recalled, explaining why he had abandoned his plan to set up an advertising agency and "make lots of money and have lots of cars." He subsequently earned a Ph.D. in political philosophy at the University of Texas at Austin, where he met John Silber, who would become the outspoken president of Boston University. Like Silber, Bennett rejected the relativism of deconstructionist philosophy in favor of an unapologetic defense of the values expressed by "Judeo-Christian tradition." Ph.D. in hand, Bennett picked up a degree from Harvard Law School. Then, at age thirty-three, he drew on his connection with Silber to obtain his first major position: director of the National Humanities Center in North Carolina, a center for humanities scholars that received grants from a small federal agency, the National Endowment for the Humanities (NEH).[8]

His traditional approach to the study of the humanities attracted national attention, winning for him the directorship of the NEH itself. His NEH nomination by President Reagan originally ran afoul of two of the most conservative members of the Senate, John East and Jessie Helms of North Carolina, who held refusal rights for federal jobs of their constituents. According to what they'd heard, Bennett was a lifelong Democrat, had a picture of Martin Luther King Jr. hanging on his wall, and had picked many a Democrat to study at the National Humanities Center. Only after the conservative Heritage Foundation reassured the Capitol Hill Republicans was Bennett's nomination confirmed.[9]

Once ensconced in his new position, Bennett quickly raised his profile—and the ire of a vocal Ivy League professoriat—by substituting conservative humanities projects for liberal ones. So visible did he become, it was only a small stretch for him to jump to the top job at the Department of Education when it became available at the beginning of Reagan's second term. Bennett fought for the nomination, upsetting his old mentor John Silber, who wanted the job for himself. Reagan chose wisely, since Bennett was as aggressive and outspoken as Silber but also had the necessary political savvy.[10]

Bennett's "three C's" gave him the tools he needed to weave together the various strands of the excellence movement's struggle to save the schools. Consistent with his "missionary streak," it was the middle C, character, about which he spoke with the greatest passion. He endorsed Bible reading and school prayer at school, saying that the courts, in separating religion from public education, had defied the wishes of the founding fathers. He wanted children to learn homilies about Washington, Jefferson, Lincoln, King, and other heroes they could emulate. Analytical classes in "values clarification" were criticized for the distance they placed between teachers and moral judgments. Sex education should stress the virtues of abstinence, not the best way to use a condom. Most urgently, the country needed "schools without drugs." On his character platform, Bennett garnered enthusiastic support from social conservatives, apoplectic opposition from cultural liberals, and front-page, sometimes even complimentary coverage from writers in the mainstream media.[11]

For all his bombast, the secretary could do little about teaching character other than urge parents, teachers, and school boards to exercise their responsibilities. But what about the first and third C's—content and choice? Here the federal government could become an active force, both by holding schools to high educational standards and by creating choice-opportunities for families. How exactly would Bennett, and those who drove his agenda forward, tackle these questions?

Former U.S. Secretary of Education William Bennett (center) marches in February 1996 side-by-side with former U.S. secretary of education Lamar Alexander, a long-shot presidential candidate. Alexander crisscrossed New Hampshire in a checkered shirt, hoping it would jump start his primary campaign.

Getty Images / Timothy A. Clary.

Origins of Accountability

The first and third C's were not obviously compatible with each other. If excellence was to be achieved by means of choice and competition, then schools needed maximum flexibility to try out alternative strategies. But if the government wanted to upgrade educational content, then it had to supervise the educational context. Clear standards needed to be erected, information about student performance had to be gathered, and consequences for failure had to be spelled out. If choice decentralized power to schools and families, content control continued the march toward centralization Horace Mann had begun.

Bennett himself resolved that internal contradiction by doing very little of either, though he preached the virtues of both while making politically unrealistic suggestions, such as asking a Democratic Congress to turn the compensatory-education program into vouchers for low-income students. That agenda fit nicely with Reagan's own desire to keep the federal government out of the schoolhouse. But Reagan's local-control doctrine, and that of his party, had fallen out of step with the times. Local governments were no longer bastions of conservative power. Judicial activism, public-sector unionism, voting-rights legislation, and progressive professionals had shifted local power to the liberal side.

Given the new local reality, Bennett was not likely to get school boards to pay much attention to either content or choice, no matter how much he proselytized. If American education was to move toward excellence, the energy would have to come from higher levels of government, pushing the excellence movement more in the direction of content than of choice. By placing primary emphasis on the first C, content, Bennett and his Republican successors were about to add a fourth C: centralization, a departure quite out of keeping with Republican orthodoxy. Could Republicans reestablish the historic virtues, as Bennett wished, by establishing a degree of national control over the schools far beyond anything Horace Mann or John Dewey had ever dreamed?

If the answer to that question would be long in coming, Republican leaders could at least build upon material that was being assembled as early as 1969. This was the year in which the federal government conducted the National Assessment of Educational Progress (NAEP)—the first of a series of national surveys of student performance in math, reading, science, and other subjects. As the years went by, it became the yardstick by which both policy makers and the news media measured the country's educational performance.

State and local school officials had been suspicious of the NAEP's accountability potential from its very beginning. Any form of testing students could easily mutate into an accountability system that would allow lay people to compare one school with another. Though worried about that possibility, school officials nonetheless agreed to participate in the NAEP survey, mainly to get the Scholastic Aptitude Test monkey off their backs. The SAT was a privately administered test used to determine a student's suitability for college admission, but it had become a public embarrassment to learn, year after year, that average student performance on the SAT was steadily falling. The decline was apparent, not real, educators insisted. Previously, only the best and the brightest had taken the SAT; now, many more high school students were participating. When that happens, average scores inevitably decline, they argued; the drop in SAT scores was a good sign, not a bad one. To prove their point, they agreed to allow administration of the NAEP to a national sample of all students—not just college-bound ones— at ages nine, thirteen, and seventeen, with the expectation that it would show progress over time, just as the title of the survey predicted.[12]

To measure national progress but nonetheless avoid any semblance of accountability, the NAEP was designed in such a way as to keep schools, districts, and states from being compared with one another. Testing was done so that no complete score for any specific individual could be retrieved. Results were reported only for broad categories: for the country as a whole, for individual ethnic groups, for each of the four regions of the country, and for various types of communities (urban, suburban, and rural). That way, nothing was divulged about specific places people were interested in—particular schools, districts, and states.

Despite the limited information it provided, the NAEP drove the accountability movement forward. Expected to convince Americans that all was well with their schools, NAEP test scores revealed no more progress than SAT scores did. Indeed, it was the NAEP, and some international tests, which the "Nation at Risk" report relied upon to document the "rising tide of mediocrity." As pressures for accountability mounted, the NAEP itself was forced to change. It began identifying the levels of performance students needed to score in order to be deemed proficient, setting a high standard that in later years would prove embarrassing to the many states that had set the bar lower. When NCLB was enacted in 2002, it did even more to turn the NAEP into a state accountability device by asking that the percentage of students proficient in math and reading be reported for each state. From New York to California, and every state in between, voters learned just how poorly their schools were doing. What had once been forbidden was now required.[13]

As the NAEP drew attention to lackluster school performance, governors and other political influentials from outside the educational establishment found it necessary to respond. Initially, the focus was on the students themselves. In several states, high-schoolers were told they would have to take more of the traditional academic courses and to pass a minimum competency test if they wished to graduate. Developments in Texas were particularly eye-catching. Businessman (and future presidential candidate) Ross Perot said athletes should be barred from interscholastic competition unless they achieved at least a C in all their courses. "There is no account-ability in the public school system—except for coaches. You know what happens to a losing coach. You fire him. A losing teacher can go on losing for thirty years," he fretted. "When I was a kid, we took geography," he bragged. "We lived at a time when you knew where everything was and couldn't afford to go there. Now every-body can afford to go there but nobody knows where it is." Perot loved to point out that Soviet students studied physics and algebra for five years. "Just hearing that would give the typical U.S. high school student a Number 4 migraine headache." Such acerbic wit grabbed headlines and mobilized public support. Not only did the Texas legislature enact a "no-pass, no-play" law for school athlet-ics, but it asked every school in the state to report average student test scores—an idea which became so popular that every Texas gov-ernor, Democratic or Republican, found a way to extend it. For George W. Bush, it would become a signature accomplishment of his gubernatorial administration, an achievement which he would tout in his first presidential campaign.[14]

In other words, Texas put into place two forms of accountability. The first—student accountability—said that students had to obtain at least a C in their courses in order to participate in sports and other extracurricular activities. Along the same lines, other states chose to hold students accountable by requiring them to pass an ex-amination in order to graduate from high school. However, states were reluctant to set the test score bar very high for fear parents would become upset that their children would not be graduating with their peers. So the test score barrier was usually set at such a low point that only very low-performing students were challenged. The second form of accountability—school accountability—asked schools to release to the public the average test score results for stu-dents on state examinations. It was this second form of account-ability that proved to be the more durable, mainly because it did not hold any specific individual accountable for performance. Neither the scores of specific students nor those of specific classrooms were identified, so neither teachers nor students were shown to be performing below expectations.

Accordingly, school accountability became popular among southern gubernatorial candidates, as it helped them bridge the black-white political gap. By promising more money for education, would-be leaders appealed to the newly enfranchised black electorate; and by insisting on school accountability in exchange for the new funds made available, they sought the support of white voters as well. The idea was pushed in Kentucky, Tennessee, North Carolina, and Florida, and in 1986 the entire National Governors Association (NGA) endorsed greater school accountability. "To sum it up," said Tennessee governor and NGA chairman Lamar Alexander, "the Governors are ready for some old-fashioned horse-trading. We'll regulate less, if schools and school districts will produce better results." A few years later, Alexander would become the secretary of education. Even before his arrival, President George H. W. Bush and the fifty governors issued a joint proclamation committing themselves to "national performance goals . . . that will make us internationally competitive." Shanker hailed the plan as "bold and comprehensive. More so than any President or Secretary has come up with yet." Bush then asked Congress to create a national council that would invite students to take a national test which would meet "international standards."[15]

The Accountability Challenge

Traditionally, accountability had been left to the teachers in their classrooms. Teachers gave students grades, from A to F. They decided whether to promote a child from one grade level to the next. They did not allow a student to graduate until he or she had passed the required number of academic subjects. That old-fashioned accountability system made teachers *and* students responsible. If teachers gave out a failing grade or did not recommend promotion, they had to explain to colleagues and supervisors that the fault was the student's, not their own. If such within-school accountability operated mainly behind closed doors, it worked well enough in a country consisting mainly of small schools, small districts, small communities, and local school boards.

That old-fashioned system of accountability was breaking down under pressure from progressive and democratic reformers. F's are discouraging and perhaps racist, school boards were told, and a child who is kept back is removed from his or her peer group— something that should not happen even to a lazy or disorderly child. To fix the situation, A-to-F grading schemes were dropped in favor of more ambiguous ones, promotion to the next grade became virtually automatic, and high school diplomas were conferred on nearly all those who attended class more or less faithfully. That not only gave students a break; it did much the same for teachers. Since they no longer needed to determine if students had learned enough, teachers were freed from teaching anything specific. The impact on students was profound, Shanker felt: "Whenever I gave an examination or a quiz or told kids to bring in an essay, the whole class shouted out, 'Does it count? Does it count?' We have an educational system in this country in which nothing counts."[16]

As traditional accountability was breaking down, the case for more centralized forms of assessment gained strength. Now that teachers and principals were no longer the authorities, others had to clarify what it was that students needed to learn. Statewide tests had to be devised so that the legislature could see whether or not the students had learned the required material. Information had to be gathered annually, so that students' progress could be tracked. The degree of centralization was beyond anything that even the most progressive of reformers had ever attempted.

School accountability is tricky business, however, because students both vary in their ability and learn as much out of school as within it. Expecting every school to bring its students up to a certain level of performance is not unlike expecting hospitals to ensure that everyone is both minimally healthy and has a lengthy lifespan. While doctors and hospitals are increasingly being held accountable for diagnosing medical conditions and selecting the most appropriate treatment, those accountability expectations generally take into account the patient's health and willingness to comply with medical advice. A school accountability designed along similar lines would hold schools and teachers responsible for the gains in learning students make from the beginning to the end of the year.

It is not easy to gauge student performance from the beginning to the end of a year, however, because many students move from one school to another even within a single year. Besides, governors and legislatures have been eager to obtain results quickly, and building tests that can measure growth in learning takes both time and careful attention to test design. So the new state accountability laws usually eschewed information on the learning growth of each student from year to year in favor of gathering simple report cards from each school that gave the average math and reading scores of all students in each grade at the end of each school year or the percent deemed proficient in these subjects. But such numbers often said less about the quality of the instruction at the school than about the students' family backgrounds. Without a growth-based measuring stick, schools were being held accountable in a way that was as misleading as holding a hospital accountable regardless of the medical condition of its incoming patients.

An even more challenging question involved the curriculum students were expected to know. Bennett himself did not find that question particularly difficult. The American people, he declared, "are emphatic and consistent about what it is that our children should be taught in math, what should be taught in science, what should be taught in history." That might be accurate when one is speaking of just the early years of schooling. Most Americans probably expect first-graders to learn to recognize common words and numbers, do single-digit adding and subtracting, read simple material, and write short sentences.[17]

But when it comes to high school, reaching agreement can be challenging. European and Asian countries do set national examinations, so the problem is tractable. But in a country with a pluralist, fragmented, locally controlled school system where the federal government's educational role has been mainly that of a rights reformer, consensus is not so easily obtained. For a brief moment immediately following Bennett's term in office, it appeared that President Bush and Secretary Alexander were, with the help of the nation's governors, on the point of securing congressional agreement to a set of national standards, which would form the basis for a test students would be invited to take. Had that effort succeeded, it is just possible a voluntary test could have evolved into a gold standard that could have shaped the excellence movement for decades to come. But what seemed possible in 1991—as the president was reaching the very height of his popularity, with his triumphs in Europe and the Persian Gulf—vanished as quickly as the president's high approval ratings. A Democratic Congress, smelling victory in the upcoming election, was not about to give a Republican president a political freebie.

So resolution of the standards question was turned over to the Clinton administration. Having been an accountability advocate in Arkansas, the new president initially pursued the Bush agenda with only modest changes. But he soon encountered powerful opposition from both the left and the right. On the left, Clinton continued to have Shanker's backing, but most educators, including the NEA and most civil rights groups, did not want all students held to a single national standard—at least not until the federal government gave schools a lot more money. Union leaders, employing the same arguments they had used in equity and adequacy lawsuits, deplored any suggestion that common expectations should be set for all students unless massive federal aid was forthcoming. Breaking with his fellow educators, Shanker argued: "We don't abolish medical school exams because not everyone has had the opportunity for top-notch pre-med education." But much to Shanker's dismay, Clinton dropped the idea of national standards and a national test, substituting a requirement that states create their own standards.[18]

Proponents of national standards took another hit once conservatives realized just how national standards might be deconstructed by the new educational professoriat. During the waning days of the Bush administration, the Department of Education, along with the NEH, the same agency Bennett had once headed, gave a group at the University of California in Los Angeles (UCLA) the job of drafting the history standards that were to be adopted. All was well and good until the contents of the UCLA-prepared standards became known. At that point the United States, as one headline put it, came to "the end of history," or at least the end of history standards. The first salvo was launched by Lynne Cheney, who had succeeded Bennett as NEH director and who had agreed to fund the UCLA group in the first place. She denounced the negative portrait of the United States to which children would be exposed under the new curricular guidelines. "Imagine an outline for the teaching of American history in which George Washington makes only a fleeting appearance and is never described as our first president," she began. Instead, students were encouraged to "analyze the achievements and grandeur of Mansa Musa's court" in Africa, or to hold a mock trial of John D. Rockefeller in which he would be charged with "unethical and amoral business practices." The standards were rife with other alleged imbalances as well: "Harriett Tubman, an African-American who helped rescue slaves by way of the underground railroad, is mentioned six times. Two white males who were contemporaries of Tubman, Ulysses S. Grant and Robert E. Lee, get one and zero mentions, respectively." McCarthyism was condemned sixteen times, but Stalin's crimes were not mentioned.[19]

Other voices rushed to the UCLA group's defense. A Columbia University professor responded in a way John Dewey would have approved: "There's never a moment when an historical question is settled, about which over time there is not some debate. . . . The process of revising and reinterpreting history is what historical scholarship is all about." Or, as one history teacher involved with the project explained, "History is very messy, and kids have to get in there and wrestle with the material." UCLA's project leader defended the outcome by explaining the process: "We had an open, democratic process and listened respectfully to all points of view." Summing up the debate, a writer for the *New York Times* concluded: "As Oscar Wilde put it, 'the one duty we owe to history is to rewrite it.'"[20]

Teaching that kind of postmodern relativism to elementary and high school students might have pleased a few professors, but it made little political sense to the Clinton administration—at least not after November 1994, when Republicans, thought to be firmly in the doghouse, captured control of Congress just as the report was being released. Shanker, too, was appalled. It was a "travesty," he said, to call "white people . . . evil and oppressive, while Genghis Khan is [portrayed as] a nice, sweet guy just bringing his culture to other places." At last finding a cause to rally around, the U.S. Senate condemned the standards by a vote of ninety-nine to one. The UCLA-recommended standards were revised to make them more palatable and eventually became available for states that wanted to use them. But Congress reasserted its preference for local control, and all attempts to write a national curriculum were abandoned. The Clinton administration gave up the effort to hold *students* accountable, and *school* accountability requirements were so watered down that many states simply ignored the legislation's testing requirements. It was up to the next administration to move the accountability agenda forward.[21]

No Child Left Behind

Clinton's successor, George W. Bush, willingly assumed the task. In his election campaign, accountability had helped the Republican elephant to steal the Democratic donkey's educational backpack. Accordingly, Bush placed school reform near the top of his legislative agenda, and within a year of his inauguration he had signed a bill into law that centralized power over education in ways that went far beyond anything that had preceded it. The unforgettable title: No Child Left Behind.

According to NCLB requirements, each state had to set curricular standards in reading and math (and, later, in science), design a set of tests aligned with those standards, determine the level of proficiency students were to reach each year, and test all students in grades 3–8 and again in high school. By 2014, all students were expected to reach the proficiency standard set by each state. In the intervening period, each school had to show that the percentage of its students deemed proficient was steadily increasing—at an annual pace that would bring it up to 100 percent proficiency by 2014. Key subgroups of students within the school—ethnic minorities, low-income students, and the disabled, among others—were expected to show gains that would bring them up to the same level of proficiency.[22]

The Bush administration managed to smuggle a little school choice into the law as well, despite the fact that the law could not be passed without the support of Democrats, for whom "parental choice" and "school vouchers" were loaded terms. In cases where schools failed to make adequate yearly progress (AYP) for two years in a row, parents had the option of sending their child to another public school in the same school district. In cases where schools failed three years in a row, parents had the option of picking an outside private vendor who was to provide extra educational services, usually an after-school program. Finally, if a school failed for five years in a row, then the school was to be reconstituted. None of these options came close to anything resembling school choice, as defined by its proponents. But their inclusion gave the appearance of having fulfilled a campaign pledge.

After passage, NCLB had some successes. States that had promptly implemented NCLB provisions saw the test scores of their students rise by a larger increment than did those in the laggard states. Students who were given after-school services seemed to have learned more than those who did not participate.[23]

But the accountability glass was more than half empty. What was missing was more significant that what it contained. For example, the way in which NCLB chose to hold schools accountable failed to create a level playing field. By expecting all schools to arrive at the same level by the year 2014, it expected more of schools serving the disadvantaged than those whose students had already received the educational basics at home. An excellent school serving inner-city students could be—and was—identified as a failure, while a weak suburban school, capitalizing on its clientele, passed. As a result, NCLB called some schools failing when they were doing at least as well as other schools given a pass. In Florida, there was a 30 percent probability that students were learning more at a failing school than at one given a passing grade. An umpire who called balls and strikes with that kind of error rate would soon be fired—even in the Little League.[24]

Not only did NCLB's accountability lens provide misleading information about school quality within a state, but it totally distorted comparisons among states. The cause of the distortion: allowing each state to establish its own standards and its own definition of proficiency, thereby generating fifty different meanings of the same concept. The word "standard" originally referred to the flag or emblem carried high in battle in order to martial a fighting force toward a fixed objective. If standard-bearers marched off in various directions, they led portions of the battle force toward divergent objectives, opening the army to flank attacks. So they had to be utterly reliable and consistent. Accordingly, "standard" came to mean something that was fixed, such as the specific metal-weight for an official coin or the unchanging value of a precious metal against which the value of paper currency could be compared.

It is thus an oxymoron to hold schools accountable to more than one standard, as is the case under NCLB, which allows each state to establish its own standard, no matter how widely it diverges from some national definition. A very few states—Massachusetts, Maine, South Carolina, Missouri, and Wyoming—have defined proficiency as rigorously as the world standard set by those who administer international tests. But standards in most states fall far short of that international mark—North Carolina, Oklahoma, and Tennessee being the most extreme laggards. So, according to official definitions, Johnny can be a proficient reader in North Carolina but will cease to be so should he cross the border into neighboring South Carolina.[25]

So varied are state standards that the rigor of a state's proficiency definition is a better predictor of the percentage of schools said to be "failing" (not making AYP) than the overall quality of education in the state, as estimated by NAEP scores. In Massachusetts, for example, 43 percent of the students failed to make AYP, despite the fact that the state has the highest-performing students in the country. Why? Because Massachusetts has one of the highest standards in the country. Conversely, only 7 percent of the schools in Tennessee are failing, though the state ranks near the bottom in terms of school performance. Why? Because Tennessee has one of the lowest operational definitions of proficiency in the country.

As for NCLB's choice-provisions, they were designed to fail. To obtain the requisite Democratic backing for the law, Bush had backed away from his campaign promise to give vouchers to students attending failing schools. Nor could a child attending a failing school be given the choice to attend another school outside the district he lived in. Congress was not about to ask white suburbanites to admit minority students from failing central-city schools any more readily in 2002 than the Supreme Court had been in 1974 (see Chapter 4). Instead, the law simply gave parents of students at twice-failing schools the opportunity to attend another public school within the same school district—so long as that school was not also failing. Even the minimal amount of choice left in the law was barely put into effect. Most local districts made it difficult for parents to change schools, forcing choosers to jump through many bureaucratic hoops before giving them limited options from which to pick. Five years after NCLB's enactment, fewer than 1 percent of all eligible students were participating in the choice program.[26]

NCLB gave students access to supplemental educational services offered by private providers, if their school failed for three years running. In 2006, this option was exercised by about 10 percent of eligible students, most of whom attended after-school programs at which additional instruction was given in small classroom settings. Several years later, the program seemed to be growing in size, fairly popular among disadvantaged families, and marginally successful. Although this can hardly be faulted, it seems odd that NCLB, after all the trumpeting, had become little more than an after-school program.[27]

Politically, accountability remained a popular goal; but in practice, NCLB had many flaws. Still to be determined is whether its imperfections are temporary glitches, or whether accountability will be the latest reform gone completely awry. In principle, the current system can be patched. National standards can be set, measuring sticks can be better designed, and more appropriate consequences for failure can be devised. But if this is true in principle, politics precludes such a solution. The accountability system we have today grew not like Topsy but according to political rules. It is accountability in appearance, not in fact—exactly what one would expect if the vested interests do not wish to be held responsible.[28]

Bennett himself seemed ambivalent as to whether accountability could drive excellence. "The key to excellence is local control," he always argued. A faithful Reaganite, he never did propose a national curriculum, national standards, or a national testing regime. When judged by his actions as secretary, Bennett seems to have thought the federal role was mainly hortatory, not anything as concrete and convoluted as No Child Left Behind. When he retired to the private sector, he instead became for a while a player in the fast-developing world of virtual education.[29]

School accountability implies centralized control, whereas excellence requires flexibility, autonomy, and imagination. Admittedly, school accountability was an essential step, an avenue that needed exploration before other approaches could be tried. It shed a bright light on the performance of the American school. It shifted attention from dollars and teacher credentials to the amount students were learning. It documented the stagnation of the educational system as we know it. It showed the futility of the attempts to transform education by top-down regulation. But it distracted attention from the student—the person who, in the end, is the one primarily responsible for his or her education.

Student Accountability

From its inception, the excellence movement was trying to address the boredom, complacency, and misdirection to be found in the secondary education system. "A Nation at Risk" was focused on the problems of the American high school. Shanker's push for national standards had the same focus. "It's like the Olympics," he said. "There's an external standard that students need to meet, and the teacher is there to help the student make it," he continued. "Imagine saying we should shut down a hospital and fire its staff because not all of its patients became healthy—but never demanding that the patients also look out for themselves by eating properly, exercising, and laying off cigarettes." Yet neither the Clinton administration's accountability plan nor NCLB contained any indication that students should be responsible for their own education. Schools were instead held accountable for their clients, regardless of the students' willingness to attend to their own education.[30]

NCLB might have asked students to learn certain material before being passed on to the next grade and, certainly, before graduating from high school. That would have restored much of what had been lost when the old-fashioned accountability system was dismantled. National examinations are given in the last years of secondary school in many European and Asian countries. The tests are based on subject matter for which a good deal of preparation is necessary. The higher the performance, the better the chance the student has of obtaining a good job or gaining access to higher education. The exams drive the secondary-school curriculum, and the evidence is strong that students in such countries learn more math and science than in countries, like the United States, that have no such examinations. Despite success abroad, there have been few attempts to create such a national examination in the United States. Progressive reformers were more taken with the SAT, said to be a test for which one did not have to study. Nor did a demanding test have much appeal to the rights reformers, who feared low performance by minority students. Neither were teachers thrilled about having to show that their students could perform well on a national examination. Among union leaders, only Shanker lent the idea his support.[31]

Some states toyed with minimum competency tests that students needed to pass before graduation. Unlike the European and Asian examinations, which could be passed at multiple levels, the minimum-competency tests challenged only the few low-performing students at risk of not passing. In strong contrast to his backing for the European testing model, Shanker gave no support to the minimum-competency examinations, which he thought meaningless. "The political system can't support a high rate of failure," he pointed out. If the minimum-competency tests were probably better than nothing, since they raised the performance of those at greatest risk, they still fell hopelessly short of introducing excellence into American education.[32]

PART THREE

SIGNS OF RESURRECTION

CHAPTER 9

James S. Coleman and Choice Theory

Families use whatever resources they can to get a good education for their children. If they cannot use the performance and behavior of their children to do so, they use money or racial exclusion.

—James S. Coleman, "Some Points on Choice in Education," *Sociology of Education,* 65 (October 1992)

Excellence was seldom to be found in 2006, when David Ferrero, an officer of the Bill and Melinda Gates Foundation, reviewed five first-hand, book-length accounts of teaching and learning at individual high schools. In one account, a rookie teacher, telling her own story, "struggles to establish authority in her classes and generally fails; . . . her students ritually defy her, going so far as to openly declare their intention to get her fired for the sheer sport of it." At another school, "numerous attempts" by well-meaning, hardworking teachers fail "to coax students out of their shells, engage them in important issues, and motivate them to perform on tests." On and on, such tales go. A powerful but hostile peer group seemed in charge of the learning process.[1]

According to Cornell economist John Bishop, the problem begins in middle school, where "nerds" are harassed. "Studiousness is denigrated . . . in part because it shifts up the grading curve and forces others to work harder to get good grades. . . . Victims of nerd harassment hardly ever tell their parents, their siblings, or their friends. Most accept the proposition that . . . acting like a dork is bad. . . . Complaining to a teacher is self-defeating. Squealing on classmates only exacerbates [the situation]."[2]

The problem did not appear suddenly at the beginning of the twenty-first century. Fifty years earlier James Coleman, reflecting on his own adolescence, had detected something quite similar and then provided a sociological explanation for the phenomenon.

James S. Coleman

Born in 1926, Coleman began his graduate studies in sociology at Columbia University in 1951, one year before Dewey died at the age of ninety-two. The two intellectuals had had much in common. Both came from ordinary, small-town families, but they both had entrepreneurial spirit, tremendous energy, and personal fortitude that belied their surface modesty. Neither was a brilliant lecturer, but both were kind, gentle, supportive mentors, surrounded by devoted graduate students. Like most Americans, both were pragmatists—concerned less about systematic theory than about learning what worked in practice. Neither saw his work on education as the centerpiece of his life's work. Dewey was a philosopher; Coleman, a social theorist and mathematical model–builder. Yet neither man would have made as lasting a contribution, were it not for his work on schools.

Despite the similarities, Dewey and Coleman walked in contrasting intellectual worlds. If Dewey's thinking was shaped by Rousseau, Hegel, and the Romantic tradition more generally, Coleman's owed more to two Scottish empiricists: David Hume and Adam Smith. The "Emile" of significance to Coleman was not Rousseau's mythical child but Emile Durkheim, a sociologist whose point of departure was not the state of nature but a well-defined community context. Coleman's work was more disciplined than was Dewey's.

Trained in survey research and modern analytic techniques—random sampling, systematic data collection, rigorous comparisons—taking hold at Columbia, Coleman was able to test his ideas in ways unavailable to Dewey. Most important, Dewey and Coleman had separate agendas: Dewey's ideas shaped the public schools of the twentieth century; Coleman deconstructed what Dewey had built.

Unlike Dewey, Coleman never became a household name, yet his impact on American education has been immense. At his memorial service in 1995, New York senator Daniel Patrick Moynihan observed that the man they were remembering was among "a very small number of people who end up defining a major part of the intellectual agenda for their times. Their work is both so powerful and so well argued . . . that others are inspired to focus on these same issues." Coleman's impact was not without its ironies, however. His research served the civil rights movement King had begun but also the reaction that was to follow. His studies first accelerated and then helped put the brakes on school desegregation. A part of his work has been taken to mean that schools are insignificant, while another part suggests they are decisive. Coleman himself saw no contradictions.[3]

We know few details about Coleman's early educational experiences, in part because Coleman himself wanted us to believe that at age twenty-five he had sprung directly from the head of—well, not Zeus, but Robert Merton and Paul Lazarsfeld, two men in Columbia's Sociology Department whom many students thought had god-like qualities. Reflecting back on what seems to have been something like a conversion experience, Coleman said: "I left a job as a chemist . . . and took on a new life. . . . The transformation was nearly complete. Except for my wife (and other kin who lived far away in the Midwest and South), I shed all prior associations. . . . [After] the resocialization I underwent at Columbia from 1951 to

1955 . . . I was a different person." It was Merton's social-theory course that did the trick, "a conversion experience for those of us eager for conversion."[4]

The grandson of an evangelical preacher, Coleman certainly knew the religious meaning of the concept he was invoking. But his first twenty-five years left more of a mark on him than he was willing to acknowledge. Born in Bedford, Indiana, he began high school in Greenhills, Ohio, a place he wrote about almost wistfully: "School life had, for a few of us, a more academic focus, in retrospect surprisingly so." Shortly thereafter his father took a job as a factory foreman in Louisville, Kentucky, a city that had two public high schools for boys: "Male (with a college preparatory curriculum) and Manual (with vocational and pre-engineering curricula)."[5]

Coleman adjusted to his new school by becoming a member of the school's football team. The "boys who counted in the school," he writes, "were the first-string varsity football players," because "Male and Manual were locked in a fierce football rivalry that culminated every Thanksgiving Day but flavored the whole school year." He was quickly drawn in. "[The] environment had shaped [his] own investment of time and effort, intensely focused on football, although arguably [his] comparative advantage lay elsewhere." Otherwise, high school "failed" him. Apart from an eleventh-grade algebra class, he could not find anything "to excite my interest and capture my full attention." One day, while hitchhiking to football practice, he thought longingly: "If only they would not destroy in us the interest with which we came to school, I would ask for nothing more." Only when Coleman arrived at Columbia did he find faculty members with a "personal (that is, selfish) interest in some of their students. They seemed to be interested in those students in a way I had never felt since the ninth grade," perhaps because "graduate students help bring professors closer to immortality."[6]

He nonetheless attended a small college, before joining the Navy in the middle of World War II. After his discharge, he used his benefits under the voucher-like GI Bill to earn a B.S. degree in chemical engineering from Purdue University. Though he was then hired by Eastman Kodak in Rochester, New York, Coleman was still a frustrated product of Manual High, a technician who wanted a more intellectual challenge. Despite his limited resources, he made a dramatic career decision to pursue a Ph.D. in sociology. Rejected by Harvard and Michigan, he won admission to the overcrowded program at Columbia.

He could not have been more fortunate. In 1951, Paul F. Lazarsfeld was using newly developed quantitative techniques to look at practical topics: mass media, advertising and political campaigns. At the same time, Robert K. Merton was systematizing his sense of the ironic—unexpected things happen for reasons no one anticipates—to which he gave the rather pompous label "latent-function theory." Coleman drank from both professorial wellsprings, but it was Merton who "provided the inspiration for it all." In his italicized words: "I worked *with* Lipset, worked *for* Lazarsfeld, and *worked to be like* Merton." Like Merton, Coleman viewed the world with an outsider's irony: things are not as they seem, and consequences differ from what is expected. At a personal level, Merton endeared himself to Coleman the day he asked the young man about his dissertation plans. Told that none had been devised, Merton suggested that Coleman simply use the chapters he had drafted for a study of trade unions he was writing in collaboration with Seymour Martin Lipset, the department's up-and-coming assistant professor. Acting on this advice, Coleman had his thesis completed just three years after matriculation. Shortly thereafter, he submitted a research proposal to the U.S. Office of Education's new Cooperative Research Program.[7]

Until this point, nothing in Coleman's early career indicated he would become the premier education sociologist of the twentieth century. No one at Columbia specialized in educational sociology, a field Coleman disparaged as languishing in the cellar of the discipline. But as he was ruminating over possible topics for a federal grant proposal, Manual High came up one night at a dinner party the Colemans were hosting for Martin Trow (coauthor, with Coleman and Lipset, of the trade union study) and his wife. The Trows had attended elite schools where sports were subservient to academics, not only in the schools' official focus but also in the students' interests and social relationships. How different from Manual High![8]

Turning the conversation into a research proposal, Coleman laid out a plan to study several schools in Illinois, near the University of Chicago, where Coleman had been hired as an assistant professor. The book that emerged, *The Adolescent Society,* which is as much a theoretical commentary on Manual High as an analysis of ten schools in Illinois, remains Coleman's masterpiece.[9] According

James Coleman giving a lecture at the University of Chicago.
University of Chicago News Office.

to Coleman, the focus at these schools was on sports stars, cheer-leaders, and other members of the leading crowd, known more for smart dressing than for smarts per se. Those who studied hard and got good grades were edged to the social sidelines. For those who excelled scholastically, success must appear to have been "gained without special efforts, without doing anything beyond the re-quired work." Otherwise, one is socially isolated by "the crowd." Ostensibly, schools are educational institutions, but their latent function is social and quite inimical to educational purposes. It is the way in which U.S. schools are organized that is the problem, Coleman says. They resemble jails, the military, and factories: all of these institutions are run by an "administrative corps" that makes demands upon a larger group (students, prisoners, soldiers, work-ers). In response, the larger group develops a set of norms that gov-ern the choices individuals make. "The same process which occurs among prisoners in a jail and among workers in a factory is found among students in a school. The institution is different, but the de-mands are there, and the students develop a collective response to these demands. This response takes a similar form to that of work-ers in industry—holding down effort to a level which can be main-tained by all. The students' name for the rate-buster is the 'curve-raiser,' . . . and their methods of enforcing the work-restricting norms are similar to those of workers—ridicule, kidding, exclusion from the group." With his typical irony, Coleman dedicated the book "To my own high school, du Pont Manual Training High School, Louisville, Kentucky."[10]

What Coleman had identified at Manual High intensified when the civil rights revolution changed the balance of power between student peers and those in authority. To make things worse, teach-ers were now workers, too, their jobs protected by collective bar-gaining. To maintain order, a political bargain was struck, in a pro-cess described by Arthur Powell and his colleagues in their book *The Shopping Mall High School*. Students and teachers agreed to comport themselves properly, so long as expectations were minimal. Students chose courses that were easy, that met at convenient times, and that included their friends. They did homework, provided there wasn't too much. One boy said he deliberately arranged his schedule to avoid homework, so he would have time to "work, play, and be with my friends." They never complained when little was expected of them. "Why should we? We just want to get out." They thought their teachers probably felt the same way. The teachers were "goof-offs" just like the students, and were just as eager for the schoolday to end, so they could begin their second jobs. Avoidance treaties were mutually advantageous: like had found like.[11]

Within integrated high schools, the way in which the peer group shaped motivation acquired a racial coloring. African American students who focused on their studies and achieved high grades were accused of being "Oreos"—black on the outside, white on the inside. Academically oriented Hispanic students had to endure similar insults. Resistance and indifference to schooling knew no racial boundaries, however. "No more important finding has emerged from the inquiries of our study," wrote Theodore Sizer about a school with mostly white students, "than that the American high school student, *as student,* is all too often docile, compliant, and without initiative."[12]

Coleman III and the Emergence of School Choice Theory

That school choice should be the solution to complacency and disengagement in public education is hardly obvious. Students at "shopping mall high schools" have had a plethora of course options. Giving them a choice of school would merely stretch that concept one step further. Yet Coleman, after exploring "academic games" and other progressive ideas, thought school choice was the best strategy for addressing the fundamental problems he identified at Manual High. If parents and students owned the schools that they attended—because they had a choice of which school to attend—then they would no longer resemble workers in a factory or prisoners in a jail.

That parents should have a choice of schools is not a modern idea. The seventeenth-century theorist John Locke urged families to take responsibility for educating their children. Thomas Paine wanted the government to pay the costs, but he left school choice up to parents. John Stuart Mill proposed government-funded choice in order to have both universal education and instruction within a family's religious tradition. Horace Mann's celebration of the public school as nation builder eclipsed such thinking, however, so the idea of choice had to be reinvented in a modern guise.

In 1955, just one year after the *Brown* decision, Coleman's colleague at the University of Chicago, Milton Friedman, had made the initial case for publicly funded vouchers that parents could use at the school of their choice. When schools are being run as local public monopolies, he said, they lack sufficient incentive to respond to consumer demand or to search for ways to improve. If parents had vouchers, schools would have to compete with one another for student enrollment. "Government . . . would give each child, through his parents, a specified sum to be used solely for paying for his general education," Friedman proposed. "The parents would be free to spend the sum at a school of their own choice, provided it met certain minimum standards. . . . The result . . . would bring a healthy increase in the variety of educational institutions available and in competition among them."[13]

Though persuasively formulated, Friedman's proposal soon had a blot on its escutcheon that the school choice movement is still trying to erase. In an embarrassing aside, Friedman admitted that "there can develop exclusively white schools, exclusively colored schools, and mixed schools. Parents can choose which to send their children to." Though Friedman said he deplored racial segregation, he also opposed government efforts aimed at coercing parents to send their kids to racially mixed schools, asking those "who oppose segregation and racial prejudice . . . to try to persuade others of their views." A number of southern state legislatures actually tried to preserve segregation by introducing a voucher program. Though federal courts quickly ruled such statutes unconstitutional, the damage had been done, and civil rights groups ever since have been wary of school vouchers.[14]

After those abortive attempts to use vouchers for segregationist purposes, Friedman's proposal languished for years. Yet, ironically enough, the struggles over desegregation kept the choice idea alive, as choice became one of the few successful tools that helped to integrate schools with minimal conflict. School boards created choice-based "magnet schools" that attracted a racially balanced set of students from across the district. When early experiments proved successful, the Nixon administration, with support from Democrats in Congress, gave such schools extra funding, and the idea spread. By 2000, more than 5,000 magnet schools had been created throughout the country. Districts also tried out a range of proposals giving families the opportunity to choose a school outside their residential neighborhood. A few suburban school districts agreed to accept, voluntarily, a limited number of students from central-city school districts. In places that adopted the "open-enrollment" plan, parents indicated their preferred school among all those in their district. Those parental choices that facilitated racial integration were given the edge. Public-school choice acquired a progressive patina—so much so, that a conservative Supreme Court would, in 2007, forbid choice plans that gave an edge to one race over another. These magnet schools and open-enrollment plans were still nothing but distant cousins to Friedman's voucher proposals, however. The choices were managed by school districts, were limited to public schools, and gave only limited scope to parental preference. Competition among schools was virtually nonexistent. Despite the growing interest in school choice, vouchers remained but a conversation piece for a few policy wonks.[15]

And then, in 1981, Coleman wrote his third major report, identified here as Coleman III. Two years previously, Coleman and his colleagues at the University of Chicago had been asked by the National Center for Educational Statistics to extend the work begun in Coleman I. The study was to be more than a single-shot survey along the lines of Coleman's earlier work. Instead, several rounds of data were to be collected. A nationally representative sample of high schoolers were to be tested as sophomores and then again as seniors, after which they would be followed into college and the labor force. In this way, Coleman expected to find out how much students learned between their sophomore and senior years, as well as the impact of schooling on college attendance and labor force participation. Coleman also convinced the U.S. Department of Education, which was funding the study, to look at private schools as well as public ones. He now got his chance to see if private and public schools across the country were as different from one another as Manual High differed from those elite schools his friends at Columbia had attended.

The survey of some 70,000 students at more than 1,000 high schools was conducted in the spring of 1980. Working at his usual extraordinary pace, Coleman reported his team's findings back to the government that same September, even as a presidential election campaign was in full swing. After the election was over and the Reagan administration had assumed office, the results from the first round of data collection were released. Coleman reported that sophomores in Catholic schools performed at higher levels than those in public schools, apparently showing in practice what Friedman had argued in theory. In education circles, it was about as dramatic as the first proof of Einstein's theory of relativity. Coleman explained his findings by claiming that students at Catholic schools benefited from the "social capital" surrounding the religious school: parents knew and supported one another as they attended Mass and participated together in other religious activities. As another group of sociologists put it: "Catholic schools benefit from a network of social relations, characterized by trust, that constitute a form of 'social capital.' . . . Trust accrues because school participants, both students and faculty, choose to be there."[16]

The attacks on Coleman III were no more polite and detached than the attacks on Coleman II. The day it was released, "people entering the auditorium were handed leaflets attacking the study." The executive director of the National Association of Secondary School Principals insisted that the study used "incomplete data inappropriately applied." The *New York Times* chided Coleman for publicizing his results, saying that "sociologists invite trouble" when they seek "the stardom of advocacy based on their fallible predictions." Its news reports quoted Coleman out of context in order to give the impression that he himself thought "the study was deeply flawed and that [he] was retreating from his conclusions," though Coleman had said nothing of the sort. A number of professors and education experts denounced the report. One called it a "premature" report of "an ax-grinding nature." Fumed one Harvard faculty member, "While the findings are wrapped in a mantle of social science research, the report is inconsistent with the notion of disciplined inquiry," curiously objecting to the fact that "the findings are presented quite plainly." Another set of critics opened their essay with: "The methods and interpretations used by [Coleman and his colleagues] fall below the minimum standards for social-scientific research."[17]

A good deal of the rhetoric can safely be ignored, but two criticisms were valid. (1) Students at fee-charging private schools cannot easily be compared to those attending free public schools, because they come from families who are willing to pay for their children's education. Although Coleman III adjusted for parental education and many other family background characteristics, that adjustment did not necessarily take into account the greater educational commitment of parents who were willing to pay for their children's education. (2) The study showed that sophomores in private school performed at a higher level, but it did not prove that they had learned more there. It was possible that the children who were being sent to private school were, to begin with, more capable students.

Coleman and his colleagues replied to these criticisms two years later when the second round of "High School and Beyond" data became available. This time, they were able to show that students in private schools had learned more between their sophomore and senior years than their counterparts in public school had. The findings calmed the skepticism of the more reasonable of their critics.[18]

Coleman and his colleagues made some errors. They might have decided to withhold their results until they'd gathered information on student gains in achievement in high school, not just the initial sophomore scores. And they made various methodological errors, as frequently happens when one is undertaking an innovative project. But the biggest tactical errors were made by Coleman's opponents. By relentlessly attacking Coleman III, they helped to place school choice on the national political agenda. What had been an academic debating point during the 1970s became, in the 1980s, a part of the national conversation.

The Controversy Continues

As a faculty member at Chicago, I was able to observe the Coleman III controversy at fairly close hand, and I began taking a careful look at parental choice as a potential reform strategy. When visiting Stanford, I learned that political scientists John Chubb and Terry Moe were helping to design a survey of administrators and teachers working at the schools included in the Coleman III study. The two wondered whether school morale and mission might be crucial for learning, even if money and materials were not.

Recognizing the potential of their study, I asked Chubb and Moe to join me at the Brookings Institution when I became the director of its governmental studies program in 1983. Seven years later, their study, *Politics, Markets, and America's Schools,* showed that private schools were more effective because they enjoyed more autonomy, had a clearer mission, and asked more students to take academically challenging courses. Private schools had the independence to concentrate on educating students, while public schools were distracted by politics, regulations, and the push and pull of interest groups, they argued.

That the moderately liberal Brookings Institution appeared to have endorsed school choice provoked much controversy. Al Shanker attacked the work as "irresponsible" and "dangerous." The union-connected Economic Policy Institute insisted that "Chubb and Moe were motivated to defend conclusions formed in advance of their empirical work." Harvard professor of education Richard Elmore minced no words at all: Chubb and Moe substitute "rhetorical facility and ideology for a . . . serious understanding of the subject," he claimed, warning readers against "analytic skill deployed in the service of an ideological position." Gene Glass and Dewayne Matthews complained that Chubb and Moe's work did not have "the validity of randomized experiments"—a fair criticism, but one that was true of virtually every other education study of that time.[19]

What was being said in academic corridors was much worse. At the time the work was published, I had already left Brookings for Harvard, where I was asked to help with a search for a senior education scholar for the university's Kennedy School of Government. When the committee recommended Chubb's appointment to the Kennedy School faculty, a nationwide campaign was mounted against the appointment. Letters were received from education school professors across the country, many of them making points more political than substantive. When the appointment was not made, the event gave credence to Coleman's observation, some years earlier, that scholars "hesitate to ask research questions which might lead to results that would elicit disapproval by . . . colleagues. . . . The stakes are not trivial. I think of a sociologist who, during the fervor of the 1960s, asked the wrong questions . . . and subsequently failed to get tenure." Energized by the events, I accepted an offer in 1996 to become the founding director of Harvard's Program on Education Policy and Governance, set up over strong opposition from elements elsewhere within the university. More excitement was yet to come.[20]

Even before accepting this position, I had begun to take a look at the nation's first school voucher program, in Milwaukee, Wisconsin. The Milwaukee story is laid out more fully in the next chapter. For now, it is enough to know that initially a small number of students were given vouchers to attend private schools, so long as those schools did not have a religious affiliation. John Witte, a professor at the University of Wisconsin, had evaluated the initiative, concluding that parents loved their new schools but that student learning had not improved. Inasmuch as most of Milwaukee's secular schools were not yet well established, the finding was not particularly surprising. But I became intrigued by the collected data when I realized that hidden within the evaluation was information that could be used to conduct a randomized field trial (RFT), the very thing Glass and Matthews had found wanting in the Chubb-Moe investigation.

RFTs are thought to be the gold standard for scientific investigations. Harvard's former president, Larry Summers, who later served as a top economic adviser to the Obama administration, called them one of the five greatest research inventions of the twentieth century. Certainly, they have revolutionized medical research and practice. To test the effectiveness of a new medication, individuals are randomly assigned to one of two groups. The first is given the experimental pill, the second a placebo. If the health of the pill group improves but that of the placebo group does not, the pill, if otherwise safe, may be marketed. If the health of the two groups remains essentially the same, the pharmaceutical firm has to go back to the drawing board, since medications cannot be marketed unless an RFT demonstrates that they are both effective and safe.

In Milwaukee, private schools had been asked to admit students by lot if the number of applicants exceeded the available space. Witte had collected data on those admitted via the lottery, as well as on those who failed to win the lottery. A comparison of the two groups was tantamount to conducting an RFT along the lines done in medical research. When Witte released the data upon which his evaluation was based, a graduate student, Jay Greene, and I took a closer look at the results from the RFT that had accidentally been conducted. Our preliminary analysis showed that vouchers had no effect on student performance. Since I had never before conducted an RFT, I shared these results with three Harvard colleagues: Frederick Mosteller, the statistician renowned for one of medicine's premier RFTs; Christopher Jencks, who knew the complexities of education data sets; and Don Rubin, the country's leading RFT statistician of the day. The group was notably unimpressed. Rubin, never a man to mince words, said our analysis was simply wrong. But he generously offered to help—even to the point of asking one of his graduate students, Jiangtao Du, to assist with the project, using the design Rubin recommended. Within days, Rubin's recommended analysis provided an answer consistent with Coleman III. The Milwaukee voucher program, after three and four years, had a clearly positive impact on student performance in math and a smaller but still detectable one in reading. Jay Greene and I released the paper reporting these findings two weeks before the

American Political Science Association (APSA) met in September 1996.[21]

One cannot generalize much from a study of a few hundred Milwaukee students, but we were delighted to discover that newspapers nationwide thought the results were newsworthy. Then came the retribution from union commentators, public school officials, and various academics. It was said that the private schools had cheated when conducting the lottery—a charge for which there was no basis. They accused us of releasing our results before the APSA meetings, even though the association requires that all papers be made available a month before the sessions begin. Critics said we had presented the results in a misleading way in the *Wall Street Journal* in order to make it appear that the effects for math and reading were the same, when in fact the impact in math was twice as large. Unfortunately, this particular charge was deadly accurate. The newspaper's editors had constructed a misleading graph without our knowledge.

It was much more fun to read the accusation, repeated again and again, that we had orchestrated our release with Republican party leaders so as to coincide with Robert Dole's endorsement of vouchers at the Republican National Convention. In fact, we were Democrats who had had no contact with any Republican officials at all. A press officer had advised us to hold the study until after the Republican convention, because reporters would be so absorbed with covering the convention that they would ignore the study. But we had an obligation to distribute the paper prior to the upcoming APSA convention, which required an immediate release of the findings.

No one likes to have one's reputation impugned by a battery of critics and reporters as willing to make personal attacks as to offer substantive criticism. But all the controversy yielded one beneficial consequence: it gave me the opportunity to raise the money that enabled us to conduct three additional RFTs. My colleagues and

I studied privately funded voucher programs in New York City, Washington, D.C., and Dayton, Ohio. This time, we had many more participants, and students could attend any private school of their choice, religious or secular. We conducted the lotteries ourselves, so we could be sure students had in fact been randomly given the opportunity to receive vouchers if they wished. The project fully occupied our program at Harvard for the next six years. In the end, we found that vouchers had no impact on the test score performance of white and Hispanic students, but after three years they had a strongly positive impact on the performance of African American students. We explained our finding by saying that African Americans had the most limited school choice of all, because they had few economic resources and faced discrimination in the housing market. As a result, their choice of residence—and of the public schools that served their neighborhoods—was severely restricted.[22]

Since our findings differed by ethnic group, we were criticized by both camps in the voucher debate. Advocates of vouchers said we had looked at the short-term impact of small-scale interventions, which proved nothing about the long-term impacts of a large-scale voucher intervention such as Friedman had proposed. Opponents did not hesitate to question our personal integrity. In one of the more temperate critiques, Arizona education professor Gene Glass accused us of giving "social science theory a bad name" for conducting a randomized field trial—even though only a few years previously Glass had attacked Chubb and Moe for *not* using that methodology. We responded as best we could, taking satisfaction from the fact that our work was being given Colemanesque treatment.[23]

Ideas and Interests

Ideas acquire political potency when they have something concrete to build upon. Just as the accountability movement was driven forward by the lack of progress identified by the National Assessment of Educational Progress, so the school choice movement gained impetus from a series of studies indicating that schools which survived in the marketplace were more effective than those operated by the government. Friedman offered a theory as to how schools benefit from competition; but until some empirical information could be assembled around the theory, it remained ensconced within an ivory tower.

Yet empirical information is always open to dispute. In the study of human behavior, no methodology is so foolproof, no investigation is so carefully done, and no finding is so well established that critics cannot find a flaw. When a study has potential political impact, those with a stake in the issue will search for methodological errors that can be used to challenge the results. In this way, entrenched interests hope to protect themselves from threats that the new ideas pose.

In the case of school choice research, it is not difficult to find flaws and limitations. Quite apart from the research designs and statistical methods that became the staple of academic and public commentary, the studies are limited by the fact that they can look only at school choice as it exists at the time of the study, not at the choice system that proponents want to create. For example, all the comparisons of public and private schools looked at a world in which public education was free while private schools charged tuition. But in a Friedman-like voucher program, all schools would be privately operated and all students would receive public funding. For that reason if no other, a voucher system would look entirely different from anything that exists today. Currently, private schools compete against public schools that are free to the consumer, and for this reason private schools necessarily focus on niche markets: the well-to-do, the religiously devout, and the socially conservative. In a full-scale voucher world, private schools would receive as much government support as public schools and as a result would undoubtedly cast a much wider net. Comparing public and private schools today thus cannot tell one very much about the way schools would look if funding arrangements were entirely different.

Nor do the studies give any hint as to the political viability of a system of school choice. Would the public support a system of choice? On the one hand, choice fits well with parents' desire to customize their children's schooling to their specific needs. On the other hand, it runs contrary to a deep-seated, centuries-long shift toward more central control over schools. Could anything as radical as what Friedman proposed reverse such a long-standing trend? Even if parents longed for greater control over their children's education, wouldn't other interests be able to block proposals for change? Public education is a large, expensive industry that employs millions of people and issues contracts worth billions of dollars to outside vendors. Any proposal to radically restructure that system is likely to encounter intense resistance. When real-life school choice proposals are fashioned, they are likely to be altered by the politics of choice. They may bear little resemblance to the ideal that Friedman envisioned.

CHAPTER 10

The Practice of Choice

It is ironic that the American system of higher education, with generous taxpayer support, provides . . . choice in the selection of colleges, while in elementary and secondary education, which is compulsory for all, there is choice for so few. All parents, not only the affluent, must be able to exercise greater choice in what, where, and how their children learn.

—William J. Bennett, *Our Children and Our Country: Improving America's Schools and Affirming the Common Culture* (New York, 1988)

Ideas, once strengthened by research, acquire even more potency when they are given a real-world trial. When Kentucky's legislature responded favorably to a court ruling that its funding policies were constitutionally inadequate, it jump-started a national legal adequacy movement. When magnet schools proved they could further racial desegregation, the choice movement gained impetus. If school vouchers could be successfully introduced in practice, they might have an impact well beyond anything conceived by Milton Friedman or James Coleman. At least, that was the hope of a number of school voucher enthusiasts in Wisconsin.

Milwaukee: The Nation's First—and Last?—Voucher Program

States are "laboratories of democracy," said Supreme Court justice Louis Brandeis. On the whole, the observation exaggerates state capacities to innovate, but it nicely fits the Badger State, the place where fearless public servants have often ventured into unknown policy territory. Wisconsin was the first to try out unemployment insurance, the first to reform its welfare system, and, in 1990, the first to run an urban school voucher program, which within eighteen years would expand to include upwards of 18,000 students in more than 120 schools.[1]

A bipartisan, biracial coalition was necessary to make this happen. Republican governor Tommy Thompson, a presidential aspirant, had designed a welfare reform plan so successful it became the model for the Clinton administration's reforms. The governor wanted to achieve something comparable in education. Drawing upon Coleman's research, he proposed a number of pilot school voucher plans. But the state legislature, responding to pressure from the teacher unions, rejected each proposal the governor made. It did, that is, until black legislator Polly Williams and community organizer Howard Fuller persuaded the governor to support a targeted, low-income voucher plan for Milwaukee. Inspired by the Black Power movement, they had previously asked that a separate all-black school district be formed within the city. Only then, they believed, would black children be taken seriously. When that idea failed, Williams and Fuller found ways of fitting Thompson's voucher idea to their agenda. They had also enlisted the help of Democratic mayor John Norquist, the well-endowed Bradley Foundation, and many leaders active in the Milwaukee Chamber of Commerce. The *Milwaukee Journal-Sentinel* was converted from hostility to supportive neutrality. Behind the scenes, a "mom and pop" policy advocacy operation, run by Susan and George Mitchell, conducted policy analyses and mobilized parents.

Even a potent coalition that crossed the left-right political divide was able to institute a sizable voucher program only gradually and with great difficulty. The breakthrough in 1990 was limited to just 1,500 low-income students, and only secular private schools, just 10 percent of all private schools, could participate in the program. But it did move school choice from the drawing board to a living, practical reality. The school choice coalition now had a group of parents—and several schools—with a stake in school choice.

In 1996, when Republicans won control of both the legislature and the gubernatorial chair, they expanded the program to a maximum of 15,000 students and allowed religiously affiliated schools to participate. Once the expansion survived court scrutiny, the program steadily grew and the enrollment limit was raised to 22,500 students.

Throughout the two decades since the program was enacted, political controversy has been rife. The Wisconsin Education Association (the state's largest teacher organization) and the pro-voucher coalition have fought each other on every front. Both have secured strong partisan support, so that divisions in the legislature have fallen almost exactly along party lines. When one party is in control of the House and the other is in control of the Senate, key legislation stalls until a compromise can be reached on the voucher question. Both sides have shown the capacity to defeat key but vulnerable members of the state legislature. Both sides have sought to sway the Milwaukee school board, and power has fluctuated back and forth over the years. When the pro-choice coalition wins the upper hand, it builds ties between public and voucher schools, creates charter schools, and gives parents greater choice among schools within a decentralized public school system. Policies move in the opposite direction when the unions and their allies recapture control of the board.

Most dramatically, the voucher question has been thrashed out in the Wisconsin courts. Union-backed plaintiffs filed suit against the inclusion of religious schools in the program, arguing that it violated the constitutional prohibition on the "establishment of a religion." Defendants replied that vouchers did not establish any religion, so long as parents had a choice of both religious and secular schools. The trial judge ruled in favor of the plaintiffs, thereby postponing the inclusion of religious schools in the voucher program for two years, during which time the Bradley Foundation paid for the cost of the vouchers. Then, in one of the voucher movement's greatest victories, *Jackson v. Benson* (1998), the Wisconsin Supreme Court reversed the trial court decision. Provided that parents had a choice of school, secular or private, no religion was being established.

Even before the victory in the Wisconsin Supreme Court, school vouchers seemed on the verge of going national. Bill Bennett had proposed that the federal compensatory education program be turned into a voucher program for the poor. Vouchers had been endorsed by Robert Dole in his 1996 speech accepting the Republican nomination for president, the event that made our Milwaukee study topical (see the previous chapter). Voucher proponents, almost by sleight of hand, had slipped a voucher bill for Cleveland through the Ohio state legislature. In Florida, Jeb Bush kept his 1998 campaign promise to offer vouchers to kids who were attending failing schools. When running for president in 2000, his brother George campaigned for a similar program. The idea won constitutional legitimacy when the U.S. Supreme Court, in *Zelman v. Simmons-Harris* (2002), ruled the Cleveland, Ohio, voucher program constitutional. Voucher bills were passed in Louisiana, Colorado, and Utah. Even Congress was persuaded to create an experimental pilot program for the District of Columbia.

Nor was that all. If a general voucher bill could not be passed, proponents pressed for vouchers for students with disabilities or students with autism. And when state legislatures were resistant to vouchers, the school choice coalition succeeded in winning tax deductions and tax credits for people who sent their children to private school. In Minnesota, individuals could deduct certain education-related expenses, regardless of whether their children attended public or private school. In Pennsylvania, corporations could get a credit if they donated money to a foundation that passed the money to children from low-income families. Arizona and Florida had their own tax credit programs.

Despite these successes, the voucher movement stalled somewhere in the first decade of the twenty-first century. Teacher unions were bitterly opposed, while polls revealed the public to be steadfastly divided or indifferent. Al Shanker's opposition was wholesale. "Without public education, there would be no America as we know it," he argued. Even vouchers for disadvantaged students were harmful. They would be "merely the nose of the camel in the tent," which would soon lead to vouchers for all. "What will be the effect of taking some of these best and brightest students out of public school?" he asked.[2]

No less important than the opposition of unions was that of similarly minded judges in state courtrooms. After the Supreme Court ruled that vouchers did not violate the Establishment clause of the federal constitution, judges found vouchers in violation of clauses in state constitutions. In Florida, it was said that Jeb Bush's voucher plan ran afoul of a clause stipulating that schools be uniform throughout the state. In Colorado, a court construed a state constitutional clause to say that all publicly funded students must attend district-run schools.

But it was not just in the courts where choice supporters hit unexpected roadblocks. In California, Washington, and Utah, voucher proposals were put on the ballot, only to be rejected by voters sympathetic to public schools and resistant to the unknown. Voucher coalitions have done slightly better in legislative chambers where deals can be made and proposals can be adjusted to offset objections, but even there vouchers have repeatedly run into trouble.

Missouri is a prototypical case in point, in part because it is a microcosm of the country as a whole, a bellwether in presidential elections. Voucher supporters in Missouri crafted their proposals to forestall opposition as much as possible. To avoid charges of partisanship and racism, the coalition found black Democratic legislators willing to lead the fight. To avoid the "v" word, especially unpopular among civil rights activists, they proposed a "scholarship" program. After encountering opposition from rural legislators, the scholarship program was limited to St. Louis students from low-income families.

But for voucher supporters, it was nothing but "St. Louis Blues." Many in the city's black community had jobs within the public school system. Much of the advertising in the potentially sympathetic African American newspaper came directly or indirectly from the public school system. Superintendents in rural communities called their Republican legislators and asked them not to undermine the public schools. With all this opposition added to that of a tight phalanx of teacher unions and school board members, the idea was rejected each time it was presented.

Nor were the results from Milwaukee as startlingly positive as advocates originally hoped. True, more students graduated from high school if they attended a Catholic or Lutheran school than if they remained in public school. True, a well-designed 2009 study found that boys learned more in the voucher schools than in the public schools (though girls learned more in public schools). True, the Milwaukee school board persuaded the union to accept changes in seniority provisions, so that principals could have more control over their teaching force. True, Milwaukee schools, faced with competition, were introducing innovations: fewer middle schools and more after-school programs. True, research suggested that student performance in public schools improved when they faced increased competition. But those positive developments were offset by evidence showing that a number of the new voucher schools were badly run, both fiscally and educationally, giving opponents horror stories to advertise. More important, none of the positive findings were spectacular enough to jump-start a national movement. The Milwaukee economy did not revive, suburbanites did not flock back to the city to take advantage of the new educational opportunities, and the achievement gap did not close. Mainly, Milwaukee failed to have a national impact because it was not obviously and overwhelmingly successful.[3]

The school voucher idea changed the conversation about schools. Its time may yet come. But two decades after the Milwaukee voucher bill was enacted, the number of students in the United States who go to school with vouchers or who are financed by a tax credit hovers around 160,000: only three-tenths of one percent of all those in school. Even the federally funded experimental voucher program in Washington, D.C., was scheduled for closing by Congress, despite evidence it was proving successful—an action taken with the full support of the Obama administration. If the school choice movement were to transform American schools, it would need to devise alternative mechanisms.[4]

Charter Schools

For many school choice theorists, vouchers are canonical: they produce the full-throated competition Friedman advocated. But a theoretically less elegant school choice innovation—the charter school —has proved to be politically more viable. Charters are privately managed organizations that receive government funding once their request for a charter has been authorized. Neither quite a public institution nor entirely a private one, charters are a middle way, a pragmatic compromise between ideal competition and none at all. In 2008, only two decades after the idea was first proposed, forty states were allowing applications for school charters, and more than a million students, about 2 percent of all those in public school, were attending more than 4,000 charter schools.

Nothing is more American than a charter, a contract that binds two parties to agreed-upon terms. It was a charter that Queen Elizabeth gave to Sir Walter Raleigh, according him full control over the dominions he would call Virginia (after the "Virgin Queen"). And it was a charter granted to Dartmouth College that Daniel Webster so eloquently defended in a classic property rights case argued before the Supreme Court. Could a charter also be the tool that would transform America's schools?[5]

Charter Theory

An unknown Massachusetts education professor named Roy Budde thought so. In 1988 he proposed that districts, upon request, grant charters to teachers at individual schools. They would have the autonomy to manage their affairs, so long as they lived up to their agreement with the district's board. Al Shanker, who had never forgotten his early annoyance with school principals, endorsed the idea, giving it a national audience: "One of the things that discourages people from bringing about change in schools is the experience of having that effort stopped for no good reason."[6]

The idea jumped to Minnesota when Joe Nathan, an NGA consultant, and Ted Kolderie, head of a Minneapolis think tank, asked Shanker to help them develop the concept. The two radicalized Budde's idea by recommending that statewide and regional agencies, not just local districts, be given the authority to sponsor charters, and by allowing anyone, not just local teachers, to apply for a charter. In his widely read book, Nathan also said that charters should be free of virtually all state regulations, other than those agreed upon in the charter. Charters would have no religious affiliation, would become schools of choice that had no attendance boundaries, and would be funded on the same basis as district schools. Charters would be subject to renewal every three to five years. In other words, they were to be neither public nor private, but some kind of hybrid. Although they would be privately owned and managed, they would receive public dollars and be subject to public scrutiny.[7]

Surprisingly, charters have enjoyed an acceptance and popularity that vouchers never achieved. By 2009, more than ten times as many students were attending charters as were receiving vouchers. When charters and vouchers were first launched nearly twenty years ago—charters in Minnesota in 1991, vouchers in Wisconsin one year previously—a detached observer could easily have anticipated exactly the opposite pattern. After all, the voucher concept was already well known in 1990, championed by Nobel Prize–winning economist Milton Friedman and endorsed by U.S. secretary of education Bill Bennett. Charters had been proposed by political unknowns: Budde, Nathan, and Kolderie. The Wisconsin governor who launched vouchers, Tommy Thompson, was a rising star who would later become George W. Bush's secretary of Health and Human Services, while Minnesota's Rudy Perpich was an oddball Minnesota governor with no political future. Meanwhile, Al Shanker, seeing the idea ratchet out of teacher control and sensing its potentially adverse impact on the collective-bargaining process, had turned coat and called charters a "gimmick."[8]

Vouchers originally enjoyed more than just the brand-name imprimatur. Their constituency was much more solidly based, as well. Private schools eligible to participate in a voucher program were already serving 10 percent of the student population; most of them were Catholic schools, which Coleman had found superior to public ones. Yet private schools, especially Catholic ones, were operating on the financial edge, and the pressure gave them every incentive to push hard for a government-funded voucher program. The many families sending their children to private school had equally compelling reasons for favoring vouchers: they needed help paying tuition costs. Meanwhile, charters had neither a track record nor a definable constituency that could lobby for government help.

Nor did charters hold much of an advantage over vouchers as an idea or an ideal. Except in one crucial respect (discussed below), neither the case for nor the case against charters was any stronger than the arguments for or against vouchers. Just as Friedman claimed that vouchers would free schools to innovate while allowing competition to sort the best from the worst, Nathan said that "part of the path toward progress involves introducing more competition into public education." But if free-spirited competition is the goal, vouchers are much to be preferred over a system of regulated charter schools.[9]

Similarly, the case against charters is little different from the one made against vouchers. A system of unconstrained charter schools, just as a comprehensive voucher plan, would let families pick their school and schools select their students. Both forms of mutual selection could in the long run generate social hierarchies that perpetuate inequalities. As with vouchers, charter schools can also be charged with undermining the common school, a unifying element in a pluralistic society. Nothing in Nathan's principles or in most state charter laws prevents schools from catering exclusively to the cultural predispositions of ethnic groups, language groups, or other parochial viewpoints. Currently, one can find bilingual charters that teach students in Spanish, Arabic, Hebrew, and other foreign tongues. Early on, a *New Republic* columnist condemned such schools in words no less sweeping than those used to attack voucher schemes: "Public money is shared money, and it has to be used for the furtherance of shared values, in the interests of *e pluribus unum*. Charter schools and their like are definitionally antithetical to [the] American promise. They take from the *pluribus* to destroy the *unum*."[10]

The threat posed to traditional public schools is much the same, regardless of whether a system of vouchers or a system of charters is put into place. In either case, the money follows the child when a family leaves a district school, and that district must make do with less. If the numbers leaving the district are sizable, some district schools may have to close. The most resourceful families, moreover, could be among the first to exit the district schools, leaving the public schools bereft of sources of political and social support. Given the threat, districts and their employees should have been as opposed to charters as vouchers.

Charters in Practice

Yet for several reasons, charters have never provoked an equally intense opposition. Most important, charter schools do not have to reckon with the charge that they are unconstitutionally establishing a state religion. Vouchers for low-income families are not unconstitutional either, the Supreme Court said in *Zelman*. But that decision came in 2002, after years of bitter legal controversy—and lower-court rulings to the contrary—that in the meantime had tainted vouchers as somehow un-American. It did not help vouchers that the controversy over their enactment came at a time when the two major political parties were dividing ever more sharply along religious lines, with Republicans garnering strong support from social conservatives, both Catholic and evangelical—the very religious groups with the largest number of private schools—while Democrats were disproportionately securing support from secularists and mainline Protestants. Though abortion and gay rights were the mainstay of the partisan controversy, vouchers still found themselves caught up in the country's most ideological public discourse.

Lacking a religious identity, charters never aroused the same passions. The most energetic of the secular interest groups—People for the American Way—relentlessly attacked all voucher proposals, but one searches in vain for a critical reference to charter schools on their website. Meanwhile, social conservatives, while not opposing charters, were less than enthusiastic about the ban on religious instruction at charter schools.[11]

Charters were also spared the opprobrium that tarred vouchers from their earliest days, when they were used as a tool for racial segregation in the South. Even though segregation by voucher never became operational, civil rights groups acquired a visceral hatred for the concept. It became the "v" word that could not be pronounced with a favorable accent in any politically correct circle of opinion. Charters never became the "c" word.

Nor did it hurt that charters had an ambiguous pedagogical identity. On the one side, Joe Nathan, Minnesota's charter school handmaiden, was an educational progressive who thought children learned best when freed from standard routines. In his book *Charter Schools,* he wrote extensively about a Minnesota cooperative called New Country School. "[It] does not have classrooms or even classes in the traditional sense, [but] all twenty-one of the randomly selected students I talked with . . . felt they were learning more than they did in their previous schools."[12] The charters that belong to the Essential Schools Coalition, inspired by the work of Theodore Sizer, former dean of the Harvard School of Education, are likewise as progressive as anything Dewey's followers could have wished. On the other side, conservatives could celebrate the paternalistic charters, which are pursuing a pedagogical strategy more reminiscent of the nineteenth-century little red schoolhouse than anything resembling Dewey's Laboratory School. The best-known such schools—the Knowledge Is Power Program (KIPP), the Seed School, and Uncommon Schools—have created highly structured routines with student uniforms, strict rules, and numerous drills and chants familiar to my parents and grandparents. Charters have taken many other forms as well: single-sex schools, schools for the performing arts, schools for science and technology, bilingual schools, schools for the disabled, schools for dropouts, and virtual schools where learning takes place online. Unlike vouchers, used mainly by students attending Catholic or Christian schools, charters have acquired a blurred image ranging across the pedagogical and political spectrum.[13]

Free of a segregationist history and any religious connections, charters found it easier to win bipartisan support than vouchers did. It is true that Republican governors and legislators did the most to champion the cause within state capitols. But seven years after the Minnesota charter law was approved, charter legislation has been enacted in more than forty states and the District of Columbia, a rapid advance inconceivable without support from both sides of the political aisle.[14]

Charters have had bipartisan support on the national level as well. In addition to steadfast Republican advocates, Democratic presidents and presidential aspirants have given at least lip service to the idea. President Clinton signed legislation that helped to defray the capital costs of starting a charter school. Though funding levels were trivial, the symbolism was not. Subsequent Democratic presidential candidates—Gore, Kerry, and Obama—favored the idea, and Obama's secretary of education, Arne Duncan, asked states to raise the limits on the number of charter schools that could be formed. Similarly, liberal media outlets—among them the *New York Times*, the *Boston Globe*, and the *San Francisco Chronicle*—cautiously endorsed charters, despite their oft-expressed distaste for vouchers. Even paternalistic charters were praised in the media mainstream. The *Washington Post*'s education columnist Jay Mathews penned a full-length, praise-filled book entitled *Work Hard. Be Nice.* The title was the KIPP school motto.[15]

Public opinion generally reflects the nature of the conversations taking place in the society at large. On vouchers, the public divides almost exactly down the middle, with an overwhelming majority taking a clear stand one way or the other. Forty percent say they support "using government funds to pay the tuition of low-income students whose families would like them to attend private schools," while 40 percent oppose the idea. Only 20 percent take a middle-of-the-road position that neither supports nor opposes the idea. When it comes to charters, the most striking fact is that no less than 41 percent of the public say they "neither support nor oppose" the idea. Among those who have an opinion, supporters outnumber opponents two to one.[16]

The political climate has influenced the strategies of foundations and individual donors. Voucher supporters wasted millions of dollars on counterproductive political and policy campaigns. Voucher referendums were initiated at great cost in California, Washington, and Michigan. Even the most politically astute proposals and best-funded campaigns proved ineffectual, as opponents created doubts among voters by pointing out such potential "horribles" as voucher schools for terrorists. Referenda defeats undermined legislative efforts elsewhere, when politicians became concerned that a vote for vouchers might be the last vote they cast. Two pro-voucher philanthropists, Theodore Forstmann and John Walton, tried another tack, giving millions to the Children's Scholarship Fund, which provided privately funded vouchers to low-income families across the country. The program, rushed into reality without careful analysis, had an educational impact so diffuse and difficult to evaluate that it barely pierced the policy debate.

When it came to charters, foundations and donors have spent little money on political mobilization and much more on the kinds of practical matters they do best: helping with the purchase of buildings, paying startup costs, and supporting "extras" that enhanced the curriculum. Results are visible and concrete, reinforcing donor enthusiasm. Heartwarming stories about students from low-income families who won admission to college strengthened connections between charters and foundations. The charter constituency broadened beyond those who wanted to alter public policy, and came to include the many more who just wanted to help needy students.

Quite accidentally, the voucher controversy had its own positive impact on the charter bandwagon. By capturing the attention of school districts and teacher unions, vouchers helped to create a political thicket within which fledgling charters could build their nests. Teacher unions, flatly opposed to vouchers, pulled their punches when it came to charters, perhaps because it was politically risky to oppose all forms of school choice. In its officially stated policy, the National Education Association says that it neither supports nor opposes charters per se, but insists only upon tight restrictions, such as protections for collective bargaining and the explicit approval of local school boards.[17]

By these criteria, very few (if any) state laws pass muster. Yet union opposition to many charter laws has not prevented the charter bandwagon from moving forward. Political leaders, always in search of compromise, found charters a middle way between the ideological polarities of vouchers and no choice at all. An early academic study found little connection between union strength in a state and the state's ability to shape charter legislation, despite the fact that "teachers' organizations . . . opposed strong charter laws."[18]

What remains unclear is whether charter opponents, by leaving the gate open, have allowed charter horses to roam out of control, or whether they can still fence in this threatening institution. Each year, the number of enrolled charter students has grown, and most charter schools claim application rates in excess of the number of students who can be accommodated. With the numbers now surpassing a million, charters have acquired a constituency that can be mobilized politically by their state and national associations. Charters have not grown exponentially, as do populations without a natural enemy, but neither has their trend line pointed anywhere but upward—a sign that natural enemies, though present, are currently not dominant.

The long-term outcome remains in doubt, however. Charters

could turn out to be little other than a boutique within the public school shopping mall, open and available to a passionate few, never the engine capable of transforming American education. Many states limit the number of charters that can be formed, and winning approval for a new charter can be a lengthy, burdensome task. At the local level, relations between district schools and charters are often tense. Stories abound of school districts refusing to let charters inhabit empty public school buildings, or rejecting students who want to participate in district sports programs, or restricting the flow of money to charters (when state money must first pass through district offices), or failing to transport students on district buses even when required to do so by state law. One of the most telling incidents occurred in Carbondale, Colorado. A Montessori charter school purchased its own school bus, but it could not use it because the vehicle needed to be inspected by a "specially licensed schoolbus mechanic." All such mechanics were in full-time employment by the school district, and none were allowed to take the assignment on their own time. An inspector from an adjacent school district was lined up to the job, but he called back to report he "didn't want to get involved in the politics" of another school district. When the school finally reached a working relationship with a Catholic school, a local administrator called the Colorado Department of Education "to question the separation of church and state." Not every charter school has quite such a tale to tell, but few will report the kind of smooth, cooperative relationship with local district authorities that would be necessary if charters were to be effective laboratories of educational innovation.

The biggest threat to charters is the very thing that initially worked in their favor: their own novelty. When charters first began, hopes were high that they would succeed when all else was failing. But charters, as new institutions, had much to learn, and not every new school manager was up to the task. No less than 10 percent of all charter startups have lost their charters, a number spun by supporters and critics alike. It's either proof positive that charters are failing, or demonstrated evidence that markets do in fact eliminate ineffective schools. The fact of the matter is that most of the shutdowns are the result of imprudent or fraudulent business practices, not necessarily bad pedagogy. In Arizona, it was comparatively easy to obtain a charter. By 2007, 462 charter schools were operating, and more than 13 percent of the students in public schools were attending them. But fiscal and accounting problems emerged. According to news reports, "Scores of charter companies fail to track their spending and can't produce receipts for many expenses. Some . . . inflate[d] attendance to bring in more state money." One school was so audacious as to find space in a building that also housed a topless bar. In response to these problems, Arizona in 2006 tightened its audit requirements. Altogether, eighty-three charter schools in the state closed their doors in the decade of 1996–2006.[19] Even the strongest charter school supporters began to wonder whether chartering had become too permissive in the Grand Canyon state.

Defenders of charters say that closing poor schools is exactly what is needed in American education. But even the charters that have remained open have yet to demonstrate an unequivocally positive impact on student achievement. Some studies have shown that charters in some big cities—Boston, New York, and Chicago, for example—have outperformed district schools. But studies of charters in Texas, North Carolina, and elsewhere have generated less favorable results. Admittedly, the new schools seem to be improving with the passage of time, a positive in itself. But twenty years after their founding, it is impossible to determine whether charters, on average, are outperforming the district schools that students would have been attending.[20]

For this reason, the foundation world is shifting away from supporting new startups in favor of encouraging the most successful charters to expand their operations, creating new schools along a model that has proven successful. That idea works well when a business is seeking to expand in order to realize greater profits.

But most charter schools are nonprofits. Whether those in charge have sufficient incentive to take on the task of building nationwide networks of effective charters is a question that has yet to be answered.

Equally thorny is the path by which charters can be expected to affect public schools. Charter theory slides back and forth between two poles: diffusion and competition. Joe Nathan's primary justification for charters was their capacity to serve as incubators of knowledge that would permeate the educational system.[21] But so far, one finds scant evidence that district-run schools have picked out and tried to emulate the most successful charter models. A few urban districts are moving away from middle schools in favor of old-fashioned K–8 schools, because parents, when given a choice, opt for the K–8 model. And charter school models are encouraging public schools to extend the schoolday by offering sessions both in the early morning and after school. So far, there is little sign of charter impact on public-school curricula. Students at KIPP schools are showing signs of making striking gains, but KIPP's paternalistic approach is so foreign to contemporary pedagogical theory that public schools resolutely refuse to follow suit.

Nor has competition had, as yet, a big impact on public schools. A few studies have identified some positive impacts on traditional public schools in those few places where a high percentage of students are attending charter schools,[22] and international studies have found higher levels of performance in those countries where parents have greater choice among government-funded schools. In the District of Columbia, where charters have a strong presence, superintendent Michelle Rhee has been charged with undertaking a wholesale makeover of district schools. But the charter presence is substantial in only a few parts of the country: Arizona, the District of Columbia, Albany, New York, and some cities in Ohio. Many states limit the number of charters that can be built, the number of students in a community that can attend them, and the amount of funds they can draw away from district schools. Other states require an applicant to complete a long, complex process before they charter a school. So long as charters are educating only a tiny percentage of the school-age population, they will not force public-school reform.[23]

In other words, the jury on charter schools is still out. Charters may still show that they can educate young people more effectively than district schools. Their numbers could grow at a faster pace than ever before. Their ideas could be widely adopted. But charters might also remain rarities, opportunities for a few families seeking an alternative to the neighborhood school. Rather than charters, homeschooling—the most dramatic, most potent, most radical form of choice—may prove to be the incubator of the educational future.

Homeschooling

"I never really told anybody about my music at school, only my really close friends. . . . Then [school officials] actually aired the show around the whole entire school, and that caused a lot of problems. I was a straight-A student, and all of a sudden I didn't want to go to school anymore because of the things people were saying. That's why I'm homeschooled now." So spoke twelve-year-old Cheyenne Kimball—a recording artist, the star of her own MTV show, and winner of NBC's *America's Most Talented Kid*. She is a symbol of the extent to which homeschooling has broken out of the conservative closet into the cultural mainstream.[24]

For all the talk about charters and vouchers, it is homeschooling that is the fastest-growing alternative to the country's district schools. According to the National Center of Education Statistics, the number of homeschoolers grew from around 850,000 to roughly 1.1 million in the years 1999–2003. But this figure consists only of those homeschoolers who register with the state—a number that may be little more than half of those choosing this form of schooling. In states that are keeping records, the direction is clearly upward. Virginia "had 3,816 registered homeschoolers in 1990. By 2007 the number had grown to 20,694. Maryland saw a similar growth, from 2,296 in 1990 to 24,227 in 2006." To get a sense of the extent to which homeschooling has become a widely recognized phenomenon, the journal *Education Next* asked a cross-section of Americans in 2008 if they knew anyone who homeschooled their child. No less than 45 percent said they did. Homeschooling is no longer strictly a sideshow.[25]

Nor is it anything new to the American experience. The practice was pervasive at the time the American constitution was written, and, decades later, even Horace Mann had his children schooled at home. But after schooling became compulsory in the late decades of the nineteenth century, homeschooling virtually disappeared. It revived only as an unexpected byproduct of the civil rights reforms of the 1960s. At that time, much ado was being made about a small free-thinking British school, Summerhill, which ran itself according to principles Rousseau would have admired. In its bucolic setting, children romped freely until they thought of something they wanted to study. Along these same lines, the brilliant, eccentric Ivan Illich made a name for himself by critiquing schooling as nothing other than the channeling of pliable students into a bureaucratized, dehumanized modernity.[26]

It was John Holt who made the connection to homeschooling. In *How Children Fail,* a radical critique of American schools still widely read in education schools today, Holt argued, à la Rousseau, that "compulsory schooling destroys children's native curiosity and replaces it with a self-conscious and fearful desire to please the teacher." At that time, Holt thought schools, properly redesigned, could still become educational institutions; but after a visit to Ivan Illich, a radicalized Holt put his faith in parents. In his journal, *Growing without Schooling,* he argued: "Some may feel that the schools spend too much time on what they call the Basics; others that they don't spend enough. Some may feel that the schools teach a dog-eat-dog competitiveness; others that they teach a mealy-mouthed Socialism. . . . What is important . . . [is that we] work . . . for the right of all people to take their children out of schools."[27]

If the New Left initiated the homeschooling movement, social conservatives quickly hijacked it. For social conservatives, the issue was not the imposition of conformity or the stifling of creativity, but overt instruction of a secularist ideology that ran contrary to their deepest religious convictions. They objected to the court-mandated banishing of prayer and Bible reading, biology courses that taught evolution, history courses that ignored God's control over human destiny, and health courses that encouraged contraception and abortion rather than premarital abstinence. Social conservatives also could draw on pedagogical materials prepared for Christian schools, and they could learn from one another at the evangelical churches they attended. By 1990, "somewhere between 85 and 90 percent of homeschoolers were conservative Christians."

More than one social movement has thrived under suppression, and the homeschooling movement is no exception. When children did not appear at school, local school districts inquired into their truancy, and soon there appeared in homeschooling newsletters "gripping horror stories of homeschooling families threatened by truant officers, social workers, liberal activist judges, and the National Education Association." It was by publicizing such encounters that Chris Klicka built the movement's most powerful institution, the Home School Legal Defense Association (HSLDA), started with grants from conservative foundations and nourished by its $100 annual dues, which guaranteed members legal assistance if school authorities questioned their homeschooling rights.[28]

The legal battle has been convoluted enough to keep HSLDA in business for decades. In more than one suit, its attorneys have argued that homeschooling is guaranteed by the Fourteenth Amendment right to "life, liberty, and property," pointing out that the Supreme Court had invoked that clause when it protected private schools from state closure. If parents had the right to send their child to a private school, this implied a parental right to educate their own children. Most courts, however, were unwilling to take that additional interpretive step.[29]

Nor have the courts regularly found in the First Amendment's Freedom of Religion clause the right to educate a child in the religious atmosphere of the home. The Supreme Court did find such a right when it ruled that the Amish need not send children to public school after age fourteen but could instead prepare them at home for the Amish way of life. But the nation's highest court ducked the question as to whether religious parents of younger children had that same right, and lower courts have often ruled to the contrary. Only a 1993 Michigan Supreme Court—and perhaps a California appeals court (see below)—found a First Amendment right to homeschool.[30]

So if schooling is compulsory, and if parents have no well-established constitutional right to educate their children at home, how has HSLDA succeeded in protecting the practice of homeschooling? That story, well told by Milton Gaither, is so varied and complex that it defies summary. Three things can be said in general, however. First, homeschooling is permitted in every state. Second, regulatory controls vary widely. Some states insist that parents demonstrate they are successfully following a regular curriculum, while other states merely require a statement that the child is being homeschooled. Third, homeschoolers have demonstrated their growing political clout, and public officials have become ever more wary of preventing parents from doing as they wish. Politicians have little stomach for putting a mother in jail for teaching her child, especially when that mother can call upon a well-organized, politically active group of like-minded parents to dramatize her case to a news media ready to side with a courageous individual fighting against bureaucratic or judicial power.[31]

Just how all these facts fit together is well illuminated by a 2008 California case. Rachel Long, one of Phillip and Mary Long's eight homeschooled children, had complained of maltreatment, and the child welfare officials who conducted an investigation found the children to be badly educated. A lower-court judge, following the lead of the Michigan Supreme Court, said that the parents nonetheless had a constitutional right to homeschool their children. But the state appellate court reversed the lower court and lurched decisively in the opposite direction. It claimed that California law required all homeschoolers to be taught by certified teachers.

With that decision, homeschooling was essentially outlawed throughout the entire state of California. Or so it seemed, until the HSLDA and its sister organizations demanded that the legislature clarify its intent. A petition signed by more than 250,000 people asked the California Supreme Court to "depublish" the appellate court decision. The *San Francisco Chronicle* and the *Sacramento Bee* condemned the judges' decision. Governor Arnold Schwarzenegger deemed it "outrageous," saying it "must be overturned by the [higher] courts, and if the courts don't protect parents' rights, then, as elected officials, we will." The state superintendent of instruction proposed to clarify state regulations. So negative was the reaction that the appeals court, upon further reflection, reversed itself, concluding that state law, while confusing and inconsistent, did in fact permit homeschooling after all. Even if it did not, the judges said, the denial of homeschooling might be in violation of the U.S. Constitution, given the *Yoder* decision granting the Amish the right to homeschool their teenagers. In the words of Joshua Dunn and Martha Derthick, "Much like banks that become 'too big to fail,' home schooling appears to have become too widespread . . . to be undone by a judicial opinion."[32]

Just as important, homeschooling, no longer the exclusive prerogative of the hippie left or the socially conservative right, has been hijacked once again, this time by the mainstream. To the distress of HSLDA and other social conservatives, many families who have no particular objections to the secularization of public education prefer to educate their children at home for quite practical reasons. Sophisticated families living in urban areas do not wish to send their children to dysfunctional public schools, but cannot afford expensive private ones. Child superstars—whether skaters, singers, surfers, or snowboarders—are discovering that they can pursue their dream more easily if their families, rather than the public schools, assist them with their education. "I've been in this business fifteen years," one surfboarding agent told Gaither, "and it's always been those with parents that understand the freedom and flexibility of home-schooling that go the furthest." Homeschoolers have won far more than their share of spelling and geography bees, and one find homeschooled students at any and every Ivy League college. Homeschoolers who take state exams generally outperform those who attend public school, though it is not clear whether the exam takers are representative of all homeschoolers.[33]

As homeschooling goes mainstream, the new type of homeschooler is just as likely to have had a hybrid education as students educated exclusively at home. It can mean a blend of self-teaching, learning from parents, professional tutoring, online education, group education with other homeschoolers, and involvement in community institutions for sports and musical activities. In some parts of the country, even public schools are getting into the act, offering homeschoolers enrichment classes—sign language, art, karate, and modern dance, for example. Homeschooling still has a constituency that is predominantly southern, midwestern, and western, as well as conservative, rural, and Christian. But it is no longer so exclusively concentrated in such populations that it is unconnected to a broader segment of the population. And higher-income, better-educated families are the most likely to be personally familiar with the practice.[34]

Legitimate Choice

If parental choice has hardly transformed American education, more options are available now than when the excellence movement began. Within school districts, some families have choices among magnets or other schools outside their own neighborhood. A few have chosen schools in districts other than their district of residence. A few trial experiments with school vouchers are under way—in Ohio, the District of Columbia, and, most notably, Milwaukee, Wisconsin. Charter school enrollments have steadily grown, so that they now constitute about 2 percent of the population. Homeschooling, too, is on the increase, educating 3 to 4 percent of the population. But none of these developments come close to realizing the fully competitive system Friedman had in mind.

In the world of ideas, however, something transformative has already happened. For decades, education was ever more standardized, as power shifted away from parents and communities toward centralized institutions controlled by professionals. Larger schools, larger school districts, collective-bargaining agreements, tighter bureaucratic controls, court-ordered mandates, federal regulations: all of these developments turned the eyes of local administrators away from their immediate constituency of parents and taxpayers toward rules and procedures designed by those to whom they reported. But education is now being thought of as something that must be customized to the needs and wants of families and individuals. That families should have a choice of schools is no longer just the ideology of an isolated fringe; it is now broadly accepted as a legitimate claim, despite the disputes over the form it should take. Forty states have approved charter school laws, and all recent presidents, Democratic and Republican alike, have supported federal assistance to charters. The U.S. Supreme Court found voucher plans constitutional. Homeschoolers can be found in every state, and political leaders have shown a great reluctance to interfere.

School choice has posed a challenge to professional prerogatives and has legitimized parents' right to influence their children's educational experiences. The homeschooling movement constitutes both the most profound and the most successful expression of the choice movement, as it places the parent directly in charge. But the homeschooling movement could not have survived professional criticism, had not a larger choice movement—vouchers and charters—provided a theory of choice and competition that transformed the practice of homeschooling from the unusual and occult to something closer to mainstream practice.

None of this would matter much, were it not for underlying trends forcing even more dramatic changes: the rising cost of education and the growing capacity of technological innovation. But neither could such material realities as dollars and computers transform American education, had not a new system of ideas about choice and competition, jump-started by Coleman and propagated by Bennett, legitimated a form of schooling that was family centered, rather than professionally focused. American education was about to be transformed again—but now, for the first time, in a profoundly new way.

CHAPTER 11

Julie Young and the Promise of Technology

So long as we insist on teaching all students the same subjects in the same way, progress will be incremental. But now for the first time it is possible to individualize education—to teach each person what he or she needs and wants to know in ways that are most comfortable and most efficient.

—Howard Gardner, Harvard Graduate School of Education, *Foreign Policy*, May–June 2009

As I first approached the handsome new quarters of Florida Virtual School (FLVS), near Orlando's Valencia Community College, nothing told me that I was about to enter the nerve center for one of the state's largest schools. The four-story, rectangular, well-windowed structure is devoid of markings or ornamentation save for the massive number 2145—presumably the structure's address, not an estimate of the year virtual education is to be fully realized. A sign insists that the property is private, as indeed it is, for the school leases its space. Valencia students are warned that their cars might be towed—and even legitimate visitors have their worries, because no parking places have been set aside for them.

Stepping out of the second-floor elevator, I entered a vast waiting area, seemingly half the length of a football field. Visible in the distance was a single, very substantial desk, approximately where a goalpost would stand. As the day progressed, I moved from one capacious office to another, all of them decked out with large, well-appointed work stations and sizable meeting areas enjoying the Sunshine's State's prized natural resource. Florida Virtual School is clearly doing very well. I was regularly informed that the furnishings had been donated and the school's lease costs less than the rent previously paid for cramped quarters within the Orange County school system.[1]

Starting in 1997, the state-operated Florida Virtual School began on a small scale. Six years later, it had only 11,500 course enrollments. But by 2008, more than 116,238 courses had been completed and the projection for 2010 was nearly 200,000.[2]

To be translated into full-time pupil equivalents, those numbers must be divided by twelve (to account for the twelve courses high school students are expected to take each year), so the numbers are more modest than they first appear. But the trajectory has been steep enough to make Florida Virtual the most successful internet-based school in the country. It began as a high school, but now offers courses to those in middle school as well. Though initially offering only supplemental courses, today it gives students the opportunity to complete their entire education on line. They can even wear FLVS alumni sweatshirts and drink from alumni mugs. The school's operating budget in 2007 came to approximately $50 million. The school and its chief executive officer, Julie Young—the school eschews "superintendent," "principal," and other standard public-school monikers—have won just about every distance learning award invented. According to the plaques in the FLVS entrance hall, the United States Distance Learning Association gave the school awards in 2000, 2002, 2003, 2005, and 2007, and the organization has inducted Julie Young into its Hall of Fame. In 2008, the Center for Digital Education gave Florida top ranking after conducting a nationwide review of state support for online learning. The Pioneer Institute, a Massachusetts think tank, selected Florida Virtual as the grand-prize winner of its 2008 Better Government competition.

Educational-technology expert Bill Tucker has suggested that Florida Virtual is "perhaps one of the most important reform stories" in education. That assessment may be premature, but online schooling for middle and high school students has definitely become more than an odd item in the curiosity shop. In 2008, according to a report by the North American Council for Online Learning, thirty states had statewide or state-led programs and there were 170 virtual charter schools nationwide. The number of students was estimated at more than a million—a 47 percent increase over the 2006 figure. If the numbers and trajectory are accurate, virtual enrollments will soon rival those of charter schools. One (admittedly speculative) projection has half of all high school courses in 2019 being taught online.[3]

Disruptive Innovation

If technology is to pave the road ahead, it will come as a great relief to those who have led education's excellence movement. Progress toward excellence has been lurching slowly along a bumpy, bog-filled dirt road. By the end of the twenty-first century's first decade, it seemed to have reached a dead end, either of its own making or the result of a blockade constructed by school districts, teacher unions, and other vested interests. The drive for accountability has lost its way in a morass of misdirection, mismeasurements, and meaningless rewards and penalties. Brick-and-mortar schools are held accountable, but real people—teachers and students—almost never are. The choice movement built a few bridges into the future, but their size and strength are not yet able to carry the excellence movement's heavy freight. Still, choice and accountability, if coupled to technology, have the potential to create a more productive educational system.

Elementary and secondary education cannot turn the excellence corner, so long as the industry remains labor-intensive. The monies that can be reasonably anticipated in the next decade or two will hardly be enough to keep the quality of the system, as currently designed, from eroding further. If education could become a more capital-intensive industry, one where technological innovation progresses as rapidly as in other sectors of the economy, fewer teachers and other employees would be needed, and each employee could be better compensated. But is this a system that could transform American education?

More than one thoughtful scholar has serious doubts about such a possibility. Stanford professor Larry Cuban found that when computers were introduced into the classroom, they were used mostly by teachers, and then largely for administrative purposes. When students used a computer, it was mainly for word processing. A "small percentage" of teachers did become "serious or occasional users" of new technology, but even these teachers seldom "alter customary practices." That might be due in part to teachers' unfamiliarity with new technologies, Cuban conceded. But even if teachers were to become better trained, he still did not expect "core teaching and learning practices" to rely on anything other than "very familiar" models (such as self-contained classrooms), even into the middle of the twenty-first century.[4]

Cuban's argument will resonate with many. If led by excellent teachers, face-to-face learning experiences have a vitality, intensity, and immediacy that can inspire students and leave a lasting impression. Students can be exposed to diverse ideas and opinions that allow them to clarify their own thinking and understand better how the life experiences of others color their outlook. When all students have read the same book yet interpret the material in different ways, each person, in direct, rapid-fire conversation with others, gathers a richer understanding of the text's meaning. Cuban even thinks "our current excessive focus on technology use in schools" could threaten "historic civic idealism and broad social purposes public schools serve in a democracy."[5]

As broadening an experience as a classroom can be when teachers are outstanding and students are fully engaged, Cuban's arguments may be overstated. Too many classrooms are as enervating as those that prompted John Dewey to start his Laboratory School, or the ones that bored James Coleman at Manual High in Louisville. Social interaction in most high schools may not produce "historic civic idealism" as often as it creates a status hierarchy in which sports stars and cheerleaders come first, nerds last.

But even if Cuban is more correct than Coleman, even if the public school is the melting pot of democracy, even if learning on a machine cannot come close to learning in an idyllic, pastoral setting where the student sits at one end of a log with the teacher on the other end, online instruction is undoubtedly still better than no education at all. This is the crux of Clayton Christensen and Michael Horn's fascinating argument as to how, exactly, technology is about to change American education. In their view, some innovations establish themselves by providing a new product at low cost to someone who had nothing in the past. Their favorite example is the transistor, first successfully used for tinny, battery-run, pocket-sized Sony radios that teenagers loved—not because they were as good as the sophisticated RCA vacuum tube radios their parents had, but because young people now had their own radios, something that enabled them to listen to their own music, something they could take with them wherever they went, something they could listen to in their bedrooms in the middle of the night when no one else could hear. From such lowly beginnings, the transistor steadily improved until Sony captured the mainstream market, driving RCA out of business.[6]

Christensen and Horn believe that the same thing can happen—and in fact is happening—in American education. Online education is currently in its pocket radio stage—not exceptionally good, certainly not as good as an excellent face-to-face classroom experience. But online education is better than very bad education, or none at all. And there are many situations where bad or nothing is the only alternative. Consider the talented person in a rural community who would like to take an Advanced Placement course in physics, chemistry, or calculus. Few students at the school want to take the course, and the school district has decided it cannot afford—probably cannot even find—a capable teacher for esoteric subjects only a few students will take. For that young person, online education is better than nothing. Much the same can be said for the high school dropout who has come to hate his local school but still wants to get a high school diploma. Furthermore, online education may be the only kind of education realistically available for a person with a physical or emotional disability that precludes regular attendance in a classroom. And homeschooling makes more sense—and very probably improves in quality—when parents need not rely on their own resources but can purchase courses, lectures, and materials online.

Even now, online education at the college level is proving to be competitive with the classroom experience. According to a Babson College survey funded by the Sloan Foundation, nearly 4 million students in 2007, about 20 percent of all students in postsecondary schools and twice the number six years previously, were taking at least one course online—that is, a course where at least 80 percent of the content is provided over the Web. Growth is particularly rapid—an average yearly compound growth rate of 24 percent—in junior and community colleges, where most students are pursuing a two-year program and are usually commuting to school from their homes or their job sites. Growth is also rapid—22 percent compounded annually—among those pursuing master's degrees. Some for-profit colleges—Phoenix University and the Apollo Group, for example—have won national visibility for their online course offerings, but the growth rate is actually more rapid in the public than in the for-profit sector. Significantly, it is the colleges and universities with the largest enrollments that are most aggressive in exploiting online opportunities.[7]

Most colleges and universities are not drawing artificial distinctions between their online and on-site student bodies. Instead, students can choose to mix the two to suit their individual needs and predispositions. Schools that provide a variety of good-quality courses online gain a competitive advantage over those that do not. Among other things, they can extend their reach into geographic markets previously unavailable to them.

Organized political opposition to online college instruction has melted away. A number of individual professors have condemned the rise of low-quality domestic and overseas "diploma mills," but such complaints have not generalized into a campaign against Web education per se. Neither the American Association of University Professors nor the American Federation of Teachers, which also represents a sizable number of university instructors, has raised principled objections. On its website, the AFT has laid down guide-

Julie Young, Florida Virtual School's chief executive officer, giving the keynote address at the September 2008 gathering of the school's teachers and staff members.

Photo courtesy of James Perreault, FLVS.

lines which would keep the innovation labor-intensive: "Class size should be set through normal faculty channels. . . . Degree programs should include same-time same-place coursework. . . . Close personal interaction must be maintained." But the spread of the practice has never been stalled by legal action or the threat of a strike. Inasmuch as two-thirds of all higher-education institutions in the United States now offer some courses over the Web, the genie is out of the bottle.[8]

Julie Young and Virtual Education

At the elementary and secondary level, the situation is more opaque. No one knows whether Cuban is right when he argues that technology and schools mix no better than water and oil, or whether Christensen and Horn are on to something when they claim it can disrupt education as we currently know it. But if technology is to do for education what the Sony transistor did for radio and television, then the Florida Virtual School may well be remembered as education's Sony. By revisiting the four-story building with 2145 above the entrance, we may be able to glean insights into the ways in which online education will navigate the steep hillsides and dangerous curves it will encounter in the years ahead.

Change requires a leader, of course—a John Dewey or an Albert Shanker—someone who can translate ideas into a viable reality, an individual with high ideals, personal passion, and the ability to inspire others to stay the course. At this point, one has no way of knowing whether Julie Young of Florida Virtual is destined to play such a monumental role. But as she is as able an innovator as any, I begin with her story.

Young resembles none of the heroes we have discussed. Her background is marked neither by exceptional credentials nor by unusual challenges. She has not served in a state legislature, as did Horace Mann, or earned a Ph.D., as did John Dewey, Bill Bennett, and James Coleman. Nor was she the scion of a prominent minister, as was Martin Luther King Jr. Deprivations are likewise absent from her life. She was not the child of a broken marriage, as was Bennett, or restless at school, as Shanker and Coleman often were. Neither did she reject her religious heritage (she wore a Cross the day I interviewed her), as did Mann, Dewey, Shanker, and Coleman.

She attended high school in Lexington, Kentucky, where James Coleman, by his own account, wasted his time playing football instead of being challenged by teachers. But while Coleman was a Lexington outsider, Young felt at home there as a child. Her mother was devoted to raising three children and fixing up their homes so they could be sold at a profit, while her father moved steadily up the ladder to become the president of one of Lexington's more prominent banks.

Everything about Julie Young's early years is redolent of normalcy. When asked to participate in sessions devoted to explaining how women can be successful in the workplace, she says she is embarrassed by her inability to identify something unusual about her past. Her one educational disruption was caused by her own insistence that she switch, in fourth grade, from the city's most upscale Catholic school to the local public school. That such successful, loving parents as Julie's would let their youngest daughter talk them into a move contrary to family tradition testifies to the child's self-assertiveness and tenacity. The next year, however, Julie was bullied unmercifully, an experience she says has helped shape her management style and educational philosophy. So family traditions won out in the end, as she happily returned to the Lexington's Catholic schools for the rest of her schooling.

Normalcy marked her college years as well. She went to Lexington's own University of Kentucky, the only college she could ever imagine attending, the same university her father and brothers went to. Years later, she told her alumni magazine that she loved "the whole Greek experience" and had "great memories" of her days "with her sorority sisters in Alpha Gamma Delta." She chose the same elementary-education major many other young women selected as their area of concentration, and she married her college sweetheart (an engineer, the very profession from which Coleman had fled). When their two boys became teenagers, she said that she liked nothing better than to watch them participate in two of the great southern pastimes, basketball and boating. When a family member calls, her cell phone plays the University of Kentucky fight song, she once told a reporter.

Nor is it just the Greek connection that hints at Julie Young's old-fashioned lifestyle at a time when other college-educated women were seeking liberation. Unlike Coleman, Young was in no rush to leave Lexington. In 1981, she took her first position as a sixth-grade teacher at Sts. Peter and Paul, an inner-city Catholic elementary school. She remembers enjoying teaching so much that she forgot to pick up her paycheck—much to her husband's bemusement. But she was willing to leave Lexington three years later, when she followed her husband to Jupiter, Florida. They returned to Kentucky for a short stint, but Julie decided she preferred Florida after all, and they ended up in Fort Myers, where he took a job with IBM and Julie found a position at Carlos Park Elementary, a perfectly ordinary neighborhood public school.

In 1989, IBM expressed an interest in working with an elementary school on a pilot technology project. Carlos Park was selected, and Young became the technology coordinator. In her own words, "My primary role became taking this school from pretty much zero or 15 percent to one of the most highly recognized elementary schools in the nation in regard to technology." Before long, she was promoted to a district-wide position, where she trained teachers in how to make better use of IBM computers than did the schools Cuban had observed. Young's IBM connection never wavered. Many years later, she would hire a former supervisor of IBM's educational services as head of Florida Virtual's Global Services department.[9]

In 1996, when her husband's job required a family move to Orlando, Julie toyed with the idea of abandoning the public school system in favor of "some type of business . . . related to education." But after a casual conversation about technology with an Orange County school board member, she was hired as an assistant principal and soon fell into what she describes as a "vat of chocolate." The local school district, by forming an alliance with the Alachua School District in nearby Gainesville, had landed a technology grant from the State of Florida. In December 1996, by which time Young had, in her words, "a résumé packed full of technological experiences as somewhat of a project manager," Orange County chose her to head up their side of the effort. The next fall, Florida Virtual offered its first classes to seventy-seven students.

A Stealth Strategy

The governing arrangements for the new project were just short of disastrous. Authority was divided between two school districts, under the direction of two school boards with two separate "principals," who had "very different ideals about how Florida Virtual School should play out," Young recalled. Alachua envisioned online education as a way of providing Advanced Placement courses, while Orange, under Julie's prodding, had a broader concept in mind. Nor was it easy to convince administrators in either district that the venture was worth the effort. "For the first two years, when I attended meetings and was introduced as the 'online lady,' there were many chuckles in the room. I don't think anybody expected this to actually last, including the folks at the [Florida] Department of Education that awarded the grant."

As luck would have it, a change in those arrangements became possible with the election in 1998 of Jeb Bush as Florida's new governor. The state now had a highly visible governor who was politically savvy, intent on education reform, and willing to take risks. After FLVS did a self-study that called for a single administrative structure, Bush backed legislation that established the school as a statewide entity with its own gubernatorially appointed board of trustees. A few years later the school was accredited.

Despite its new status, Florida Virtual was careful not to alienate local school districts. Much like an Everglades alligator, Young took a quiet, underwater approach. FLVS presented itself as a supplement to traditional schools, not an alternative. Its program was carefully crafted to fit with—not fight with—that of district schools. As the head of Florida's major teacher union put it, the school "never developed the kind of mistrust that tends to be associated with other reform ideas." The school advertised itself as offering courses not available elsewhere, or ones that did not fit well into a student's time schedule, or ones that a student had to take for a second time. Students on the verge of dropping out could be given a second chance via the virtual option. Advanced Placement courses in the more esoteric subjects were available to those in rural districts that could not afford to hire staff in those areas. Even today, FLVS publicity devotes a great deal of space to the triumphs of its Latin instruction. Similarly, the school initially pursued a "below-the-surface" financial strategy. It avoided any impingement on school district revenues by obtaining its own fixed sum in the state budget. Students could take courses from FLVS, while districts could still get their standard per-pupil allocation from the state.

That stealth strategy stood in marked contrast to the ones pursued by many other virtual schools. Wisconsin Virtual Academy is a case in point. Launched by K12, Inc., a company originally headed by William Bennett, it was granted a charter by the state's Northern Ozaukee School District, a district of falling enrollment that saw virtual education as a promising new business opportunity. The Virtual Academy offered a full-time, traditional curriculum that appealed to many homeschoolers (though the Home School Legal Defense Association saw it as a Trojan Horse that would lure homeschoolers back into public education). Northern Ozaukee and K12 split the more than $5,000 in state aid received for each of the 500 Wisconsin students who in 2004 were enrolled in the school. Other districts lost state revenue whenever any of their students enrolled in the virtual school instead of locally.

Noticing the ideological and financial issues at stake and hoping to nip the school in the bud, the Wisconsin teacher union and its ally, the state's elected school superintendent, filed a lawsuit that challenged Virtual Academy's legality on two grounds: (1) the only schools Northern Ozaukee had the authority to charter were ones that admitted students from within the district; and (2) by law, every classroom must have on site (in the student's home) a certified schoolteacher, not just a parent. The plaintiffs lost in the state trial court, but in 2007 an appeals court accepted these arguments and reversed the lower court's decision.

As soon as the appeals court ruling was handed down, Virtual Academy's parents and students marched on the state legislature, asking it to modify the statute upon which the court had relied. The next spring the legislature passed a law that allowed the chartering of virtual schools, so long as certified teacher communicated with students by email on a regular basis. Governor Jim Doyle, newly elected with hearty backing from the teacher union, threatened to veto the bill unless virtual enrollments were limited. So the two sides compromised on a statewide limit of 5,250 students, a number not much larger than the 3,000 students already attending one of Wisconsin's virtual charters. Meanwhile, the state Department of Education launched its own set of online courses. In other words, virtual education in Wisconsin survived a variety of political and legal battles, and the new legislation placed it on more certain legal footing. But so long as enrollments were tightly limited, the innovation remained corralled.[10]

FLVS's underwater strategy circumvented such opposition during the critical early years, when it was getting established. As its enrollment began to grow, however, Florida legislators began asking why they had to fund each course twice—once at the virtual school, where the course was being taken, and again at the district school, where the course was credited. Fortunately for FLVS, the Jeb Bush administration came up with an imaginative solution. The statutes were changed so that district schools, instead of receiving a per-pupil grant, received one based on the number of courses taken. If a student was taking a full load of twelve courses, of which one was taken online, Florida Virtual would get a payment equivalent to one-twelfth the allotment for a full-time student. The district would get the remaining eleven-twelfths.

Stealth was no longer a viable strategy, as the new arrangement pitted FLVS directly against district schools for state dollars. But the virtual school now had a statewide constituency and the backing of a popular governor, and, as an officer of the School Boards Association conceded, "school boards are less concerned about losing funding to the virtual school than to the various voucher programs." Even so, Florida Virtual had to agree that it could not be compensated unless a student successfully completed the course—that is, a student could not have received a failing grade or have withdrawn from the course. A student had to earn at least a D if FLVS was to be reimbursed for the course.

A Progressive Curriculum and Pedagogy

Florida Virtual broadened its constituency by offering its services to those attending private schools and even to homeschoolers, groups that Governor Bush courted and that Julie Young, a Catholic-school alum herself, could relate to. In 2008, a third of all FLVS courses were taken by students not enrolled in a public school. The school even agreed not to ask homeschooled students to do projects with other students in the class if parents objected. Reaching out to this conservative constituency had its risks, however. Not only might it arouse union and district animosities, as K12 had in Wisconsin, but by extending services to those outside the public school system, it added costs to the state's budget. Offering courses to students in religious schools also opened Florida Virtual to a potential lawsuit that objected to a possible violation of the state's Establishment of Religion clause. None of these potential risks materialized, however—perhaps because FLVS had been careful to sustain working relationships with district schools, and also because it was beneath the political radar screen at a time when Governor Bush was promoting vouchers, charters, student accountability, and other more controversial innovations. Later, the former governor reflected that "we were doing so many different things that were provocative, this didn't seem as radical."

As part of its alligator strategy, FLVS steered clear of anything like the conservative curriculum that had proved so provocative in Wisconsin, saying instead that courses were geared to the standards of the Sunshine State. The school's pedagogy, one top administrator boasted, was at first "constructivist" and then went beyond that, to a "post-constructivist" approach. In the words of the school's motto: students can learn at "any time, any place, any path, any pace." Students are even given four-week grace periods during which they can withdraw from a course without penalty, an option exercised by 25 percent of the enrollment. (If that seems high, it should be noted that more than 25 percent of ninth-graders nationwide fail to graduate from high school within the standard four-year window.)

Young's progressivism runs deeper than short-term political tactics, however. She earned her elementary-education certificate by pursuing a perfectly normal elementary-education major, and the norm for U.S. elementary education during the 1970s was strictly progressive. She avoided the conservative K12, Inc. when choosing her partner for the launch of a full-time virtual charter school in 2008. And when voicing her own educational vision, little she says resembles the conception Bennett had articulated as U.S. secretary of education. Instead of celebrating the teaching of content, she comes closer to giving it the back of her hand: "My background has been middle school and elementary school. In high school, they [are] so passionate about their content . . . and their subject area. Whereas in the elementary and the middle school . . . it was about teaching the *kids,* and the content kind of came along. . . . I started out with high school teachers saying, 'Guys, we are about teaching *kids,* not teaching content. They all learn differently, and we adjust our content to our kids.'"

Consistent with its progressive philosophy, the two most popular of the school's online courses are Life Management Skills and Health / Physical Education, both favorites of the life-adjustment movement. In Florida, high school students, to get a diploma, are required to take one physical education course (with a health component), despite the fact that research finds no beneficial impact of such laws on the extent to which students exercise or on their body mass index. Undoubtedly, hundreds of thousands of Floridians have for years hated taking required physical education courses, reviling the smelly locker rooms, and no small number have rejoiced at the opportunity to take the online version. Once enrolled, they are asked to take a trip to "Wellville," where they monitor their physical condition, develop a workout log, and learn about appropriate exercise, conditioning, nutrition, and ways to manage stress. Young admits that she gets "many questions about how it is possible to teach personal fitness online." But she goes on to defend the course by claiming it is more beneficial than similar courses taught in most district-run schools, and pointing to the "almost daily letters we receive from students and parents about how life changing the course was. We've had students write to say they lost ten, twenty, forty pounds. These are the same students who likely would have gotten nothing out of a school gym class." Still, online instruction in physical exercise is hardly intuitive, and so the offering just barely escaped the ax when the school was placed on the legislative chopping block in 2009.[11]

In addition to getting life adjustment courses out of the way, students have other quite practical reasons for taking a course from FLVS. The reason most often given, stated by 25 percent of those surveyed, was "to take a course needed to graduate on time." The other top three reasons were: (1) to raise a course grade, (2) to accelerate graduation, and (3) to supplement a homeschool education. For all the talk of serving students in remote areas or giving access to an elective not otherwise available, taking a course not offered at the district school was the reason given by only 6 percent of the students.[12]

Most of the Wellville curriculum, as well as that of the more academic courses, is, in Young's words, "predeveloped"—or, as another top curriculum officer put it, "canned." Teachers may supplement the prepared material with their own lectures, if they wish to delve more deeply into a particular subject, and of course they are expected to communicate regularly via email with students about the assignments. Books are deemphasized, except for Advanced Placement courses geared to external examinations, which require knowledge of a designated body of material. Originally, teachers were responsible for preparing their own courses, but the school discovered that curriculum development for online presentation is its own art form. So most course materials are now designed by curricular experts that regularly modify the school's offerings in light of what seems to be most appealing and most effective. "Past developments that have worked well with students," Young says, "are simple things like chunking the content and adding things like pace charts to give students simple tools to make their way through a course." One mark of the success at "canning" material at 2145 is that the school is now marketing its curriculum both to Florida school districts and nationwide, through its Global Services Division. More than 10,670 students are now enrolled in district-run virtual courses that FLVS has "franchised" for $50 per student. That sum buys professional development for teachers, curricular supplies, and of course the online program itself. Other districts and states across the country are also able to purchase the courses, and from anywhere in the world a student can take a course from Global School for $375. If a student attends full-time, that would total $4,500 a year, a very competitive price—if the quality is equivalent. But as of 2008, the number of out-of-state students ever enrolled in a FLVS course had reached only 2,240.[13]

A Business, not a Bureaucracy

Young's ability to speak the language of progressive education is certainly beneficial to her stealth strategy. But beneath her repeated assurances that online schooling is in no way designed to replace the classroom setting lurks a distaste for the pettifoggery that pervades public education. When she talks about the management of public schools, however, she is careful not to compare school bureaucracy to business entrepreneurship or to private schools, but instead contrasts her observations of high schools with the sixth-grade teaching experiences of her early career in Lexington (leaving unstated that her employer was a private Catholic school): "In the elementary and in the middle school venues that I experienced," one felt "a spirit of 'leadership is there to help and support you.' Whereas many high school teachers [today] actually see leadership as sometimes a threat, rarely as a support, and something that is 'over there.'"

Her own management style is as entrepreneurial as a high-tech startup. To build a culture that departed from the public-school norm, and to eliminate any hint of the bullying she had experienced as a child, she and her top aides initially "spent a lot of time . . . reading books together. We started with *The Magic of Teamwork*, by Pat Williams, . . . of the Magic [professional basketball] team here in Orlando. And this particular book became our Bible. . . . After that, we focus[ed] on . . . customer service, teamwork, change management." More than a decade later, it is hard not to be impressed by the cooperative, positive, problem-solving spirit at 2145.

That business-minded approach is nowhere more evident than in the policies the school follows in its hiring, compensation, and retention policies. The school's teachers live throughout the state of Florida and work from home. No collective-bargaining agreement constrains decisions to compensate or retain teachers. The school does not care at all whether teachers are working a forty-hour week or not. But instructional leaders do monitor teacher activities by checking email correspondence between teacher and student, noticing the length of time it takes for a student assignment to receive an evaluation, and asking teachers to record each time a student or parent is called (once a month being the required minimum). At a teacher-training session I observed, beginning teachers were urged to call parents within the first two weeks, just to let the student know that a teacher-parent contact had been established. I also learned that teachers are asked to identify early on those students who cannot make the grade in an online setting, so that the student can withdraw (or be withdrawn) from the course within the twenty-eight-day grace period.

Teachers begin at the same salary level, regardless of whether they have worked three years or thirty years elsewhere in the Florida school system. The 2009 beginning salary for those holding a bachelor's degree was just over $45,500 plus the standard benefits all teachers receive in the state, an above-average salary for Florida teachers statewide. It can be argued that the higher salary is justified, given the school's twelve-month contract, which requires teachers to work 231 days per year: 18 percent more days than the standard school year in Florida. Yet FLVS working conditions have much to recommend them. Teachers can work from home at times they prefer, reducing their commuting costs and giving them the freedom to move easily from professional to other responsibilities. No less important, teachers are free of hallway duties, lunch duties, and many of the other hassles of ordinary school life. Keeping track of students by email and telephone poses its own problems, of course, but it is hardly surprising that the teacher retention rate for FLVS is somewhere in the range of 90 percent.

The Accountability Problem

Efforts to evaluate the effectiveness of online instruction are still primitive, but scholars have generally reached the conclusion that such courses are no better—and no worse—than comparable courses delivered face to face. FLVS students say their online courses are as difficult as their other high school courses. Most also think instruction is as good as, or better than, that received at their local high school. More objective data seem to support the claim that FLVS is offering equivalent-quality courses. For one thing, its students score higher on state tests and on Advanced Placement tests. Yet those higher scores could be due to the attraction of online courses to more able students or to the twenty-eight-day grace period which gives less engaged students a chance to drop the course.[14]

In the end, it's not all that easy to detect whether students have mastered the material expected of them. Young says that "we are a standards-based school. A student does not complete unless they master the standards." But apart from those in Advanced Placement courses—fewer than 2 percent of all course enrollments—students take no externally proctored examinations. Teachers grade the materials students submit and phone the students once a month, calling them much more frequently if distress signals are detected. An honor code is given heavy emphasis. Early on, FLVS attempted proctored examinations, but the challenges of getting students on time to the designated location—a town library or a community college campus—proved to be a Herculean management task. So, aside from Advanced Placement courses, only FLVS' popular driver-training course requires that students pass a proctored examination—a road test—before they are properly certified.

Of course, FLVS does not differ from district schools in this regard. But the accountability issue is magnified by the fact that Florida Virtual receives no funding if students do not receive at least a D in their course. None but very tough-minded teachers will set a high barrier to passing the course when they know that they will disappoint not only their students, but also those responsible for the financial well-being of the institution. As Young admits, "I've been asked many times: How do you keep from being perceived as a school that is all about completion? Once we became funded on completion, it became an even greater challenge." Young relies upon the integrity of her teachers to meet that challenge. "The most important thing that we do is hire," she says. "And it becomes even more important in our organization, because we don't see our teachers every day. So you have to rely on the hiring process to make sure that you do get people that have integrity and an intrinsic need to succeed." When measuring whether or not a teacher has been successful, the indicators the school uses are "completion and drop rate and, you know, grades, certainly," says Young. If that's the way teachers are evaluated, they certainly need a good deal of integrity if high standards are to be maintained.

Cost-Effectiveness

Whether or not virtual education can raise the standards in American education, one certainly expects it to reduce costs. Young has long been aware that the State of Florida expects a savings from its virtual-school experiment. "We are going to have to show the state that we can serve enough students per teacher to make this . . . cost effective," she insists. "One of our tremendous leadership challenges has been pushing the envelope on the number of students a teacher can successfully teach in an online venue." In its 2007 assessment of FLVS, Florida TaxWatch concluded that state taxpayers saved money because FLVS state funding is lower per pupil and the school received no funds for capital purposes. Even though FLVS mainly serves a secondary-school population, which generally is more expensive than elementary schooling, its average per-pupil operating costs appear to be about three-fourths those of district schools—in 2009, about $6,100, as compared to about $8,500 statewide. Other virtual schools (whose quality cannot be ascertained) are yielding still higher cost savings. According to one survey of twenty such schools in fourteen states, the average per-pupil cost of online learning in 2008 was $4,300 as compared to an average per-pupil cost of $9,100 at a traditional public school in 2006.[15]

The issue came up in the 2009 session of the state legislature, when the education committee in the state senate proposed major changes in the school's operations—prohibiting, for example, the taking of virtual courses in addition to a full district load and eliminating the popular Wellville course from the online curriculum. Private vendors argued that they could do an equally good job for less. In the end, FLVS fought off all cuts, but only by agreeing to a 10 percent cut from its $6,100 per-course reimbursement for every course completed. The cut, while hardly fatal, was grating, especially since district schools avoided a similar cut.

One reason FLVS costs run as high as they do is the number of teachers in the school's stable. Rather than becoming more capital-intensive, as one might expect, Florida Virtual has roughly the same pupil-teacher ratio as district schools. The ratio varies with the subject matter, of course. Teachers of Advanced Placement courses have the smallest enrollments, while teachers of the Wellville course have enrollments as high as 200. Overall, 544 teachers were responsible for 196,450 course enrollments in the school year ending in 2008. If a teacher is typically responsible for six preparations in each semester, and if a summer term can be interpreted as a half-semester, that works out to the equivalent of twenty-five students per class—exactly what is required of district schools by the Florida constitution.

Whether FLVS runs as efficiently as possible is difficult to calculate. Any new enterprise has startup costs, and any growing business should plow its profits back into the company rather than pay fat dividends to its investors. Nothing if not entrepreneurial, Florida Virtual seems to be doing just that. Every year it hires more teachers; every year it develops a wider set of curricular offerings; and, most recently, it has begun marketing its product to states and districts nationwide. Despite its handsome quarters, the school seems as lean, healthy, and well-exercised as those students who faithfully walk the town of Wellville. In the years ahead, it may be leaner than ever.

The Coming Technological Transformation

The Florida story gives no assurance that technology will transform American education. If anything, the use of technology at FLVS resembles less the way transistors are employed today than the way they were used in 1950, when they powered squawking radios that were hidden under adolescents' pillows. Teachers phone and email students, working with them in teacher-student ratios not unlike those of brick-and-mortar schools. Costs are reduced substantially, but it is not clear that capital has replaced labor to the extent it has in the most productive sectors of the modern economy. Achievement levels have not suffered, but neither are they spurting upward. Virtual schooling today is certainly better than nothing, but it is hardly transformative.

Yet one should not underestimate the pace at which things can change, once technology takes hold. When computers were first introduced, hardly anyone imagined an Internet of worldwide proportions. When the Web was constructed, few anticipated search engines that could access vast storehouses of fact and opinion. When search engines were initiated, only the most far-sighted users anticipated the sharing of knowledge and creativity via free encyclopedias and cell phone applications.

Many questions remain unanswered, however. Will political opposition block the full utilization of technology, or subject it to needless regulation? Will opposition be so well mobilized in courts and legislatures as to limit the impact of the new tools that become available? Will political pressures structure the delivery of new technologies in ways that will preserve monopolies and limit choices to parents and students? Will schools become more transparent? Will students be held accountable? Will teachers be retained and compensated on the basis of merit? Answers to these questions will determine whether technology winds up operating as Larry Cuban expects, or disrupts the current system of service delivery, as Christensen and Horn suspect it will.

Customization

We do know that in a virtual world, education will be largely coproduced. By "coproduction," I mean the substitution of unpaid labor for paid labor. Many firms have increased their profitability by making it easy and convenient for unpaid people to assist in the distribution of the products they purchase. Safeway and Best Buy stock their shelves in convenient, attractive ways so that consumers will supply the labor of product selection and delivery to the checkout counter. Banks allow consumers to use ATM cards so that fewer paid tellers are needed. Airlines allow passengers to download their boarding passes on their home computers so that fewer agents are needed at check-in.[16]

Education has always been coproduced. A teacher cannot practice without a learner. Students learn the most when they and their peers are engaged. With new technology, educational coproduction can be accelerated. Rather than being taught by a teacher in a classroom, the student can access "predeveloped" material without any immediate intervention by an adult employee. If the material is not self-explanatory, a student can write an email to his teacher, or contact a peer, or talk with his parents or other adults, who then become unpaid coproducers themselves.

If technological innovation is done properly, students will have educational experiences designed for their specific needs. As the FLVS motto goes, they learn at "any time, any place, any path, any pace"—a customization of the educational experience that educator John Dewey would embrace. Previous attempts have fallen short. Individualized education for the disabled has bogged down in bureaucratic regulations, and schools are still trying to figure out how to reach English-language learners. Class size has not been reduced to the point that individual children can have their specific needs addressed. Technology promises to alter this situation. As one FLVS student with attention deficit disorder put it: "It's more one-on-one than regular school. It's more they're there—they're listening." A college-bound student was no less enthusiastic: "I like working by myself because of no distractions, and I can go at my own pace rather than going at the teacher's pace."[17]

Cognitive scientist Daniel Willingham provides an explanation for the power of customized learning. "Working on problems that are of the right level of difficulty is rewarding, but working on problems that are too easy or too difficult is unpleasant," he notes. Unfortunately, traditionally organized schools cannot customize the learning experience to each individual so as to achieve the optimal difficulty point. As a college-going waitress commented to me one day, "High school is being baby-sat." So it's little wonder that, as Willingham says, students don't "care much for school." As technology improves, schools can match students to their ideal difficulty point, giving them the intrinsic satisfaction that comes with a genuine learning experience. And students can be told on a regular basis just how well they are doing. Those benchmarks can also be fed back to students by computer assessments of their performance as they are completing their assignments—a practice already in place for some of the courses at FLVS. Also, curriculum specialists can use that same information to design new material when existing presentations seem ineffective: "The curriculum, the teacher's daily lesson plans, the interaction in the classroom are all on display, available for capture and replication."[18]

Replication can be global. Online courses, if not offered synchronously, are accessible regardless of space and time. One teacher—or group of teachers—can reach students scattered across the continents. That the same exact course can be offered to thousands, even millions, would seem to usher in an educational system that is more centralized than ever before. When a single teacher, just like a single pop star, can reach multitudes, one might fear the arrival of George Orwell's nightmare, with Big Brother telling us what to know and how to know it. That could happen—but the opposite is more likely. Young people are too diverse, too imaginative, too insistent on doing it their own way, too reluctant to be told what to do to accept a one-size-fits-all mass educational system purveyed over the Web. Students will differ in the history they wish to explore, the approaches to science they want to take, the novels and poetry they want to read, the languages they want to study.

Unless vested interests create monopolies, control over education will increasingly become controlled by the consumer. Each student, each household, each family will pick and choose among the endless variety of options entrepreneurs can produce. Curricular material may soon be available to consumers free of charge, as open-source development does for schooling what it has already done for encyclopedias, cell applications, and website design. Young people will set up communication systems among themselves, finding the sharing of ideas among themselves more interesting than listening to hoary figures of the past. Quite apart from peer-to-peer exchanges of information, purveyors of new products will have incentives to make material available at minimal cost, in order to get attention for their ideas, while established producers will seek to expand market share through a similar strategy. The emerging way to learn will more closely resemble the way John Quincy Adams read to his mother from the family's favorite book than the deadly dull instruction administered at Coleman's Manual High.

All of this will require that course completion and degree acquisition be separated from daily attendance in a prescribed setting. To begin with, other states will need to follow FLVS' example of letting students take a course more quickly or more slowly, depending on their situation. They will also have to fund schools by the course rather than by enrollment, as Florida does, and they might go beyond current policies by paying providers only if students demonstrate that they have learned what is expected. If such policies are put into place, students can pick and choose how, what, and where they will learn.

If courses are funded by the level of student completion and accomplishment, providers, to maximize revenue, will hire specialists to ensure that dropouts are minimized. FLVS is already doing just that. Teachers will be valued by their ability to attract students and provide a manner of instruction that allows a student to successfully complete a course—another FLVS practice. The technological sophisticates who know how to create exciting courses that convey desired content will become the captains of the industry. If the FLVS model were generalized, educators could build a highly decentralized, highly competitive, highly customized service delivery system that has the potential for continuous improvement in productivity.

In the long run, brick-and-mortar high schools may become places where they meet their friends, get help from their coaches, and engage in group activities—sports, music, theater, and other extracurricular activities. Manual High can do what it always could do very well: mount a successful football team and mobilize school spirit. At the same time, students can meet with tutors and coaches who can suggest courses and explain how to make better use of the technologies available. Such schools will not need to be vast enterprises built on the scale of Newton North, but community institutions serving young people will be needed in the future as much as they are now.

The Roadblocks

All of this *can* happen, but how and when and whether it actually *will* happen remain political questions. The battles in Wisconsin and Florida suggest that the struggle between virtual and district schools will be prolonged and complex. Part of the debate will be over the quality of virtual education. Unfortunately, that debate is currently focusing more on educational inputs than on student outcomes. Legislators and judges are paying less attention to the amount of learning that is taking place online and in classrooms than to class size, teacher credentials, and the amount of communication taking place between teacher and student. Unnecessary regulation could prevent effective substitution of capital for labor—the very thing that is essential for educational progress.[19]

It is not just school districts and teacher unions that pose a challenge to school transformation. Virtual schools themselves can throw up their own roadblocks. As soon as a virtual school gets established, it has an incentive to try to keep its monopoly on the provision of virtual services. FLVS objects to competing providers on the grounds that they will not provide the same quality of instruction. That is a real problem, of course, but the solution is to require proctored end-of-term examinations for students, not to create monopolies for "good" providers. If virtual education is left to one—or only a few—schools, it will soon lose its capacity to drive innovation.

Despite potential obstacles to genuine progress, technological innovation is likely to continue at an even faster pace than currently. The United States has a history of rejecting Luddites who oppose technological change. Demand for more efficient, more economical instruction is likely to accelerate at a time when the United States has become more sensitive to its economic limits. The public is increasingly concerned that in a flat world, the United States will be swamped by developments overseas. Admittedly, the rate of innovation throughout most of Europe and most parts of Latin America has been ponderous. Teacher unions are, if anything, even more powerful in those countries than in the United States. Nor is rapid change likely in the poorest countries most desperately in need of virtual education. There, the broadband infrastructure for online learning has yet to be built, access to computers is still limited to elites, and appropriate software packages will take longer to produce. But in many parts of Asia, online education is spreading rapidly as a way of catching up with the West.

Still, the United States can exploit inordinate advantages if it has the necessary political will. It has the concentration of technical skill needed to develop ever more sophisticated online educational programming. It has the broadband infrastructure necessary to distribute sophisticated software packages and sustain rapid Web communication between teachers and students. Its citizens have near-universal access to personal computers, notebook computers, and cell phones with Web capabilities. For at least the next decade or two, the United States will have a decisive potential advantage over most other nations.

Transparency and Accountability

Circumventing unnecessary political roadblocks does not mean that virtual education can go unregulated or should not be held accountable for its performance. Given the potpourri of courses that will be designed, virtual education needs to be transparent, common standards must be set, and an outcome-based accountability system has to be designed. One cannot expect the new virtual schools to be any more eager to be held accountable than district schools are today. FLVS is caught in an accountability—or, more exactly, lack of accountability—nexus no less complex than the one that bedevils the American high school more generally.

The issue is hardly confined to Florida. It is central to ensuring that the spread of virtual instruction becomes a vehicle for educational progress. A virtual course should not earn credit apart from an externally proctored examination, and school reimbursements should be conditioned upon successful completion of such a course. If such a policy were applied to all schools, virtual and regular alike, one would be putting into place a system of secondary education that would become more coproductive, more effective, and less costly.

Any such accountability will need to be designed differently from the way it has been done under No Child Left Behind. No school should be told that all students must be proficient by a certain year. Instead, every student should be asked to meet a demonstrated standard of proficiency before he or she moves on to the next grade. Instead of "aging out" of a grade, students will have to demonstrate a certain level of accomplishment. Students will graduate from high school when they have mastered a certain body of material. Special recognition will be given to those who perform at a more advanced level. Students will be free to seek out tutors, coaches, and resources to assist them, perhaps online but also in direct face-to-face settings, the size of the class depending on the severity of the learning deficit. Some coaches and computer programs will offer phonics and math tables and, perhaps, a "drill and kill" learning strategy. Others will use more progressive educational techniques. Parents and students can select the one that works best for them.

Accountability will be facilitated by the transparency of the courses. When a course is offered online, it is open for inspection. It becomes easier to evaluate the curriculum, identify ways of improving it, and notice techniques that might be applied in other courses as well. Since FLVS knows the precise curriculum that is being offered to each of its students, it can revise courses that are unpopular or ineffective. In this way, course transparency becomes one of the keys to continuous gains in productivity. Courses offered online can also be analyzed for their strengths and weaknesses by competitors, who can then identify ways to improve them.

Final Thoughts

Until now, school reforms have focused on elementary schooling, the part of the education system where reform is least needed, and have ignored secondary education, the sector currently in most serious disarray. The federal law No Child Left Behind tests students in grades 3 through 8, but only once after that. Most charter schools are serving students in grades K through 8. The lion's share of school vouchers has been given to children in kindergarten and elementary school. That reform energy seems misdirected. The United States does fairly well in international science and math test comparisons among nine-year-olds, less well among thirteen-year-olds, and the most poorly among high school students.

The coming technological transformation has the capacity to address the tiers of the educational system where the problems are currently the greatest. Just as FLVS was at first a high school, and only later broadened its mission to encompass students in middle and elementary schools, the many who are unhappy in high school will be the first to take up the online option, once virtual-education opportunities become more general. Yet one can expect that the middle school will not go unaffected for long, since this is also a troubled tier of the contemporary educational system. Ability to use technology, moreover, is hardly beyond the game-playing preteens, who are often better at manipulating the latest in electronic technology than their parents are.

The private sector will be altered as much as the public sphere. Already, it is reeling from the rising cost of education, making the very best in private schooling unaffordable for all but families with the highest incomes. Catholic schools are closing across the country. Once serving the vast majority of private-school students, their share, in 1994, was only 51 percent, and by 2006 it had declined to 44 percent. As technological innovation progresses, online offerings will allow private and charter schools to access more diverse subject matter than they could provide themselves. Already, Florida Virtual's courses are being taken disproportionately by students in the nonpublic sector. But if virtual schooling will at first prove a valuable supplement to private schooling, in the long run much of the private sector is at risk, as parents and students will be able to design the education they wish without incurring its high costs.[20]

One would like to conclude on an optimistic note: that virtual education will close the achievement gaps between rich and poor, black and white, native and nonnative speakers of English. Unfortunately, that will not happen, at least not initially. When technology transforms a system, the process ordinarily begins with those that are the most resourceful, competent, connected, and well-off. Once an innovation proves itself, the use of the product or service diffuses. Marginal groups in society are usually the last to adopt. Digital television was first the province of the rich, though it is quickly becoming universal in the United States. Cable and telephone companies first introduced broadband technology in upscale neighborhoods, then gradually worked outward once they consolidated their market position in these friendly locations. New medical procedures—whether life saving or life destroying—are typically tried out first on those who can be expected to respond to medical direction and have the necessary financial resources to cover the cost. New doodads (moon roofs, side airbags, XM players, mirrors that assist in backing up, and so forth) are introduced first to luxury automobiles and then expanded to cover the bulk of the fleet. The rich were the first to smoke and the first to quit.

When the initial clientele is resourceful and connected, it becomes easier for those touting an innovation to demonstrate that it is successful. Innovations acquire a patina of quality simply by virtue of those who use it. iPhones appear slick and desirable because the clever are the first to use them. Moon roofs are of little practical value, but once put on prestige cars they become prized. When trying out a new procedure, doctors want patients who have a will to live and who do as they are told. Florida Virtual outperforms district schools on a variety of external indicators, perhaps because it is attracting a better-than-average clientele.

Until now, school reformers have tried to turn standard marketing strategies upside down. Instead of first reaching out to those who could best make use of the product, reformers have focused on the needs of marginal members of society. NCLB asked schools to raise every child's performance up to a basic level of proficiency, but it said nothing about what should be done with students who had already reached that basic level. School vouchers were restricted to students from low-income families, and charter schools were concentrated in low-income neighborhoods where students were doing poorly in district schools. The aspiration has been to transform American education by directing better-quality services to those most in need.

Many of the excellence movement's political difficulties can be attributed to that laudable, if less than shrewd, decision. As Wilbur Cohen, a Johnson administration aide who is credited for the design of Medicare, once observed, "A program for poor people will be a poor program." Ignoring his advice, choice programs serving the poor have had difficulty demonstrating unequivocal signs of success. Since charters concentrate on serving the disadvantaged, high levels of proficiency are seldom shown. Vouchers are offered to the poor, but many who apply end up not making use of them, casting doubt on the demand for the product.[21]

Virtual education has moved along a different track, opening new avenues to the more ambitious and talented at least as fast as to those with fewer resources. For this reason, technological advances will not quickly obliterate the differences in the performances of ethnic or income groups. That can happen only in the long run, as technologies improve, courses are designed in more customized ways, well-designed coaching systems are put into place, and models of success become generally available. But even if outcomes become more unequal in the short run, as always happens when innovations are introduced, the *opportunity* to learn will be equalized. Access to quality courses will not depend on the price of the house you buy or the quality of the peers in your immediate neighborhood. Any student with a will to learn will have access to the best.

If the six individuals who helped to build the contemporary school system could have observed the transformation that potentially lies ahead, they would be more pleased than disappointed, though they would express some misgivings. Horace Mann would be chagrined that a common culture was not being imposed, but he would approve the creation of a truly universal system of education. John Dewey would be disappointed at the loss of the community garden, but delighted to see students playing computer games, and he, more than anyone, would understand that learning is truly child-centered only when personalized education can be made available to every student. Martin Luther King Jr. would be disheartened by growing gaps in educational achievement, but pleased to see the end of the tyranny of the segregated neighborhood and enjoy the prospect that bright African American boys and girls will have access to the same facilities as anyone else. Al Shanker, regretful that teacher unions had lost membership and influence, would appreciate the higher salaries, professionalism, and autonomy that technology has made possible for the smaller but more talented teaching population that remains. As pleased as any of the six, Coleman would welcome schools that had coaches instead of instructors, peers that played academic games with one another, and students that competed against standards instead of classmates. William Bennett would be disturbed that virtual schools focused more on pedagogy than content, but he would nonetheless remind one and all, again and again, that he was among the first to realize that virtual education could, at last, genuinely transform learning. Julie Young, in 2145, would simply join the pantheon of those who have transformed America's schools, fulfilling the prediction emblazoned on the exterior of her school's headquarters.

Abbreviations

Appendix: Figures

FIGURE 1. Trends in high school and college participation and completion, 1940–2008.

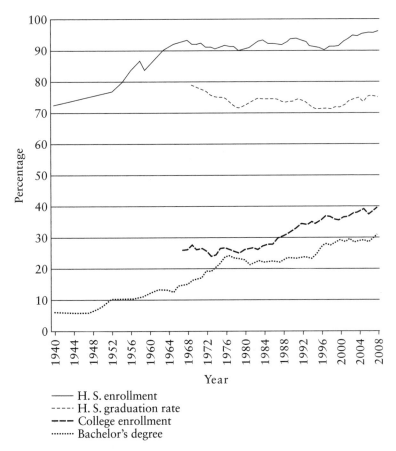

Note: High school enrollment rates for 2007 and 2008 are predicted.

Source: Digest, 2009, tables 55, 104, and 204; U.S. Census Bureau, Population Division, Education and Social Stratification Branch, *Current Population Survey, Historical Tables* (U.S. Census Bureau, 2009), table A2.

FIGURE 2. Secondary school and college completion rates in the United States and the average rate for other industrialized countries, 2006.

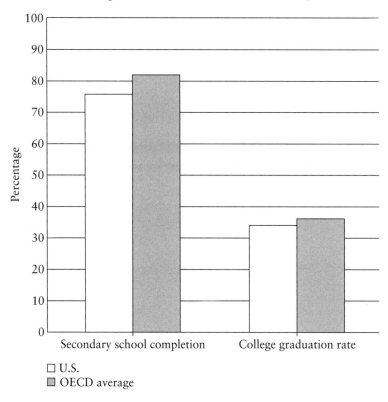

☐ U.S.
▨ OECD average

Note: The member countries that participated in the Organization for Economic Co-operation and Development (OECD) secondary school completion survey were: Czech Republic, Denmark, Finland, Germany, Greece, Hungary, Iceland, Republic of Ireland, Italy, Japan, Luxembourg, Mexico, New Zealand, Norway, Poland, Slovakia, South Korea, Spain, Sweden, Switzerland, Turkey, United Kingdom, and United States. The participants in the college graduation survey were the same countries, except for Korea, Luxembourg, Mexico, and Turkey. Austria and Portugal did not participate. Reported high school completion rates are higher in this figure than in Figure 1, because the manner in which high school graduation is calculated differs between the two figures. Figure 1 shows the number of graduates as a ratio of the seventeen-year-old population (as reported in the *Digest*), while in this figure the high school completion rate (as provided by the OECD) is the "percentage of the age group normally completing this level," which presumably takes into account diplomas received subsequent to the age of seventeen. The OECD average is calculated as the unweighted mean of the data values of all OECD countries for which data are available or can be estimated.

Source: Organization for Economic Co-operation and Development, *Education at a Glance, 2007* (Paris, 2007), tables A2.1 and A3.1.

FIGURE 3. Performance of the United States and other industrialized countries on 2003 reading and 2006 math and science assessments.

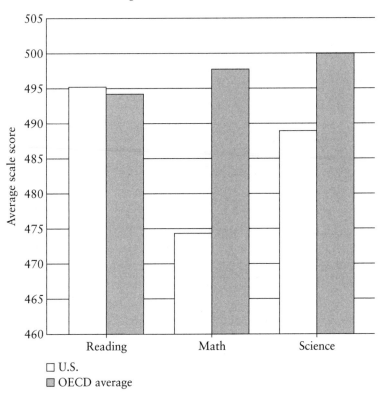

☐ U.S.
▨ OECD average

Note: The Organization for Economic Co-operation and Development (OECD) determined that 2006 U.S. reading literacy results could not be reported because of an error in printing the U.S. test booklets. The OECD average is calculated as the unweighted mean of the data values of all OECD countries for which data are available or can be estimated. The OECD member countries are: Australia, Austria, Belgium, Canada, Czech Republic, Denmark, Finland, France, Germany, Greece, Hungary, Iceland, Republic of Ireland, Italy, Japan, Luxembourg, Mexico, Netherlands, New Zealand, Norway, Poland, Portugal, Slovakia, South Korea, Spain, Sweden, Switzerland, Turkey, United Kingdom, and United States. The United Kingdom did not participate in the 2003 reading assessment.

Source: Organization for Economic Co-operation and Development, *Learning for Tomorrow's World: First Results from PISA 2003* (Paris, 2004), table 6.2. Organization for Economic Co-operation and Development, *PISA 2006 Science Competencies for Tomorrow's World* (Paris, 2007), tables 2.1c and 6.2c.

FIGURE 4. Performance of seventeen-year-olds in the United States on the reading and math components of the National Assessment of Educational Progress, 1971–2008.

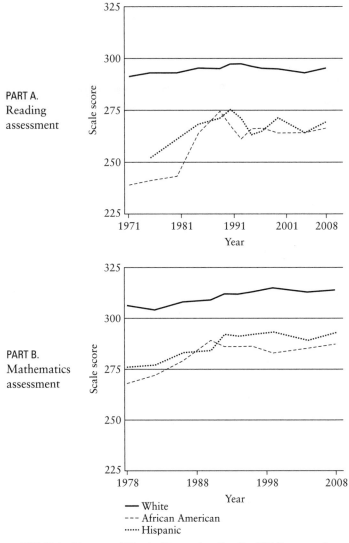

PART A.
Reading
assessment

PART B.
Mathematics
assessment

— White
--- African American
······ Hispanic

Source: NCES, *National Assessment of Educational Progress, Long-Term Trend* (U.S. Department of Education, 2008).

FIGURE 5. Total expenditures per pupil in constant dollars and pupil-teacher ratio in the United States, 1920–2006.

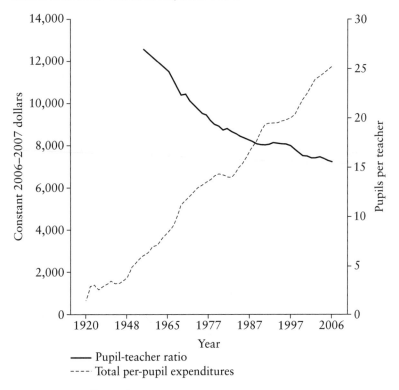

Source: *Digest,* 2009, tables 64 and 181.

FIGURE 6. Days on which local elections were held in California, 2005.

January

2	3	**4**	5	6	7	1/8
9	10	**11**	12	13	14	15
16	17	18	19	20	21	22
23	24	**25**	26	27	28	29
30	31					

February

		1	2	3	4	5
6	7	**8**	9	10	11	12
13	14	**15**	16	17	18	19
20	21	**22**	23	24	25	26
27	28					

March

		1	2	3	4	5
6	7	**8**	9	10	11	12
13	14	15	16	17	18	19
20	21	22	23	24	25	26
27	28	29	30	31		

April

					1	2
3	4	**5**	6	7	8	9
10	11	**12**	13	14	15	16
17	18	**19**	20	21	22	23
24	25	26	27	28	29	30

May

1	2	**3**	4	5	6	7
8	9	10	11	12	13	14
15	16	**17**	18	19	20	21
22	23	24	25	26	27	28
29	30	31				

June

			1	2	3	4
5	6	**7**	8	9	10	11
12	13	**14**	15	16	17	18
19	20	21	22	23	24	25
26	27	**28**	29	30		

July

					1	2
3	4	5	6	7	8	9
10	11	12	13	14	15	16
17	18	19	20	21	22	23
24/31	25	**26**	27	28	29	30

August

	1	**2**	3	4	5	6
7	8	9	10	11	12	13
14	15	16	17	18	19	20
21	22	23	24	25	26	27
28	29	**30**	31			

September

				1	2	3
4	5	6	7	8	9	10
11	12	**13**	14	15	16	17
18	19	20	21	22	23	24
25	26	**27**	28	29	30	

October

2	3	4	5	6	7	1/2
9	10	11	12	13	14	15
16	17	18	19	20	21	22
23	24	25	26	27	28	29
30	31					

November

		1	2	3	4	5
6	7	**8**	9	10	11	12
14	14	15	16	17	18	19
21	21	22	23	24	25	26
28	28	29	30			

December

				1	2	3
4	5	6	7	8	9	10
11	12	**13**	14	15	16	17
18	19	20	21	22	23	24
25	26	27	28	29	30	31

Note: Days when county, city, and school district elections were held in 2005.

Source: Institute for Social Research, Sacramento State University, "California County, City and School District Election Outcomes: 2005 Elections" (Sacramento State University, 2006), xi–xiv.

FIGURE 7. Number of school districts in the United States, 1940–2006.

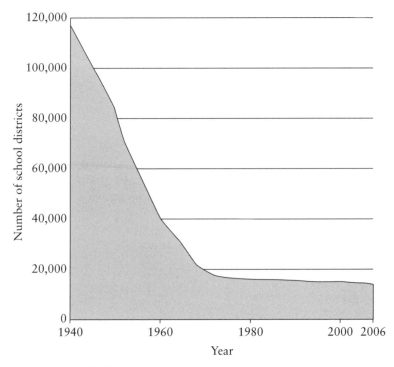

Source: Digest, 2009, table 87.

FIGURE 8. Average number of students per school in the United States, 1870–2006.

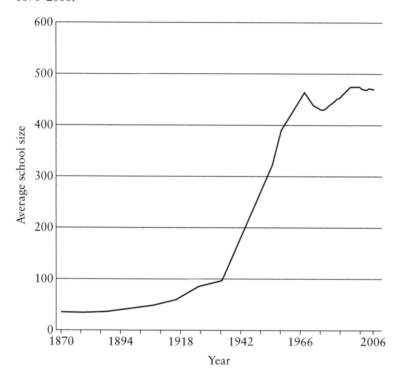

Source: Digest, 2009, tables 40 and 87. T. D. Snyder, *120 Years of American Education: A Statistical Portrait* (NCES, 1993), table 14.

FIGURE 9. Local, state and federal share of revenue for public education, 1920–2006.

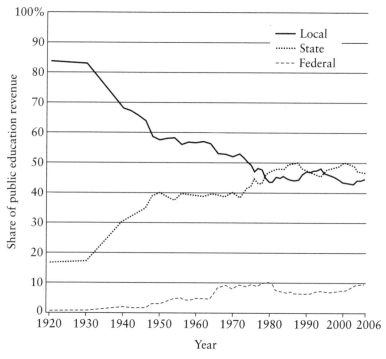

Source: Digest, 2009, table 171.

FIGURE 10. Number of states with laws requiring the certification of all teachers by the state, 1898–1937.

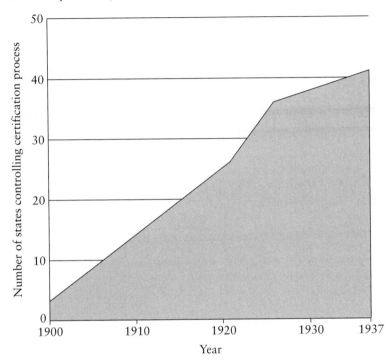

Source: David L. Angus and Jeffrey Mirel, *Professionalism and the Public Good: A Brief History of Teacher Certification* (Thomas B. Fordham Institute, 2001), table 1.

FIGURE 11. African American student enrollment in schools with a nonwhite majority, 1968–2000.

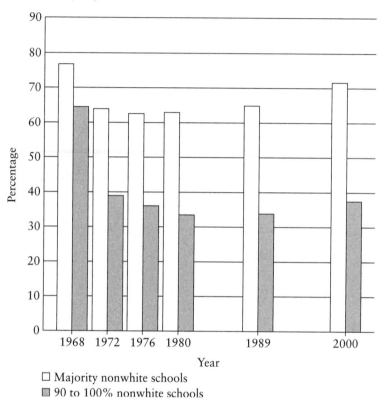

□ Majority nonwhite schools
▨ 90 to 100% nonwhite schools

Source: Charles T. Clotfelter, *After Brown: The Rise and Retreat of School Desegregation* (Princeton, N.J., 2004), table 2.1.

FIGURE 12. Length of the Milwaukee School District collective bargaining contract with the Milwaukee Teachers Union, by section, 1965, 1968, 1997.

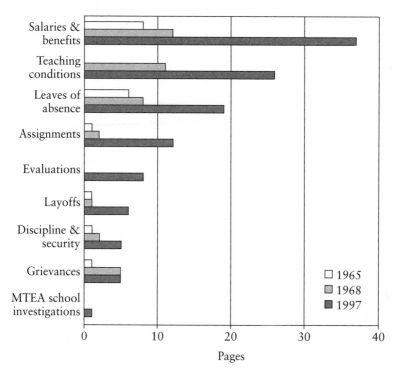

Note: MTEA is the Milwaukee Teachers' Education Association.

Source: Howard L. Fuller, George A. Mitchell, and Michael E. Hartmann, "Collective Bargaining in Milwaukee Public Schools," in Tom Loveless, ed., *Conflicting Missions? Teachers Unions and Educational Reform* (Washington, D.C., 2000), fig. 4-1.

FIGURE 13. Salary schedule for teachers with bachelor's and master's degrees, Denver school district, 2006–2007.

STEP	BACHELOR'S DEGREE	MASTER'S DEGREE
Beginning salary	$32,490	$32,960
1	34,200	34,700
2	34,460	35,100
3	34,550	36,500
4	34,730	37,860
5	35,040	39,470
6	35,260	41,150
7	36,740	42,880
8	38,290	44,690
9	39,890	46,600
10	41,590	48,600
11	43,340	50,660
12	45,190	52,840
13	47,500	55,650

Note: Generally speaking, a teacher advances one step with each year of service.

Source: "2006–2007 DCTA Salary Schedule," www.nctq.org (accessed May 14, 2009).

FIGURE 14. Wages and salary earnings of teachers, all those with at least sixteen years of schooling (bachelor's degree), and all full-time workers, 1963–2008.

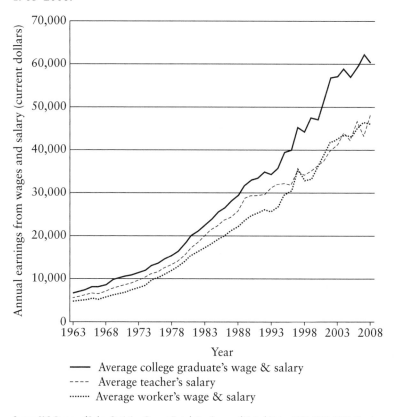

Average college graduate's wage & salary
Average teacher's salary
Average worker's wage & salary

Source: U.S. Bureau of Labor Statistics, *Current Population Survey of United States,* 1964, 1966–2008. Graph from *Our Schools and Our Future: Are We Still at Risk?* edited by Paul E. Peterson, fig. 18. Reprinted with the permission of the publisher, Hoover Institution Press, copyright © 2003 by the Board of Trustees of the Leland Stanford Junior University. Data since 2001 were supplied by Caroline M. Hoxby directly to author.

FIGURE 15. Final judgments on equity and adequacy cases by outcome, 1971–2005.

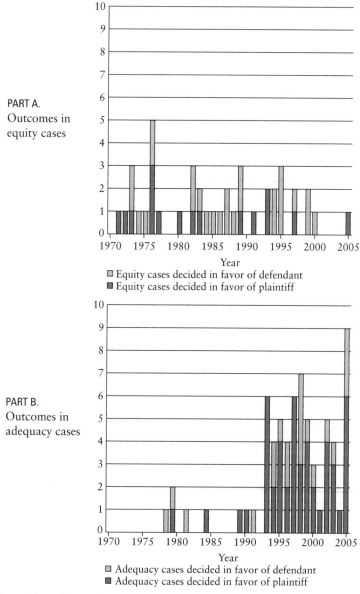

PART A. Outcomes in equity cases

☐ Equity cases decided in favor of defendant
■ Equity cases decided in favor of plaintiff

PART B. Outcomes in adequacy cases

☐ Adequacy cases decided in favor of defendant
■ Adequacy cases decided in favor of plaintiff

Source: Authors' tabulation of judgments, as compiled by Martin R. West and Paul E. Peterson, "The Adequacy Lawsuit," in West and Peterson, eds., *School Money Trials: The Legal Pursuit of Educational Adequacy* (Washington, D.C., 2007), fig. 1-2.

Notes

1. Heroes and History

1. W. Stephen Wilson, "What Do College Students Know?" *Ednext*, 8 (Fall 2008): 88.
2. Mark Aguiar and Erik Hurst, "Measuring Trends in Leisure: The Allocation of Time over Five Decades," *Quarterly Journal of Economics*, 122 (August 2007): 969–1006.
3. For a more optimistic interpretation of the evolution of the American public school, see Patricia Albjerg Graham, *Schooling America: How the Public Schools Meet the Nation's Changing Needs* (New York, 2005).
4. Leo Tolstoy, *War and Peace*, trans. Richard Pevear and Larissa Volokhonsky (New York, 2007), 604–605.

2. Horace Mann and the Nation Builders

1. Carl F. Kaestle and Maris A. Vinovskis, *Education and Social Change in Nineteenth-Century Massachusetts* (New York, 1980); Carl F. Kaestle and Eric Foner, *Pillars of the Republic: Common Schools and American Society, 1780–1860* (New York, 1983); Charles Leslie Glenn, *The Myth of the Common School* (Amherst, Mass., 1988).
2. Felix Frankfurter, concurring opinion in *McCollum v. Board of Education*, 333 U.S. 231 (1948).
3. John Locke, *Some Thoughts Concerning Education and Of the Conduct of the Understanding*, ed. Ruth W. Grant and Nathan Tarcov (Indianapolis, 1996), 48.

4. Milton Gaither, *Homeschool: An American History* (New York, 2008), chs. 1–2.

5. Ibid., ch. 2; David H. Donald, *Lincoln* (New York, 1996), 28–33.

6. "Land Ordinance of 1785" and "The Northwest Ordinance," in Henry S. Commager, ed., *Documents of American History*, 6th ed. (New York, 1958), 124, 131.

7. Thomas Paine, *The Rights of Man* (New York, 1906), 131; David Freeman Hawke, *Benjamin Rush: Revolutionary Gadfly* (Indianapolis, 1971); Benjamin Rush, "Of the Mode of Education Proper in a Republic" (1798), in *The Selected Writings of Benjamin Rush*, ed. Dagobert D. Runes (New York, 1947), 87–97; Benjamin Rush, "Plan for the Establishment of Public Schools," in Frederick Rudolph, ed., *Essays on Education in the Early Republic* (Cambridge, Mass., 1965), 6; Thomas Jefferson, "Public Education in the South," in *The Life and Writings of Thomas Jefferson, Including All of His Important Utterances on Public Questions*, ed. S. E. Forman (Indianapolis, 1900), 194.

8. Lawrence A. Cremin, *The American Common School* (New York, 1951), 87.

9. On Paine, see Robert Middlekauff, *The Glorious Cause: The American Revolution, 1763–1789* (New York, 1982), 320. On Vermont literacy, see William J. Gilmore, "Elementary Literacy on the Eve of the Industrial Revolution," *Proceedings of the American Antiquarian Society*, 92 (1982): 81–178, as cited in Carl F. Kaestle and others, *Literacy in the United States* (New Haven, 1991), 23.

10. Glenn, *Myth*, 71–72; Tyler Anbinder, *Five Points: The Nineteenth-Century New York City Neighborhood That Invented Tap Dance, Stole Elections, and Became the World's Most Notorious Slum* (New York, 2001); Jonathan Messerli, *Horace Mann: A Biography* (New York, 1972), 248–249.

11. Messerli, *Mann*, 19–20.

12. The information in this paragraph and the previous one is drawn from Messerli, *Mann*, ch. 11, quotation on 249.

13. Glenn, *Myth*, 120–121, 133.

14. Mary Peabody Mann, *Life of Horace Mann* (Boston, 1891), 231; Cremin, *Common School*, 94.

15. Messerli, *Mann*, 429.

16. W. Vance Grant, "Statistics in the U.S. Department of Education: Highlights from the Past 120 Years," in Thomas D. Snyder, ed., *120 Years of*

American Education: A Statistical Portrait (Washington, D.C., 1993), 1–4; Lawrence A. Cremin, *The Transformation of the School: Progressivism in American Education, 1876–1957* (New York, 1961).

17. See Figure 9 in the Appendix. See also Paul E. Peterson, *The Politics of School Reform, 1870–1940* (Chicago, 1985), chs. 7–8.

18. Alexis de Tocqueville, *Democracy in America,* vol. 1, trans. Phillips Bradley, Henry Reeve, and Francis Bowen (New York, 1945), 95.

19. Peterson, *School Reform,* 30; Claudia Goldin, "The Human Capital Century," *Ednext,* 3 (Winter 2003): 73–78. For further discussion of expenditures as a percentage of GDP, see Chapter 7 below.

20. *Meyer v. Nebraska,* 262 U.S. 390 (1923); *Pierce v. Society of Sisters of the Holy Names of Jesus and Mary,* 268 U.S. 510 (1925).

21. Lloyd Jorgenson, *The State and the Nonpublic School, 1825–1925* (Columbia, Missouri, 1987), 138–144; Peterson, *School Reform,* 42–44; Diane Ravitch, *The Great School Wars, New York City, 1805–1973: A History of the Public Schools as Battlefield of Social Change* (New York, 1974), chs. 1–7.

22. Peterson, *School Reform,* 29, 102–111.

23. Ibid., 47; Cremin, *Transformation,* 21.

3. John Dewey and the Progressives

1. Jay Martin, *The Education of John Dewey: A Biography* (New York, 2002), 21, 23.

2. Material in preceding paragraphs taken from Martin, *Dewey,* 36, 91–99. On Dewey's influence, see Lawrence A. Cremin, *The Transformation of the School: Progressivism in American Education, 1876–1957* (New York, 1961).

3. Martin, *Dewey,* 260–261.

4. Ibid., 186–227.

5. Charles Leslie Glenn Jr., *The Myth of the Common School* (Amherst, Mass., 1988); Martin, *Dewey.*

6. Diane Ravitch, *Left Back: A Century of Failed School Reforms* (New York, 2000), 22–24.

7. Jean-Jacques Rousseau, *Emile: Or, On Education,* trans. Alan Bloom (New York, 1979), 93, 94, 116; John Dewey, *Dewey on Education* (New York, 1959).

8. Ravitch, *Left Back,* 23–26.

9. John Dewey and Evelyn Dewey, *Schools of Tomorrow* (New York, 1962), 10; William Kilpatrick, "The Project Method," *Teachers College Record,* 19 (1918): 319–335, as quoted in Ravitch, *Left Back,* 179.
10. Ravitch, *Left Back,* 26–29.
11. Paul E. Peterson, *The Politics of School Reform, 1870–1940* (Chicago, 1985); David Tyack, *The One Best System: A History of American Urban Education,* 2nd ed. (Cambridge, Mass., 2005); Frederick M. Hess, "School Boards at the Dawn of the 21st Century: Conditions and Challenges of District Governance," Report of the National School Boards Association, 2002, 33–34.
12. Ellwood Patterson Cubberley, *Rural Life and Education: A Study of the Rural-School Problem as a Phase of the Rural-Life Problem* (New York, 1914), 186; Deborah Meier, "The Road to Trust," *American School Board Journal,* 190 (2003): 18–21.
13. Norman D. Kerr (pseudonym), "The School Board as an Agency of Legitimation," in Alan Rosenthal, ed., *Governing Education* (Garden City, N.Y., 1969), 137–172.
14. James Bryant Conant, *The Child, the Parent, and the State* (Cambridge, Mass., 1959), 38, as quoted in Paul E. Peterson and John Chubb, "Consolidate Districts, Not Schools," in "Reforming Education in Arkansas: Recommendations from the Koret Task Force," Report of the Hoover Institution, Stanford, Calif., 2005, 107–117.
15. Peterson, *School Reform,* 207–209; Paul E. Peterson, *School Politics, Chicago Style* (Chicago, 1976), 79–107.

4. Martin Luther King Jr. and School Desegregation

1. Howard Ball, *A Defiant Life: Thurgood Marshall and the Persistence of Racism in America* (New York, 1998); Juan Williams, *Thurgood Marshall: American Revolutionary* (New York, 1998); Roger L. Goldman and David Gallen, *Thurgood Marshall: Justice for All* (New York, 1992).
2. Martin Luther King Jr., *The Autobiography of Martin Luther King, Jr.,* ed. Clayborne Carson (New York, 1998), 223–227.
3. Taylor Branch, *Parting the Waters: America in the King Years, 1954–63* (New York, 1988), ch. 2.
4. Ibid., 57.

5. Ibid., ch. 2.

6. Ibid., ch. 3.

7. Ibid., 94–103.

8. Ibid., 111–114; *Brown v. Board of Education of Topeka*, 349 U.S. 294.

9. Stephen B. Oates, *Let the Trumpet Sound: The Life of Martin Luther King Jr.* (New York, 1982), 64–68; Branch, *Parting*, 124–137.

10. Branch, *Parting*; Taylor Branch, *At Canaan's Edge: America in the King Years, 1965–68* (New York, 2006).

11. James S. Coleman, Sara D. Kelly, and John A. Moore, *Trends in School Segregation, 1968–73*, Report 722–0301 of the Urban Institute (Washington, D.C., 1975), 15, 27–28.

12. Charles T. Clotfelter, *After Brown: The Rise and Retreat of School Desegregation* (Princeton, 2004).

13. Paul E. Peterson, *School Politics, Chicago Style* (Chicago, 1976), 165–169.

14. *Milliken v. Bradley*, 418 U.S. 717.

15. Branch, *Parting*, ch. 30; Clotfelter, *After Brown*.

16. Gerald Grant, *The World We Created at Hamilton High* (Cambridge, Mass., 1988), 40–44.

17. "About Shaker: General Information," City of Shaker Heights, www.shakeronline.com (accessed September 11, 2009); "David G. Molyneaux and Sue Sackman, eds., "Seventy-Five Years: An Informal History of Shaker Heights," Report of the Shaker Heights Public Library (Shaker Heights, Ohio, 1987), 78–79; "Shaker Heights Alumni Association Hall of Fame Members," Shaker Heights Schools, www.shaker.org (accessed September 11, 2009); "Nate Clements," National Football League, www.nfl.com (accessed September 11, 2009); Dale Whittington, "Achievement: State and College Admissions Testing," Accountability Report of Shaker Heights City School District, 2007–2008, www.shaker.org (accessed May 17, 2009), table 65.

18. Molyneaux and Sackman, "Seventy-Five Years"; Anne Galletta and William E. Cross Jr., "Past as Present, Present as Past: Historicizing Black Education and Interrogating 'Integration,'" in Andrew Fuligni, ed., *Contesting Stereotypes and Conflicting Identities* (New York, 2007), 15–41, quotation on 23; "The Reunion: Shaker Heights," ABC News Special, August 18, 2004.

19. Whittington, "Diversity of Student Population and Staff," Accountability Report, table 1; Whittington, "Achievement: Terra Nova

Achievement Tests," Accountability Report, tables 32–33; Whittington, "State and College Admissions Testing," Accountability Report, tables 39–40, 49–50, 65. Racial-gap calculations by Paul Peterson. Growth in Terra Nova scale scores for blacks is subtracted from that of whites and calculated in terms of the annual growth rate for all students in Shaker Heights for the grades in question.

20. John H. McWhorter, *Losing the Race: Self-Sabotage in Black America* (New York, 2000), 123–124; John U. Ogbu, *Black American Students in an Affluent Suburb: A Study of Academic Disengagement* (Mahwah, N.J., 2003); Galletta and Cross, "Past as Present," 29–30. Also, see Ronald F. Ferguson, "A Diagnostic Analysis of Black-White Disparities in Shaker Heights, Ohio," in Diane Ravitch, ed., *Brookings Papers in Education Policy, 2001* (Washington, D.C., 2001), 347–396.

21. Paul E. Peterson and J. David Greenstone, *Race and Authority in Urban Politics: Community Participation and the War on Poverty* (Chicago, 1976), 91; Harold Cruse, *The Crisis of the Negro Intellectual* (New York, 1967).

22. Branch, *Parting*, ch. 35. Kenneth Bancroft Clark, *Dark Ghetto: Dilemmas of Social Power* (New York, 1965); Stokely Carmichael and Charles V. Hamilton, *Black Power: The Politics of Liberation in America* (New York, 1967); Malcolm X and Alex Haley, *The Autobiography of Malcolm X* (New York, 1965).

23. James S. Coleman, "Reflections on Schools and Adolescents," in Jon Clark, ed., *James S. Coleman* (London, 1996), 19; Martin Bulmer, "The Sociological Contribution to Social Policy Research," ibid., 104; A. B. Sørensen and S. Spilerman, eds., *Social Theory and Social Policy: Essays in Honor of James S. Coleman* (Westport, Conn., 1993), 7; James S. Coleman, "Robert K. Merton as Teacher," in Jon Clark, Celia Modgil, and Sohan Modgil, eds., *Robert K. Merton: Consensus and Controversy* (London, 1990), 25–32.

24. "In Memoriam James S. Coleman (1926–1995): Speeches Given at the Memorial Service, 19 May 1995, in the Rockefeller Memorial Chapel, Chicago," in Jon Clark, ed., *James S. Coleman* (London, 1996), 376.

25. James S. Coleman, with E. Q. Campbell, C. J. Hobson, J. McPartland, A. M. Mood, F. D. Weinfeld and R. L. York, *Equality of Educational Opportunity* (Washington, D.C., 1966). Subsequent studies have found similar results. E. A. Hanushek, "Assessing the Effects of School Resources on Student Performance: An Update," *Educational Evaluation and Policy Analysis*, 19 (1997): 141–164; Gary Burtless, ed., *Does*

Money Matter? The Effect of School Resources on Student Achieve-ment and Adult Success (Washington, D.C., 1996).

26. U.S. Civil Rights Commission, *Racial Isolation in the Public Schools* (Washington, D.C., 1967); James J. Heckman and Derek Neal, "Coleman's Contributions to Education: Theory, Research Styles and Empirical Research," in Clark, *Coleman*, 90; Richard D. Kahlenberg, "Learning from James Coleman," *Public Interest*, 144 (Summer 2001): 62.

27. Coleman, Kelly, and Moore, *Trends*, 45, 79–80.

28. So William Shakespeare alleges in *Antony and Cleopatra*, Act II, scene 5; Marc Witkin, "Pettigrew Says Coleman's Busing Views Are Unrelated to Desegregation Studies," *Harvard Crimson*, July 22, 1975; "Calls Prof 'First-Class Fraud,'" *Chicago Defender*, December 9, 1975, 5; Noel Epstein, "The Scholar as Confuser: Or, Why the Busing Issue Is Not about White Flight," *Washington Post*, February 15, 1976; Letter to the editor by Alfred McClung Lee, *Footnotes* (American Sociologi-cal Association), 17 (May 1989): 7; Bulmer, "Sociological Contribu-tion," 114; James S. Coleman, "Response to the Sociology of Educa-tion Award," *Academic Questions*, 4 (Summer 1989): 76.

29. Diane Ravitch, "The Coleman Reports and American Education," in Aage B. Sørensen and Seymour Spilerman, eds., *Social Theory and So-cial Policy: Essays in Honor of James S. Coleman* (Westport, Conn., 1993), 136.

30. For a discussion of the impact of the compensatory education pro-grams, see Paul E. Peterson, "Making the Grade," Report of the Twen-tieth Century Fund Task Force on Federal Elementary and Secondary Education, Background Paper, 1983, ch. 4.

31. Steven Rivkin and Finis Welch, "Has School Desegregation Im-proved Academic and Economic Outcomes for Blacks?" in Eric A. Hanushek and Finis Welch, eds., *Handbook of the Economics of Edu-cation*, vol. 2 (Amsterdam, 2006), ch. 17; Katherine Magnuson and Jane Waldfogel, eds. *Steady Gains and Stalled Progress: Inequality and the Black-White Test Score Gap* (New York, 2008).

5. The Rights Movement Diversifies

1. American Civil Liberties Union, *Academic Freedom in the Secondary Schools* (New York: American Civil Liberties Union, 1968), as quoted in Gerald Grant, *The World We Created at Hamilton High* (Cam-

bridge, Mass., 1988), 51–52; for the other quotations in the first two paragraphs, see 51–54, 59, 65.

2. *Lander v. Seaver,* 32 Vt. 114, 76 Am. Dec. 156 (1859), as quoted in Abigail Thernstrom, "Where Did All the Order Go? School Discipline and the Law," in Diane Ravitch, ed., *Brookings Papers on Education Policy, 1999* (Washington, D.C., 1999), 302–303.

3. Richard Arum, *Judging School Discipline: The Crisis of Moral Authority* (Cambridge, Mass., 2003), 9–10, 79–86.

4. *Tinker v. Des Moines Independent Community School District,* 393 U.S. 503 (1969), as cited in Thernstrom, "School Discipline," 303.

5. Charles Lane, "Court Backs School on Speech Curbs," *Washington Post,* June 26, 2007, A6.

6. *Morse v. Frederick,* 551 U.S. 393 (2007).

7. Bob Egelko, "Judge Socks It to a Napa School's Dress Code," *San Francisco Chronicle,* July 4, 2007, B1; *Scott v. Napa Valley Unified School District,* 26-37082, California Supreme Court (2007).

8. Wood v. Strickland, 420 U.S. 308 (1975); *Goss v. Lopez,* 419 U.S. 565 (1975), as quoted in Thernstrom, "School Discipline," 305–306; Robert Spillane, "Comment," *Brookings Papers,* 322.

9. Richard Arum and Doreet Preiss, "Law and Disorder in the Classroom," *Ednext,* 9, no. 4 (Fall 2009): 58.

10. Arum, *Judging,* 142.

11. Richard Arum and Doreet Preiss, "Still Judging School Discipline," in Joshua M. Dunn and Martin R. West, eds., *From Schoolhouse to Courthouse: The Judiciary's Role in American Education* (Brookings, 2009), 255.

12. Gareth Davies, *See Government Grow: Education Politics from Johnson to Reagan* (Lawrence, Kansas, 2007), 166–174.

13. Ibid., 173.

14. Ibid., 181–184.

15. The previous several paragraphs are based on Davies, *See Government Grow,* ch. 7; also, see Paul E. Peterson, "Making the Grade," Report of the Twentieth Century Fund Task Force on Federal Elementary and Secondary Education, Background Paper, 1983, 120–126.

16. The law was originally known as the Education of All Handicapped Children Act, or Public Law 94-142. When the concept of "handicapped" fell out of fashion, the title of the law was changed but its basic content remained essentially unaltered.

17. *Board of Education v. Rowley,* 458 U.S. 176 (1982); Samuel R.

Bagenstos, "The Judiciary's Now Limited Role in Special Education," in Dunn and West, *From Schoolhouse,* 121–141.

18. Erik A. Hanushek and Steven G. Rivkin, "Understanding the Twentieth-Century Growth in U.S. School Spending," *Journal of Human Resources,* 32 (Winter 1997): 53; *Digest,* 2009, table 50, "Children 3 to 21 Years Old Served in Federally Supported Programs for the Disabled, 1976–77 through 2006–07."

19. Jay P. Greene and Marcus A. Winters, "Debunking a Special Education Myth," *Ednext,* 7 (Spring 2007): 70.

20. Robert Tomsho and Daniel Golden, "Educating Eric," *WSJ,* May 12, 2007, A1.

21. Ibid.

22. Ibid.; U.S. General Accounting Office, "Student Discipline: Individuals with Disabilities Education Act," Report to the Committees on Appropriations, U.S. Senate and House of Representatives (January 2001), 6.

23. Greene and Winters, "Debunking"; Tomsho and Golden, "Educating Eric."

24. John Hechinger, "'Mainstreaming' Trend Tests Classroom Goals," *WSJ,* June 25, 2007, A1.

25. Grant, *Hamilton High,* 247; Scott E. Carrell and Mark L. Hoekstra, "Domino Effect: Domestic Violence Harms Everyone's Kids," *Ednext,* 9 (Summer 2009): 58–63.

26. As quoted in Paul E. Peterson, *The Politics of School Reform, 1870–1940* (Chicago, 1985), 54–55.

27. Meyer v. Nebraska, 262 U.S. 390 (1923); Davies, *See Government Grow,* 143.

28. Lloyd Jorgenson, *The State and the Nonpublic School, 1825–1925* (Columbia, Missouri, 1987).

29. Ibid., 158.

30. *Lau v. Nichols,* 414 U.S. 563 (1974); Davies, *See Government Grow,* 143, 158–159.

31. This and the next two paragraphs follow the account in chapter 6 of Davies, *See Government Grow.*

32. Christine H. Rossell, "The Near End of Bilingual Education," *Ednext,* 3 (Fall 2003): 44–52.

6. Albert Shanker and Collective Bargaining

1. Opening quotation is from Frederick Hess and Martin R. West, "A Better Bargain: Overhauling Teacher Collective Bargaining for the 21st

Century," Report of the Program on Education Policy and Governance, Kennedy School of Government, Harvard University, 2006, 9; Eva Moskowitz, "Breakdown," *Ednext*, 6 (Summer 2006): 24; Howard L. Fuller, George A. Mitchell, and Michael E. Hartmann, "Collective Bargaining in Milwaukee Public Schools," in Tom Loveless, ed., *Conflicting Missions? Teachers Unions and Educational Reform* (Washington, D.C., 2000), 123.

2. Robert Sobel, *Coolidge: An American Enigma* (Washington, D.C., 1998), 144–145.

3. Martin R. West, "Politics, Public-Sector Unionism, and Education Policy: Explanations and Evaluations" (Ph.D. diss., Harvard University, 2006).

4. The next section draws upon Richard D. Kahlenberg, *Tough Liberal: Albert Shanker and the Battles over Schools, Unions, Race, and Democracy* (New York, 2007), 6–46, 50, 54; Richard D. Kahlenberg, "Philosopher or King? The Legacy of Albert Shanker," *Ednext*, 3 (Summer 2003): 34–39.

5. Kahlenberg, *Tough Liberal*, 54; West, "Public-Sector Unionism"; Richard C. Kearney and David G. Carnevale, *Labor Relations in the Public Sector* (New York, 2001); Joseph E. Slater, *Public Workers: Government Employee Unions, the Law, and the State, 1900–1962* (Ithaca, N.Y., 2004); Hanna Skandera and Richard Sousa, *School Figures: The Data behind the Debate* (Stanford, Calif., 2003), 106–110. AFT membership includes university faculty, paraprofessionals, and other school employees.

6. Terry M. Moe, "The Union Label on the Ballot Box: How School Employees Help Choose Their Bosses," *Ednext*, 6 (Summer 2006): 58–66.

7. Clive Thomas and Ronald Hrebenar, "Interest Groups in the States," in Virginia Gray and Russell L. Hanson, eds. *Politics in the American States*, 8th ed. (Washington, D.C., 2004), 119. Another study found teacher union headquarters, as opposed to the headquarters of other interest groups, to be the most proximate to the capitol building in most states. If propinquity is power, teachers appear to have it. "Jay P. Greene's Blog," jaypgreene.com, entry entitled "Proximity and Power," posted April 19, 2008 (accessed April 19, 2008).

8. Diane Ravitch, *The Great School Wars, New York City, 1805–1973: A History of the Public Schools as Battlefield of Social Change* (New York, 1974), 296–297, 334; Kenneth Bancroft Clark, *Dark Ghetto:*

Dilemmas of Social Power (New York, 1965), 137; Walter Thabit, *How East New York Became a Ghetto* (New York, 2003), 189.

9. Kahlenberg, *Tough Liberal*, 70–71.

10. Ibid., 81.

11. Ibid., ch. 4, especially p. 81; Maurice R. Berube and Marilyn Gittell, *Confrontation at Ocean Hill–Brownsville: The New York School Strikes of 1968* (New York, 1969); Ravitch, *School Wars*, 320–399.

12. Kahlenberg, *Tough Liberal*, ch. 5; Berube and Gittell, *Confrontation;* Ravitch, *School Wars*, 320–399.

13. Kahlenberg, *Tough Liberal*, 111.

14. Recent contributions to a rapidly growing literature on this subject include the following: Steven G. Rivkin, Eric A. Hanushek, and John F. Kain, "Teachers, Schools, and Academic Achievement," *Econometrica,* 73, suppl. (2005): 417–458; Thomas J. Kane, Jonah E. Rockoff, Douglas O. Staiger, "What Does Certification Tell Us about Teacher Effectiveness? Evidence from New York City," working paper, National Bureau of Economic Research, Cambridge, Mass., 2006; Thomas J. Kane, Jonah E. Rockoff, and Douglas O. Staiger, "Photo Finish," *Ednext,* 7 (Winter 2007): 60–67; Jesse Rothstein, "Do Value-Added Models Add Value? Tracking, Fixed Effects, and Causal Inferences," working paper, National Bureau of Economic Research, Cambridge, Mass., 2007; Thomas Kane and Douglas O. Staiger, "Are Teacher-Level Value-Added Estimates Biased? An Experimental Validation of Non-Experimental Estimates," working paper, School of Education, Harvard University, 2008; Karthik Muralidharan and Venkatesh Sundararaman, "Teacher Performance Pay: Experimental Evidence from India," working paper, Department of Economics, Harvard University, 2008; Eric A. Hanushek, John F. Kain, Steven G. Rivkin, "Why Public Schools Lose Teachers," *Journal of Human Resources,* 39 (Spring 2004): 326–354; Michael Podgursky, Ryan Monroe, and Donald Watson, "The Academic Quality of Public School Teachers: An Analysis of Entry and Exit Behavior," *Economics of Education Review,* 23 (2004): 507–518; Susanna Loeb, Linda Darling-Hammond, and John Luczak, "How Teaching Conditions Predict Teacher Turnover in California Schools," *Peabody Journal of Education,* 80, no. 3 (2005): 44–70; Todd R. Stinebrickner, "An Empirical Investigation of Teacher Attrition," *Economics of Education Review,* 17 (April 1998): 127–136; Peter Dolton and Wilbert van der Klaauw, "The Turnover of

Teachers: A Competing Risks Explanation," *Review of Economics and Statistics,* 81 (August 1999): 543–550; Charles Clotfelter, Elizabeth Glennie, Helen Ladd, and Jacob Vigdor, "Would Higher Salaries Keep Teachers in High-Poverty Schools? Evidence from a Policy Intervention in North Carolina," working paper, National Bureau of Economic Research, Cambridge, Mass., 2006; Eric A. Hanushek and Steven G. Rivkin, "How to Improve the Supply of High Quality Teachers," Paper presented at the Conference on Education Policy, Brookings Institution, Washington, D.C., 2003.

15. Caroline M. Hoxby and Andrew Leigh, "Pulled Away or Pushed Out? Explaining the Decline of Teacher Aptitude in the United States," *American Economic Review,* 94 (May 2004): 236–240; Sean P. Corcoran, William N. Evans, and Robert M. Schwab, "Changing Labor Market Opportunities for Women and the Quality of Teachers, 1957–1992," working paper, National Bureau of Economic Research, 2002.

16. James Vaznis, "Hub Teachers Reject Public Service Corps," *Boston Globe,* April 3, 2009.

17. Michael Podgursky, "Is There a 'Qualified Teacher' Shortage?" *Ednext,* 6 (Spring 2006): 26–32.

18. Kane, Rockoff, and Staiger, "Photo Finish."

19. Kate Walsh, "Union Influence in State Politics," *Ednext,* 10 (February 2010), forthcoming; *Digest,* 2009, table 68, "Highest Degree Earned, 2003–04" (see Figure 13 in the Appendix); Dan Goldhaber, "The Mystery of Good Teaching," *Ednext,* 2 (Spring 2002): 50–55.

20. William G. Howell, Martin R. West, and Paul E. Peterson, "What Americans Think about Their Schools," *Ednext,* 7 (Fall 2007): 23.

21. The material for this section, including quotations, is taken from Paul E. Peterson and Daniel Nadler, "What Happens When States Have Genuine Alternative Certification?" *Ednext,* 9 (Winter 2009): 70–74.

22. Howell, West, and Peterson, "Americans Think," 22; Barack Obama, "A Complete and Competitive American Education," Remarks made before the U.S. Hispanic Chamber of Commerce, March 10, 2009.

23. Albert Shanker, *NYT,* December 22, 1985 (advertisement).

24. Robert M. Costrell and Michael Podgursky, "Teacher Retirement Benefits," *Ednext,* 9 (Spring 2009): 58.

25. Michael Mannino, "Deferred Retirement Compensation for K–12 Em-

ployees: Understanding the need for Pension Reform," Report of the Independence Institute, Golden, Colorado, 2008.

26. Podgursky, "'Qualified Teacher' Shortage"; Michael Podgursky and Robert M. Costrell, "Peaks, Cliffs, and Valleys," *Ednext*, 8 (Winter 2008): 22–28.

27. Hess and West, "Better Bargain," 31. Also, see Frederick M. Hess and Martin R. West, "Strike Phobia: School Boards Need to Drive a Harder Bargain," *Ednext*, 6 (Summer 2006): 39–48; George B. Sanchez, "LAUSD Targets Teacher Shields," *Los Angeles Daily News*, April 22, 2009.

28. Brian Jacobs and Lars Lefgren, "When Principals Rate Teachers," *Ednext*, 6 (Spring 2006): 59–64; Obama, "Complete and Competitive."

29. Erin Einhorn and Carrie Melago, "Parents Say: If Tests Don't Tell Whether Teachers Deserve Tenure, What Does?" *New York Daily News*, April 10, 2008; Adam Lisberg and Erin Einhorn, "Teacher Tenure Plan's 'Just an Outrage,' Fumes Bloomberg," *New York Daily News*, April 7, 2008; Elizabeth Green, "Mayor, Teachers Square Off over Tenure Decision Language," *New York Sun*, April 7, 2008; Sanchez, "LAUSD Targets."

30. *Digest*, 2009, table 64, "Public and Private Elementary and Secondary Teachers, Enrollment, and Pupil/Teacher Ratios." Also, see Figure 5 in the Appendix.

31. For reviews of the literature, see Eric A. Hanushek, "The Failure of Input-based Schooling Policies," *Economic Journal* 113 (2003): F64–98:

32. Howell, West, and Peterson, "Americans Think," 24.

7. Money and the Adequacy Lawsuit

1. Ralph Ranalli, "How Much Does 154.6 Million Buy?" *Boston Globe*, April 1, 2007; Rachana Rathi, "North Financing Questions Persist," *Boston Globe*, March 23, 2008; Rachana Rathi, "School Bills Apt to Add Up," *Boston Globe*, April 6, 2008.

2. *Digest*, 2009, table 181.

3. *Digest*, 2009, table 78; Robert M. Costrell and Michael Podgursky, "Teacher Retirement Benefits," *Ednext*, 9 (Spring 2009): 58–70.

4. *Digest,* 2008, table 80.
5. *Digest,* 2009, table 80. Jay P. Greene and Daryl Hall, "The CEO Horizon Scholarship Program: A Case Study of School Vouchers in the Edgewood Independent School District, San Antonio, Texas," Report 01-42 of Mathematica Policy Research, Washington, D.C., 2001.
6. Eric A. Hanushek and Steven G. Rivkin, "Teacher Quality," in Eric A. Hanushek and Finis Welch, eds., *Handbook of the Economics of Education* (Amsterdam, 2006), 1051–1078.
7. Eric A. Hanushek and Steven G. Rivkin, "How to Improve the Supply of High-Quality Teachers," *Brookings Papers on Education Policy* (Washington, D.C., 2004), 7–44. On the boosting of teacher salaries in the early years of collective bargaining, see Paul E. Peterson, *School Politics, Chicago Style* (Chicago, 1976), 212; Stephen Cole, *The Unionization of Teachers: A Case Study of the UFT* (New York, 1969).
8. Jonathan Kozol, *Savage Inequalities: Children in America's Schools* (New York, 1991), 54.
9. Arthur Wise later published his thesis as *Rich Schools, Poor Schools: The Promise of Equal Educational Opportunity* (Chicago, 1968).
10. John E. Coons, William H. Clune III, and Stephen D. Sugarman, *Private Wealth and Public Education* (Cambridge, Mass., 1970); Gareth Davies, *See Government Grow: Education Politics from Johnson to Reagan* (Lawrence, Kansas, 2007), ch. 7, especially 200 and 206, and ch. 8, which contains a full discussion of the politics of school finance during this period.
11. Martin R. West and Paul E. Peterson, eds., *The School Money Trials* (Washington, D.C., 2007); *Serrano v. Priest,* 5 Cal. 3d 584, 487 P2d 1241 (1971); Eric Hanushek, ed., *Courting Failure: How School Finance Lawsuits Exploit Judges' Good Intentions and Harm Our Children* (Stanford, Calif., 2006); *Brown v. Board of Education,* 347 U.S. 483 (1954).
12. Quotes in preceding paragraphs and this one are from Davies, *See Government Grow,* 207–217; *San Antonio Independent School District v. Rodriguez,* 411 U.S. 1 (1973).
13. Martin R. West and Paul E. Peterson, "The Adequacy Lawsuit: A Critical Appraisal," in West and Peterson, *Money Trials,* 5–6.
14. *Robinson v. Cahill,* 303 A.2d 273 (1973).
15. Frederick M. Hess, "Adequacy Judgments and School Reform," in

West and Peterson, *Money Trials,* 165. The first two quotations are from Hess, the second two from the court opinion, *Rose v. Council for Better Education,* 790 S.W.2d 186 (1989).

16. West and Peterson, *Money Trials,* 346–358; *Campaign for Fiscal Equity v. State of New York,* 86 N.Y.2d 307 (2005).

17. For a discussion of Coleman's study, see Chapter 5; for recent research, see James J. Heckman and Alan B. Krueger, *Inequality in America: What Role for Human Capital Policies?* (Cambridge, Mass., 2003).

18. Joe Williams, "The Non-Implementation of New York's Adequacy Judgment," in West and Peterson, *Money Trials,* 195–212.

19. William G. Howell, Martin R. West, and Paul E. Peterson, "What Americans Think about Their Schools," *Ednext,* 7 (Fall 2007): 23–24; William G. Howell and Martin R. West, "Is the Price Right? Probing Americans' Knowledge of School Spending," *Ednext,* 8 (Summer 2008): 36–41.

20. Christopher Berry, "The Impact of School Finance Judgments on State Fiscal Policy," in West and Peterson, *Money Trials,* 213–240.

21. Robert M. Costrell, "The Winning Defense in Massachusetts," in West and Peterson, *Money Trials,* 278–306; Joshua Dunn and Martha Derthick, "Adequacy Litigation and the Separation of Powers," ibid., 322–344; *Horne v. Flores,* June 25, 2009, slip opinion.

22. Berry, "Impact," 227–231.

23. William J. Baumol and William G. Bowen, *Performing Arts: The Economic Dilemma* (New York, 1966), 171.

24. Ibid., 42; U.S. Department of Commerce, Bureau of Economic Analysis, table 2.5.5, "Personal Consumption," www.bea.gov/bea.

25. United States Census Bureau, *Statistical Abstract of the United States, Bicentennial Edition: Historical Statistics of the United States, Colonial Times to 1970,* table 3.2. The year 1902 is the first for which information is available. Change in the percentage of GDP spent on education may fluctuate with the size of the particular cohort of young people going through school.

26. Caroline M. Hoxby and Andrew Leigh, "Pulled Away or Pushed Out? Explaining the Decline of Teacher Aptitude in the United States," *American Economic Review,* 94 (May 2004): 236–240; Sean P. Corcoran, William N. Evans, and Robert M. Schwab, "Changing Labor Market Opportunities for Women and the Quality of Teachers,

1957–1992," working paper, National Bureau of Economic Research, 2002.

8. William Bennett and the Demand for Accountability

1. National Commission on Excellence in Education, *A Nation at Risk: The Imperative for Educational Reform* (U.S. Department of Education, 1983). *William J. Bennett, Our Children and Our Country: Improving America's Schools and Affirming the Common Culture* (New York, 1988), 224.
2. William J. Bennett, "The War over Culture in Education," Lecture 341, Heritage Foundation, Washington, D.C., September 5, 1991, www.heritage.org (accessed August 15, 2007).
3. Bennett, *Our Children,* 16.
4. Paul Manna, *School's In: Federalism and the National Education Agenda* (Washington, D.C., 2006), 57.
5. Ibid., 54.
6. Andrew Rudalevige, "No Child Left Behind: Forging a Congressional Compromise," in Martin R. West and Paul E. Peterson, eds., *No Child Left Behind? The Politics and Practice of Accountability* (Washington, D.C., 2003), 23–54.
7. Bennett, "The War over Culture."
8. Edward B. Fiske, "Reagan's Man for Education," *NYT Magazine,* December 22, 1985, 31.
9. Bennett, *De-Valuing,* 19–25.
10. Bennett, *Our Children.*
11. Fiske, "Reagan's Man."
12. Richard Rothstein, *The Way We Were? The Myths and Realities of America's Student Achievement* (New York, 1998).
13. Paul E. Peterson and Frederick Hess, "Few States Set World-Class Standards," *Ednext,* 8 (Summer 2008): 70–73.
14. "Humorous Quotes Attributed to Ross Perot," www.workinghumor.com (accessed September 30, 2009); H. Ross Perot, "Wake Up, America," *Washington Post,* November 20, 1988, D11; Joan Walsh, "The Truth about Texas School Reform," www.salon.com (accessed August 15, 2007).
15. "Time for Results: The Governors' 1991 Report on Education," Re-

port of the National Governors' Association, Washington, D.C., 1986; Richard D. Kahlenberg, *Tough Liberal: Albert Shanker and the Battles over Schools, Unions, Race, and Democracy* (New York, 2007), 332.

16. Ibid., 329.

17. Fiske, "Reagan's Man."

18. Kahlenberg, *Tough Liberal*, 336; for more detail, see Chester E. Finn, Jr., *Troublemaker* (Princeton, N.J., 2008), 173–180, 204–208.

19. Lynne V. Cheney, "The End of History," *WSJ*, October 20, 1994, A22.

20. Keith Henderson, "The Making of History Standards," *Christian Science Monitor*, November 18, 1994, 15; James Atlas, "Ways to Look at the Past (Or Did It Really Happen?)," *NYT*, November 13, 1994, 3.

21. Kahlenberg, *Tough Liberal*, 340; Diane Ravitch and Arthur Schlesinger Jr., "The New, Improved History Standards," *WSJ*, April 3, 1996, A14.

22. Rudalevige, "No Child."

23. "Answering the Question That Matters Most: Has Student Achievement Increased since No Child Left Behind?" Report of the Center on Education Policy, Washington, D.C., 2007; Ron Zimmer et al., "State and Local Implementation of the No Child Left Behind Act, Volume I: Title I School Choice, Supplemental Educational Services, and Student Achievement," Report of the RAND Corporation (Washington, D.C., 2007).

24. Paul E. Peterson and Martin R. West, "Is Your Child's School Effective? Don't Rely on NCLB to Tell You," *Ednext*, 6 (Fall 2006): 76–80.

25. Paul E. Peterson and Frederick M. Hess, "Keeping an Eye on State Standards: A Race to the Bottom?" *Ednext*, 6 (Summer 2006): 28–29.

26. William G. Howell, "One Child at a Time," *Ednext*, 4 (Summer 2004): 26–31; Paul E. Peterson, "Making Up the Rules as You Play the Game," *Ednext*, 5 (Fall 2005): 42–48.

27. Siobhan Gorman, "Selling Supplemental Services," *Ednext*, 4 (Fall 2004): 30–36.

28. William G. Howell, Martin R. West, and Paul E. Peterson, "What Americans Think about Their Schools," *Ednext*, 7 (Fall 2007): 12–26.

29. Bennett, *De-Valuing*.

30. Kahlenberg, *Tough Liberal*, 322, 338–39.

31. Ludger Woessmann, "Central Exit Exams and Student Achievement: International Evidence," in West and Peterson, *No Child Left Behind?* 292–323.

32. Kahlenberg, *Tough Liberal,* 328; Thomas S. Dee, "The 'First Wave' of Accountability," in West and Peterson, *No Child Left Behind?* 215–241.

9. James S. Coleman and Choice Theory

1. David Ferrero, "High School: Tales from the Inside," *Ednext,* 6 (Spring 2006): 76–80, reviews the following books: Elizabeth Gold, *Brief Intervals of Horrible Sanity: One Season in a Progressive School* (New York, 2003); Meredith Maran, *Class Dismissed: A Year in the Life of an American High School, A Glimpse into the Heart of a Nation* (New York, 2000); Michael Bamberger, *Wonderland: A Year in the Life of an American High School* (New York, 2004); Elinor Burkett, *Another Planet: A Year in the Life of a Suburban High School* (New York, 2001); Edward Humes, *School of Dreams: Making the Grade at a Top American High School* (Orlando, Fla., 2003).

2. John H. Bishop, "Nerd Harassment, Incentives, School Priorities, and Learning," in Susan Mayer and Paul E. Peterson, eds., *Earning and Learning* (Washington D.C., 1999), 232–233.

3. "In Memoriam James S. Coleman (1926–1995): Speeches Given at the Memorial Service, 19 May 1995, in the Rockefeller Memorial Chapel, Chicago," in Jon Clark, ed., *James S. Coleman* (London, 1996), 377. Moynihan quotes from a fax sent to him by an anonymous individual in the federal government.

4. James S. Coleman, "Columbia in the 1950s," in Bennett M. Berger, ed., *Authors of Their Own Lives* (Berkeley, Calif., 1990), 75, 98.

5. James S. Coleman, "Reflections on Schools and Adolescents," in Clark, *Coleman,* 17.

6. Coleman, "Reflections," 17; Coleman, "Columbia," 97; James S. Coleman, "Robert K. Merton as Teacher," in Jon Clark, Celia Modgil, and Sohan Modgil, eds., *Robert K. Merton: Consensus and Controversy* (London, 1990), 26.

7. Coleman, "Columbia," 100–102; James S. Coleman, "Merton," 31; James S. Coleman, "The Sidney Hook Memorial Award Address: On the Self-Suppression of Academic Freedom," *Academic Questions,* 4 (Winter 1990–1991): 21.

8. Coleman, "Reflections," 17.

9. James S. Coleman, *The Adolescent Society: The Social Life of the Teen-*

ager and Its Impact on Education (Glencoe, Ill., 1961); James S. Coleman, "Academic Achievement and the Structure of Competition," *Harvard Educational Review,* 29 (Fall 1959): 330–351.

10. Coleman, "Academic Achievement," 343. The longer quotation comes from James S. Coleman, "The Adolescent Society," *Ednext,* 6 (Winter 2006): 42.

11. Arthur G. Powell, Eleanor Farrar, and David K. Cohen, *The Shopping Mall High School: Winners and Losers in the Educational Marketplace* (Boston, 1985), 19.

12. John U. Ogbu, *Black American Students in an Affluent Suburb: A Study of Academic Disengagement* (Mahwah, N.J., 2003); Ronald Ferguson, "A Diagnostic Analysis of Black-White GPA Disparities in Shaker Heights, Ohio," *Brookings Papers on Education Policy,* (Washington, D.C., 2001), 347–414; Roland Fryer, "'Acting White': The Social Price Paid by the Best and Brightest Minority Students," *Ednext,* 6 (Winter 2006): 52–59; Theodore R. Sizer, *Horace's Compromise: The Dilemma of the American High School* (Boston, 1984), 54.

13. Milton Friedman, "The Role of Government in Education," in Robert Solo, ed., *Economics and the Public Interest* (New Brunswick, N.J., 1955), 144.

14. Ibid., 131n.

15. *Community Schools v. Seattle School District,* 551 U.S. 701 (2007). Peter Tice et al., "Trends in the Use of School Choice," NCES (2006), 5.

16. Anthony S. Bryk, Valerie E. Lee, and Peter B. Holland, *Catholic Schools and the Common Good* (Cambridge, Mass., 1993), 314; for extensions of the "social capital" concept, see Robert Putnam, *Bowling Alone: The Collapse and Revival of American Community* (New York, 2000); David Campbell, *Why We Vote: How Schools and Communities Shape Our Civic Life* (Princeton, N.J., 2006).

17. Edward B. Fiske, "School Study Didn't Push Key Point, Coleman says," *NYT,* April 26, 1981, Sec. 1, Pt. 1, 40. Diane Ravitch, "The Coleman Reports and American Education," in Aage Sorensen and Seymour Spilerman, eds., *Social Theory and Social Policy: Essays in Honor of James S. Coleman* (London, 1993), 138; Scott D. Thomson, "Initial Comments, Responses to Scholars to the Coleman Report," Report of the School Research Forum, Education Research Service, April 1981, 40; Ravitch, "Coleman Reports," 138–139; Robert Crain, "Initial Comments, Responses to Scholars to the Coleman Report," Education

Research Service, School Research Form, April 1981, 33; Anthony Bryk, "Disciplined Inquiry or Policy Argument?" *Harvard Educational Review,* 51 (November 1981): 507; Arthur S. Goldberger and Glen G. Cain, "The Causal Analysis of Cognitive Outcomes in the Coleman, Hoffer and Kilgore Report," *Sociology of Education,* 55 (April–July, 1982): 103, 121.

18. Christopher Jencks, "How Much Do High School Students Learn?" *Sociology of Education,* 58 (April 1985): 128–135.

19. Muriel Cohen, "The Choice Is Made," *Boston Globe,* March 24, 1991, 65; Jeanne Allen, "Serving Up a Skewed Look at Parents and School Choice," *Washington Times,* November 10, 1993, A21; Richard Elmore, review of *Politics, Markets, and America's Schools,* by John E. Chubb and Terry M. Moe, *Journal of Policy Analysis and Management,* 10 (Autumn 1991): 694; Gene V. Glass and Dewayne A. Matthews, "Are Data Enough? A Review of Chubb and Moe's *Politics, Markets, and America's Schools," Educational Researcher,* 20 (April 1991): 24–27.

20. Coleman, "Self-Suppression," 20.

21. Jay P. Greene, Paul E. Peterson, and Jiangtao Du, "School Choice in Milwaukee: A Randomized Experiment," in Paul E. Peterson and Bryan C. Hassel, eds., *Learning from School Choice* (Washington, D.C., 1998), 335–356. Similar impacts are observed by Cecilia Rouse, "Private School Vouchers and Student Achievement: An Evaluation of the Milwaukee Parental Choice Program," *Quarterly Journal of Economics,* 113 (May 1998): 553–602.

22. William Howell and Paul E. Peterson, with Patrick Wolf and David Campbell, *The Education Gap,* rev. ed. (Washington, D.C. 2006).

23. John Merrifield, *The School Choice Wars* (Lanham, Md., 2001); for citations and brief discussion, Howell et al., *Education Gap,* 298, n. 2; Gene V. Glass, review of *The Education Gap,* by William Howell et al., *Contemporary Sociology,* 32, no. 5 (2003): 642–643. For the reply to the most extended critique of *The Education Gap,* see Howell et al., *Education Gap,* 209–219 and Appendix E.

10. The Practice of Choice

1. Robert Costrell, "Who Gains, Who Loses? The Fiscal Impact of the Milwaukee Parental Choice Program," *Ednext,* 8 (Winter 2008): 62–

69. On the growth of the voucher program in Milwaukee, see Paul E. Peterson, "School Choice in Milwaukee Fifteen Years Later," in Paul Hill, ed., *Charter Schools against the Odds* (Stanford Calif., 2006), 71–101.

2. William G. Howell, Martin R. West, and Paul E. Peterson, "The 2008 *Education Next*–PEPG Survey of Public Opinion," *Ednext*, 8 (Fall 2008): 12–26; Richard D. Kahlenberg, *Tough Liberal: Albert Shanker and the Battles over Schools, Unions, Race, and Democracy* (New York, 2007), 236–237.

3. Jay P. Greene and Ryan H. Marsh, "The Effect of Milwaukee's Parental Choice Program on Student Achievement in Milwaukee Public Schools," Report 11 of the School Choice Demonstration Project Comprehensive Longitudinal Evaluation of the Milwaukee Parental Choice Program, Department of Education Reform, School of Education, University of Arkansas, 2009.

4. Patrick Wolf, et al., "Evaluation of the DC Opportunity Scholarship Program: Impacts after Three Years," Report of the U.S. Department of Education, Institute of Education Sciences, National Center for Educational Evaluation, 2009; Robert Tomsho, "School-Voucher Movement Loses Ground after Democratic Gains," *WSJ*, March 26, 2009; Greg Toppo, "More Black Lawmakers Open to School Vouchers," *USA Today*, May 5, 2009.

5. *Trustees of Dartmouth College v. Woodward*, 17 U.S. (4 Wheat.) 518 (1819).

6. Joe Nathan, *Charter Schools: Creating Hope and Opportunity for American Education* (San Francisco, 1996), 63.

7. Ibid., 2–4, 6. For a discussion of the role played by Budde and Shanker, see ibid., ch. 2.

8. As quoted in Kahlenberg, *Tough Liberal*, 314–315.

9. Nathan, *Charter Schools*, 83.

10. As quoted in Kahlenberg, *Tough Liberal*, 314–315.

11. The People for the American Way website contains sixteen critical references to school vouchers, but charters appear only once—in the title of a newspaper article quoted for other purposes. See www.pfaw.org (accessed January 22, 2009).

12. Nathan, *Charter Schools*, 36–37.

13. Nancy Faust Sizer and Theodore R. Sizer, "A School Built for Horace: Tales from a Start-Up Charter School," in Paul E. Peterson, ed., *Choice*

and Competition in American Education (Lanham, Md., 2006), 172–181; David Whitman, "An Appeal to Authority: The New Paternalism in Urban Schools," *Ednext*, 8 (Summer 2008): 52–58.

14. Bryan C. Hassel, *The Charter School Challenge* (Washington, D.C., 1999), 1, 25–27.

15. Jay Mathews, "Work Hard. Be Nice.: The Roots and Reality of the Knowledge Is Power Program," *Ednext*, 9 (Spring 2009): 28–35.

16. William G. Howell, Martin R. West, and Paul E. Peterson, "The 2008 *Education Next*–PEPG Survey of Public Opinion," *Ednext*, 8 (Fall 2008): 20.

17. National Education Association website, www.nea.org (accessed January 25, 2009).

18. The conflict in Carbondale, Colorado, is described in Joe Williams, "Games Charter Opponents Play," *Ednext*, 7 (Winter 2007), 13–18; Hassel, *Charter School Challenge*, 27–28.

19. "Annual Survey of America's Charter Schools," Report of the Center for Education Reform, Washington, D.C., 2007; Pat Kossan, "Arizona Lax on Charter Schools," *Arizona Republic*, September 2, 2007; Bruce V. Manno, "Charter School Politics," in Peterson, *Choice and Competition*, 169; Lewis C. Solmon, Kern Paark, and David Garcia, "Does Charter School Attendance Improve Test Scores? The Arizona Results," Report of the Center for Market-Based Education, Goldwater Institute, Phoenix, Arizona, 2001. Also, see discussion in Brian Gill, P. Mike Timpane, Karen E. Ross, Dominic J. Brewer, and Kevin Booker, "Rhetoric versus Reality: What We Know and What We Need to Know about Vouchers and Charter Schools," Report of the RAND Corporation, Santa Monica, Calif., 2001, as revised in 2007, 100–101.

20. Atila Abdulkadiroglu et al., "Informing the Debate: Comparing Boston's Charter, Pilot and Traditional Schools," Report of the Boston Foundation, 2009; Caroline M. Hoxby and Sonali Murarka, "New York City Charter Schools: Who Attends Them and How Well Are They Teaching Their Students?" *Ednext*, 8 (Summer 2008): 54–61. For a review of the literature on charter school effectiveness, see Gill et al., "Rhetoric versus Reality." Also, see Caroline Minter Hoxby and Jonah E. Rockoff, "The Impact of Charter Schools on Student Achievement," working paper, Department of Economics, Harvard University, Cambridge, Mass., 2004; Kevin Booker, Brian Gill, Ron Zimmer, and Tim R. Sass, "Achievement and Attainment in Chicago Charter Schools,"

Technical Report of the RAND Corporation, Santa Monica, Calif., 2008. For critiques of charters, see F. Howard Nelson, Bella Rosenberg, and Nancy Van Meter, "Charter School Achievement on the 2003 National Assessment of Educational Progress," Report of the American Federation of Teachers, Washington, D.C., 2004; Martin Carnoy, Rebecca Jacobsen, Lawrence Mishel, and Richard Rothstein, *The Charter School Dust-Up: Examining the Evidence on Enrollment and Achievement* (Washington, D.C., 2005).

21. Mark S. Granovetter, "The Strength of Weak Ties," *American Journal of Sociology,* 78 (May 1973): 1360–1380.

22. Caroline M. Hoxby, "Do Vouchers and Charters Push Public Schools to Improve?" in Peterson, *Choice and Competition,* 194–205.

23. Martin West and Ludger Woessmann, "'Every Catholic Child in a Catholic School': Historical Resistance to State Schooling, Contemporary Private Competition and Student Achievement across Countries," Report of the Program on Education Policy and Governance, Kennedy School of Government, Harvard University, 2006; Martin R. West and Ludger Woessmann, "School Choice International: Higher Private School Share Boosts National Test Scores," *Ednext,* 9 (Winter, 2009): 54–61.

24. Milton Gaither, "Homeschooling Goes Mainstream," *Ednext,* 9 (Winter, 2009): 11.

25. Ibid., 12; Howell et al., "2008 Survey," 19.

26. David Skinner, "Libertarian Liberals: When the Left Was (Sometimes) Right," *Ednext,* 5 (Fall 2005): 74–80; Diane Ravitch, *Left Back: A Century of Battles over School Reform* (New York, 2001), 398; Alexander Sutherland Neill, *Summerhill: A Radical Approach to Child Rearing* (New York, 1960); Ivan Illich, *Deschooling Society* (New York, 1971).

27. This and the following paragraphs, including quotations, are drawn from Gaither, *Homeschooling,* 123, 127, 142, 163.

28. Ibid., 162–163.

29. *Meyer v. Nebraska,* 262 U.S. 390 (1923); *Pierce v. Society of Sisters,* 268 U.S. 510 (1925).

30. *Wisconsin v. Yoder,* 406 U.S. 205 (1972); Gaither, *Homeschooling,* 178.

31. Gaither, *Homeschooling.*

32. Joshua Dunn and Martha Derthick, "Home Schoolers Strike Back: California Case Centers on Parents' Rights," *Ednext,* 8 (Fall 2008): 11.

33. Gaither, "Homeschooling Goes Mainstream," 13.
34. Ibid., 14–15.

11. Julie Young and the Promise of Technology

1. The opening paragraphs of this chapter are a revised version of Paul E. Peterson, "Virtual School Succeeds: But Can We Be Sure about the Students?" *Ednext,* 9 (Summer 2009): 5.
2. "A Comprehensive Assessment of Florida Virtual School," Final Report of the Florida Tax Watch Center for Educational Performance and Accountability, Tallahassee, Fla., 2008, 9; Personal interview, George Latimer, chief financial officer, Florida Virtual Schools, May 12, 2009.
3. Anthony Picciano and Jeff Seaman, "K12 Online Learning: A 2008 Follow-Up of the Survey of U.S. District School Administrators," Report of the Babson Survey Research Group, Wellesley, Mass., January 2009; Bill Kaczor, "Florida Leading in Virtual Learning," *Herald-Tribune,* August 19, 2007; Clayton M. Christensen and Michael B. Horn, "How Do We Transform Our Schools?" *Ednext,* 8 (Summer 2008), 17; Clayton M. Christensen, Michael B. Horn, and Curtis W. Johnson, *Disrupting Class: How Disruptive Innovation Will Change the Way the World Learns* (New York, 2008).
4. Larry Cuban, *Oversold and Underused: Computers in the Classroom* (Cambridge, Mass., 2001), 171, 175.
5. Ibid., 189, 190, 197.
6. Christensen and Horn, "Transform Schools," 12–19.
7. I. Elaine Allen and Jeff Seaman, "Online Nation: Five Years of Growth in Online Learning," Report of the Babson Survey Research Group, 2007.
8. "A Virtual Revolution: Trends in the Expansion of Distance Education," Report of the American Federation of Teachers, Washington D.C., 2001, 19.
9. The discussion of Julie Young and Florida Virtual School comes from the following sources: Bill Tucker, "Florida's Online Option: Virtual School Offers Template for Reform," *Ednext,* 9 (Summer 2009): 13–19; Robin Roenker, "UK Grad Julie Young leads the Florida Virtual School—the Nation's Largest Pre-collegiate Online School," *Kentucky Alumni Magazine* (Winter 2004), 11–13; "Governor Crist Praises

Florida's Virtual Education for Leading the Nation," Press Release, Florida Department of Education, December 9, 2008; "Leading in Program Technology Interview with Julie Young," prod. by Keith Gleinman, November 25, 2005, Education Development Center, Northeast and the Islands Regional Technology in Education Consortium, www .neirtec.org (accessed March 30, 2009); Interviews with FLVS administrators: Pam Birtolo, FLVS Chief Learning Officer, Hooy Sagues, FLVS Chief Strategist and Policy Officer, Joy Smith, FLVS Chief Development Officer, and Andy Ross, FLVS Vice President, Global Services Division, March 17–18, 2009.

10. Josh Dunn and Martha Derthick, "Virtual Legality: Unions and Home Schoolers Attack Internet Education," *Ednext* 6 (Fall 2006), 11; Patrick Marley and Stacey Forster, "Doyle OKs Aid for Virtual Schools," *Milwaukee Journal-Sentinel*, April 7, 2008.

11. Students pursuing a three-year (instead of four-year) college-bound high school degree are exempt from the physical education requirement. The course on physical fitness is described on the Florida Virtual School website as follows: "By taking this course you will feel the difference, both physically and mentally. You will start by assessing your current physical condition. You will keep a workout log to measure your progress. In addition, you will have a great personal trainer (your teacher) who will help you set realistic goals and reach your potential health-related objectives. As you travel through the virtual town of Wellville, you will learn about exercise, conditioning, diet and nutrition, and managing stress. You and your trainer will develop a fitness program tailored to your individual needs. As you make progress, you will feel your energy level increase. By the end of the course, you will have developed the kind of healthy habits that will last a lifetime." See www.flvs.net (accessed January 10, 2009). For the Julie Young quote, see "TravelinEdMan," Blog post of Curt Bonk, www.travelinedman .blogspot.com (accessed May 10, 2008).

12. Tucker, "Florida's Online," 14.

13. Bonk, "TravelinEdMan."

14. Tucker, "Florida's Online."

15. The expenditure for Florida district schools is for the year 2007, the latest year for which that information is available from the NCES—see Common Core of Data, *National Public Educational Financial Survey,*

2008, table 8; Katie Ash, "Experts Debate Cost Savings of Virtual Ed," *Education Week,* March 18, 2009, 1. The comparison does not take into account the special education services offered at a regular school.

16. Elinor Ostrom, "Crossing the Great Divide: Co-Production, Synergy, and Development," in Peter Evans, ed., *State-Society Synergy: Government and Social Capital in Development* (Berkeley, Calif., 1997), 85–118; Elinor Ostrom and James Walker, "Neither Markets nor States," in Dennis C. Mueller, ed., *Perspectives on Public Choice: A Handbook* (Cambridge, 1997), 35–72.

17. Kaczor, "Florida Leading."

18. Daniel T. Willingham, *Why Don't Students Like School? A Cognitive Scientist Answers Hard Questions about How the Mind Works and What It Means for the Classroom* (San Francisco, 2009), 10; Bill Tucker, "Laboratories of Reform: Virtual High Schools and Innovation in Public Education," Report of the Education Sector (Washington, D.C., 2007), 1, 4.

19. Terry M. Moe and John E. Chubb, *Liberating Learning: Technology, Politics, and the Future of American Education* (San Francisco, 2009); Personal interviews, Latimer, Young.

20. Paul E. Peterson, "Thorough and Efficient Private and Public Schools," in Eric Hanushek, ed., *Courting Failure: How School Finance Lawsuits Exploit Judges' Good Intentions and Harm Our Children* (Stanford, Calif., 2006), 195–234; NCES, *Characteristics of Private Schools in the United States: Results from the 2005–2006 Private School Universe Survey,* 2008; also, see Peter Meyers, "Can Catholic Schools Be Saved?" *Ednext,* 7 (Spring 2007): 12–21.

21. George A. Clowes, "The Only Solution Is Competition: An Exclusive Interview with Milton Friedman," *School Reform News,* December 1998. Friedman attributed the quotation to Wilbur Cohen.

Index

55, 64, 65, 138, 188, 191, 193. *See also* Laboratory School
University of Illinois, 41, 108
University of Kentucky, 237, 238, 244
University of Michigan, 39
University of Texas, 141, 161
University of Vermont, 39
University of Wisconsin, 197
U.S. Constitution, 21, 33, 97, 141, 225; Establishment clause, 207; First Amendment, 84, 224; First Amendment, Freedom of Religion clause, 224; Fourteenth Amendment, 33, 51, 57, 89, 140, 223; Fourteenth Amendment, Due Process clause, 33, 51, 89; Fourteenth Amendment, Equal Protection clause, 51, 57, 89, 139, 141
U.S. Department of Education, 133, 193
U.S. Department of Health, Education, and Welfare (HEW), 60, 100, 101
U.S. Office of Education, 30, 44, 158, 187
U.S. Supreme Court. *See* Supreme Court, U.S.
Utah, 206, 207

Valencia Community College (Orlando, Fla.), 229
Vermont, 25, 80; Burlington, 38
Vietnam War, 81, 82
Virginia, 222; Fairfax County, 85
Virtual education, 178, 229, 236–239, 241, 249, 256–258, 260, 262, 263. *See also* Florida Virtual School; Wisconsin Virtual Academy
Voucher programs: Thomas Paine and, 24; Bush presidencies' support

of, 159, 174, 177; Milton Friedman and, 191; Milwaukee, 197, 198, 203–209, 227; effect on student performance, 198, 200; private schools and, 211, 215; public support and demand for, 215, 216, 262; referendums, 216; unions and, 217; constitutionality of, 228

Wagner, Robert F., Jr., 110–112
Walsh, Kate, 122
Walton, John, 216
War on Poverty, 134, 138
Warren, Earl, 56, 57, 62, 90, 139
Washington, Booker T., 69
Washington, George, 25, 162, 172
Washington (state), 207, 216; Tacoma, 94
Washington, D.C., 19, 59, 89, 90, 125, 127, 139, 153, 156, 160, 200, 206, 209, 215, 220, 227
Weaver, Reg, 123
Webster, Daniel, 210
Weinberger, Caspar, 124
Weingarten, Randi, 128
Weller, Charles, 23
West Virginia, 59
Wieman, Henry, 55
Williams, Pat, 247
Williams, Polly, 204
Williams College, 161
Willingham, Daniel, 253, 254
Wisconsin, 23, 94, 203–205, 211, 227, 241, 243, 256; Cazenovia, 94; Eau Claire, 105; Madison, 94; Milwaukee, 105, 197–199, 204–206, 208, 209, 227
Wisconsin Education Association, 205
Wisconsin Virtual Academy, 240, 241